D0371782

Inside Cuba Today

The Sierra Maestra Mountains have always been Cuba's remote and mysterious southern frontier. The fact that they housed Fidel's successful guerrilla band gives them great romantic appeal as the birthplace of the Revolution.

Inside Cuba Today

by Fred Ward

CROWN PUBLISHERS, INC.   *New York*

Copyright © 1978 by Fred Ward

All rights reserved. No part of this book may be reproduced or utilized in any form or by any means, electronic or mechanical, including photocopying, recording, or by any information storage and retrieval system, without permission in writing from the publisher. Inquiries should be addressed to Crown Publishers, Inc., One Park Avenue, New York, N.Y. 10016.

Printed in the United States of America

Published simultaneously in Canada by General Publishing Company Limited

Library of Congress Cataloging in Publication Data

Ward, Fred, 1935-
    Inside Cuba Today.

    Includes index.
    1. Cuba. I. Title.
F1758.W37   1978   972.91   77-15528
ISBN 0-517-53192-5
ISBN 0-517-53193-3 pbk.

To our children—Kim, Chris, Lolly, and David—
in the loving hope that they may grow up in a world where
people have learned to be good neighbors

WARREN CENTRAL HIGH SCHOOL LIBRARY

2.64
972.91
849
15,697

ACKNOWLEDGMENTS

The material which follows was all personally gathered during seven separate visits totalling six months inside Cuba. The interviews to obtain background information and quotes were all gathered at the scene. Included with these was a wide-ranging private interview with Fidel Castro, which produced the chapter-heading quotations.

After my first reporting on Cuba appeared in *National Geographic* magazine, I was surprised and disappointed at the response from the Cuban exile community and the inability of many of them to accept any positive information about the country. It is not my role as a journalist to report biased information, but to report accurately all the relevant facts that might increase understanding. Because of the unique access I have had to Cuba, I feel this book offers the kind of view that will be increasingly important if rational decisions are to be made about its future in relation to ours. Events in the past year have moved even faster toward normalization of relations than the most optimistic observer would ever have thought. Decisions on these moves should only be made with the fullest background possible, and to shield one's eyes from the truth, whatever it may be, serves only the demons of ignorance.

Many people helped in my quest. My wife, Charlotte, was always a stalwart support with encouragement and generous hours of editing and proofreading. Senator James Abourezk opened many doors and was of great assistance. Teófilo and Esther Acosta, formerly with the Cuban U.N. Mission, and René Mujica with MINREX in Havana were tireless in their help. Gil Grosvenor, Joe Judge, Bob Gilka, and Jim Cerruti at *National Geographic* supported the Cuba project when I needed it. To all, and to many others, I give my heartfelt thanks.

F.W.
1977

Introduction

> In Cuba after the Revolution, people who hated the
> state saw a new form of state and identified with it.
> Everybody was able to say, like Louis XIV, "I am the State."
>
> —*Fidel Castro*

It is altogether possible that Cuba is the most controversial nation on earth. Other countries may be regarded unemotionally, but in the vortex of passions that have swirled around the island's recent history, only strong opinions remain. Cuba has seemed like a magnet to problems, having traded one troubled era for the next, only to be cast into despair after each new wave of hope. The current leaders, operating the first and only Marxist government in the Western Hemisphere, constantly boast that the country has finally found its path and is successfully solving its problems in the only way possible, as a socialist state. In contrast, the United States, most of the American people, and a very vocal Cuban exile community living mainly in south Florida, insist just as strongly that Fidel Castro and his government have stolen democracy from the Cuban people, have enslaved them within the Communist web, and have sold out their future to the Soviet Union. The fact that conclusions about a single set of conditions vary so widely can only mean a serious lack of communication and enormous difficulties in interpreting the true status of life in Cuba today. Attempting to answer some of the questions becomes much like dancing in quicksand—with each step, one gets in a little deeper.

Many people have said facetiously that there would be some truth in anything written about Cuba. Even to that there is some truth. For Cuba today is changing its face and attitudes so rapidly that it is virtually impossible to have the latest information. Even more important, since the country has been ruled from the first day of the Revolution's success in January, 1959, until December, 1976, without any formalized government, Cuban policy has been, in reality, what Fidel Castro said it was on any given day. In light of this fact, it is far easier to understand why positions have altered so many times in so many directions. Castro is a volatile character, full of intellectual curiosity, anxious to try new ideas, as impatient as a child with concepts that do not seem to work. Following the actions of this government by trial and error makes convoluted reading.

There have been some stabilizing consistencies. From the earliest days, movement toward social reforms has been evident. Castro has insisted on the need for agrarian reform; his plan was mildly stated in 1953, revised in his broadcasts from the Sierra Maestra in 1958, and put into practice in even different forms in 1959. His desire for reform was known for years, although the character of the law turned out to be considerably altered. Most important, from the time of Castro's announcement regarding his conversion to Marxist-Leninist thought in 1961, Cuba has moved on a steady course toward socialism and communism.

Cuba today once again faces a pivotal event. Having successfully outlasted all the dire predictions of downfall, she is embarking on a flirtation with the archenemy colossus to the north, only ninety miles away. The time has come, the Cubans say, when the United States must face reality, recognize their country for what it is and what it plans to remain, and get on with the job of incorporating Cuba fully into the hemisphere once more.

Only a more confident Castro, and a more "institutionalized" revolution, would express such an idea. The Cuban government now feels sufficiently safe to actually deal with "Yankee imperialism," which has been so convenient as a whipping boy to keep revolutionary enthusiasm peaked. It will be somewhat more difficult to be quite so blatant in attacks against the United States when she is an important trading partner and her tourists pack the beaches.

In one *Washington Post* article, Fidel Castro was described as an "America Freak," devouring all available information about his neighbor. Similarly, Americans are abnormally interested in this fascinating island that is almost as large as all the other Caribbean islands combined. Whenever a visitor returns from Cuba, he is inundated with the same questions: "What's it truly like down there?" "Are the people poor and starving?" "Do they really hate Americans?"

Cuba defies categories. If a revolution can be personalized, then the Cuban Revolution can be called an ongoing, living revolution. It is still young, and kept deliberately so by massive propaganda efforts and emotion-boosting celebrations. Over half the people on the island have been born since the heady days when Fidel and his enthusiastic bearded guerrillas triumphantly marched into Havana and promised a bright new world for all Cubans. Since then the raw edge of emotional stress has been a constant companion as the loyal Cuban followers of Fidel Castro have experienced agrarian and urban reform laws, lived through the Bay of Pigs invasion, feared the consequences of the Missile Crisis of 1962, seen the great sugar harvest fail, accepted rationing as a part of life, watched families torn apart as over half a million citizens voluntarily went into exile, and pledged themselves to a complete social revolution setting out to build a "New Society."

The Cuban exile community in Florida and other vocal anti-Communist groups are quick to say that the Cuban experiment is a failure. The economy is a shambles, there are food and other shortages, the people are enslaved by the system, children are forced to work for the state, there is no free press or dissent, and the Soviet Union pulls the strings which make the puppet Cuba send troops into Africa. Cubans reply that they are extremely glad to have gotten rid of their former thieves, prostitutes, graft-ridden public officials, gamblers, and robbing privileged class and are just as happy to see them in the United States causing someone else trouble. Both charges are worthy of some consideration.

In fact, Cuba is not about to collapse. It is, however, in serious economic trouble simply because the government has chosen to live beyond its means. The desire to industrialize and construct the New Society in as short a time as possible means that more money has to be spent than is available. Such a temptation is an obvious one and easily understood. Cubans were beneficiaries of U.S. capital and technology for years and now want to skip over as many of the normal development steps as they can in order to bring about industrialization in one generation that would normally cover several decades. Payment for this dream is creating some severe dislocations in the economy. Sugar still remains the principal crop and normally produces 80 percent of the island's export money. Continuing drought threatens to decrease the output, and the disastrous 1976 plunge in world sugar prices to seven cents a pound has thwarted the government's first Five-Year Plan, already estimated to be 1–1½ years behind schedule. Nickel is the only other product of great value, with a pair of old and inadequate on-line factories now handling the available ore. New plants are years in the future. Fishing is a growing export factor, but it is still too early to determine the impact it will have now that 200-mile coastal limits are in effect and Cuba lacks productive fishing grounds within her boundaries. Finally, there is the Soviet aid, amounting to up to $2 million a day. The Soviet Union buys Cuban sugar over the world market price and sells oil under the international price. Cubans are grateful for the help, but some grumble while asking, "At what cost to us?"

Then there is the military. Estimates are that 200,000 of Cuba's 9½ million people are in the armed forces. Adult males up to age forty are in the reserves, and the civilian militia includes about everyone else. Even though the Soviet Union gave Cuba the equipment for Cuba's army, navy, and air force, keeping it up is at local expense. Also, having so many men on active duty means a constant peso drain to house, feed, and keep them, plus the loss of the incomes they would have if they were free to work in the normal job market. Some sources claim that Cuba has the most powerful military in all of Latin America, including the largest nations of Brazil, Argentina, and Chile. When all the latest Soviet tanks, supersonic jet fighters, air-to-air, surface-to-air, and surface-to-surface missiles are on military parade, it is easy to agree with the boast.

For most observers in the 1950s, the least likely candidate of all Latin American countries to turn to communism was Cuba. After all, it enjoyed a higher standard of living than almost all of them, was relatively industrialized, had a booming U.S. tourist trade, and was located tantalizingly close to the Florida Keys. However, intermixed with that was a sizable quantity of discontent, particularly among the less privileged. The land and commercial holdings tying U.S.-Cuban interests together were viewed in the United States as a symbol of security, but in Cuba the young revolutionaries saw them as a stranglehold on their pride and their future. That discontent would forever alter the nature of Western Hemisphere relationships.

Contents

Acknowledgments   vi

Introduction   vii

1   The Pearl of the Antilles   1
2   Working and Living Conditions   15
3   The Home Life   33
4   The Mass Organizations and the Communist Party   55
5   The Economy   81
6   Education   95
7   Public Health   115
8   The Arts, Entertainment, Cinema, and Sports   129
9   Tourism   155
10   Sugar   178
11   Agriculture, Cattle, Tobacco, and Fishing   194
12   Industry   216
13   The U.S. Naval Station at Guantánamo Bay   226
14   The Government of Cuba   235
15   Fidel Castro   254
16   Cuba, the United States, and the World   280

Index   306

Havana and the Malecón provide a spectacular view for the new occupants of the old U.S. Embassy. Taken from the roof terrace of the building, it is a scene not enjoyed by Americans since relations were broken in 1961.

For many, watching the sun set behind the Havana skyline remains a favorite pastime. The old U.S. Embassy, now housing the U.S. Interest Section in the Swiss Embassy, is the building to the far right.

The Pearl of the Antilles

> . . . the loveliest land that human eyes have beheld.
>
> *—Christopher Columbus*
> *October, 1492*

Havana—oh, the memories that word recalls. For anyone over forty, Havana excites a cornucopia of emotions. There were the old world charm, the Spanish buildings, "Old Havana," the "Sin Capital of the World," the sexual exhibitions, "America's Playland," unrestricted gambling, long, beautiful beaches, easy girls everywhere, tropical nightlife, romance under the stars, beautiful hotels, "America's Sugarbowl," and machine guns at the airport.

To a younger generation, Havana means something entirely different. Now it is the seat of the first and only Marxist government in the Western Hemisphere, the home of Fidel Castro, the site of those hours-long harangues, and the source of endless fascination for Americans who are ending a generation of isolation from their southern neighbor.

Havana is all those physical things and much more. Of course, the gambling and flesh-peddling are gone, some of the first casualties of the revolutionary government in 1959. What remains is a city of charm and beauty, located on a sweeping arc of land, intercepted by a large, naturally protected harbor. Many of the buildings need paint and plaster now, victims of the shortages of the system, but the graceful skyline remains and many *habaneros* wander nightly along the Malecón to watch the orange fireball set behind high-rise apartments.

Havana is a city of about 2 million people, a size that makes it the largest metropolitan area in the Caribbean. As such, it houses over a fifth of Cuba's population. Its mass and importance have always made it alluring for Cubans, draining the countryside of people and resources. At the time of the Revolution, over half the country's doctors, for example, practiced in Havana, to the detriment of the remainder of the island. Now, with the central planning and control that Marxism brings to a country, Cuba is deliberately de-emphasizing Havana. Doctors are assigned to spend time away from cities (usually their first two years of practice), new housing and industries are located in rural areas, and a concerted effort continues to build up undeveloped regions like the Isle of Pines and distribute the population more evenly.

Even with decentralization, Havana is still thriving and alive. The plan seems to be to have the capital hold its present population instead of growing at the island's rate. Cuba had about 6 million people in 1959 and has already jumped to 9½ million. With half again as many people in a generation, tremendous pressures have been placed on all areas of service—food, housing, consumer goods, etc. It continues to be very difficult to industrialize and care for the extra people simultaneously.

Yet the government seems unconcerned about birth control. Family planning instructions are offered and all types of contraceptives are free and available, but there is no pressure to use them. As the Cubans point out, their island is large, 759 miles from the western end of Pinar del Río to Point Maisi in Oriente. That is almost as far as New York to Chicago, while the current population is a little more than New York City itself. So, for the time being, they seem satisfied with their population growth. Much like the Chinese, they consider people their most valuable asset. Those children scampering along the narrow streets of Old Havana, playing the Cuban passion, baseball, with a scrap piece of lumber and a tattered, stringy ball, are looked upon not as a handicap, but as the future of the Revolution. Interestingly, as people become more aware of the possibilities of controlling family size and, because of state retirement funds, Cubans no longer have to depend on their children for security in old age, and the birth numbers are dropping even without a government policy. The first year of the Revolution produced 191,000 live births. A steady climb resulted until 1965, when a peak of 256,014 births was reached. Since then the totals have declined to the 1976 figure of 187,353.

Part of the attractiveness of Havana continues to be the rows of pastel-colored stucco buildings along palm-lined avenues. But since the wait for paint and maintenance materials often exceeds two years, the fine old mansions have a slightly shabby look on close inspection. With very few exceptions, the grand homes were vacated in the early 1960s, when over half a million Cubans fled the new communism to exile, mainly in Miami. Since they were required to leave all household goods behind, the homes remained furnished. Naturally, they are still used today, although for other purposes. The luxury home areas of Vedado, along Fifth Avenue in Miramar, and in Country Club and Cubanacan are still Havana's fashionable neighborhoods. Vacated homes and their furnishings were inventoried and reassigned as multi-family dwellings, schools, dormitories, day-care centers, offices, protocol homes for official visitors, etc. Mystery stories abound about the houses, since many exiles supposedly buried their family treasures in the walls or underground in the yards. Recently, a long ball from a sandlot baseball game hit an old home, dislodging three loose bricks and 30,000 pesos hidden behind them. Before they left, a few people with foreign connections donated their estates to the embassies of other countries, and the homes are now used as diplomatic residences. Some of the homes taken by the government were turned over to the Ministry of Foreign Affairs to accommodate other embassy personnel.

At first glance Havana looks much as it did before the Revolution, almost as if time had stood still for twenty years. The buildings, houses, hotels, and streets have hardly changed since 1959. On the ride into Havana from José Martí Airport, a tourist may experience a strange Rip Van Winkle sensation. Today's visitor looks around and suddenly realizes that the streets are filled with old U.S. automobiles. These ancient bailing-wire beauties are a credit to Cuban ingenuity, and a sight to behold. Only on old TV shows can such a repository of "Detroitiana" be seen in such a concentrated area. Nostalgic Americans usually stand around on a busy intersection to watch Packards, DeSotos, Studebakers, Kaisers, an occasional Edsel, and a remarkable coughing, clanging collection of 1959 Chevrolets, Buicks, Cadillacs, Dodges, Plymouths, and Fords creak by, 1959 being the last year that American cars were imported. They are far too prized

Cars are so old and parts so scarce in Cuba that breakdowns are the rule.

ever to let die, though the sun and salt air and spray take their toll on the bodies. No car is junked, even after a serious accident; it is pirated. Irreplaceable parts are fabricated, no matter how complicated. Only when all efforts to revive an aging beauty have failed must the owner take it to a government shop that disassembles it piece by piece and puts the usable parts back into circulation. One result of this process is that Cuban cars are the strangest arrays of mismatched components to be found in the world. Some indescribable vehicle will approach, and a knowledgeable viewer can note perhaps a Cadillac grill, a basic Chevrolet chassis, and maybe one Plymouth fender. A rusting body may be riddled with so many holes that it is possible to see the driver inside through the doors and for him to see outside through the floors. Motors and transmissions are mixed among makes with complete abandon.

The old U.S. relics are certainly not the only cars on the road in Cuba—just the most interesting. Traffic is light because cars are so difficult to buy. Only professional people are allowed on the buying list. It is an incentive to excel in work and a privilege granted by the government. Doctors, engineers, the lead dancers in the National Ballet, certain government officials, and other key people are able to buy cars. The autos imported for this purpose (and the numbers are small) are usually compact Fords and Chevrolets made in Argentina, some Volkswagens, Fiats from Italy and the Soviet Union, and Alfa Romeos. The government also imports some Soviet cars for official use in addition to the standard Falcons and Chevrolets that are now so common. An entire new taxi fleet is in service, and is composed of the U.S. makes from Argentina.

Cuba limits the numbers of automobiles for various official reasons. First, there is insufficient money to pay for them. A recent order for more Argentinian models had to be cancelled when lowered sugar prices severely curtailed the funds available for foreign purchases. Next, Cuba imports most of her oil from the Soviet Union. (A tiny new oil-drilling operation on the north coast just east of Havana is producing some crude oil, but not much.) Even though Cuba buys at under the current world oil price, paying the power bill for electricity, industry, cars, and trucks is still a considerable drain on the economy. Fidel Castro told the author that Cuba will never be an automobile society like the United States, even if she could someday afford it. He said oil should be used in petro-chemical industries for the benefit of people and not burned for the convenience of pollution-producing cars.

The one place where a single automobile becomes an inconvenience and two make a traffic jam is in the narrow streets of Old Havana. Just as in New York, the typical delay is coming up behind a stopped truck. There is no room to pass, even by driving over the sidewalks, which is what the motorbikes do.

The remaining charm and legacy from the Spanish still line these streets. A number of the old stone buildings have been in constant use since Havana was the gathering port for the Spanish treasure fleet. Old Havana runs from the harbor almost to the old capitol building. The capitol looks familiar to Americans since it was patterned after the one in Washington. After the Revolution, its legislative function was dissolved and the country was run by an appointed revolutionary council. The building is now a science center and recently housed a massive Soviet science exhibit that included manned spacecraft, housewares, and heavy industrial equipment. Old Havana was

The cathedral of Havana and its impressive stone square were centers of life for much of colonial Cuba's history. Now the building is decaying through lack of attention, with weeds gaining footholds between the towers' large blocks. Services are still regularly conducted for the few left who seek religion.

originally built inside the harbor mouth, which was guarded by forts on either side of the water. A heavy iron chain was drawn across at night to keep foreign boats out. As was the fashion of the day, the city was protected by a stone wall, remnants of which remain by the water.

Just inland from the harbor is Cathedral Square, dominated on the northern side by the grand old Cathedral of Havana. Even though the cathedral appears closed, with its massive doors bolted shut and weeds growing from the cracks of its crumbling façade, a small side door admits worshipers to mass on Sundays, Mondays, Wednesdays, Fridays, and Saturdays. Outside, the cobblestone area directly in front of the church is always a busy center. Just to the left of the cathedral, in a building that has had numerous uses over the centuries, is the Patio Restaurant with its breezy open-air tables in front and lovely fountain inside. Legend has it that when the structure was a home, the first mango tree in the New World was planted where the fountain now splashes. Across the square from the restaurant is the graphic arts workshop, where almost every afternoon artists can be seen creating their designs on large smooth stones and then transferring the forms to paper. Mainly revolutionary in style, the prints sell for about $30.

Many travelers correctly note that Spanish cities tend to look alike. Some of the striking similarities are intentional. Rather than leave development to chance, King Philip II issued an ordinance on architecture in 1573. The edict laid out in fine detail how new towns should be planned. For instance, ". . . . the main plaza should be in the center of the town and of an oblong shape, its length equal to 1½ times its width, as this proportion is best for festivals in which horses are used and other celebrations. . . . it shall be no smaller than 300 feet long . . . or bigger than 800 feet long . . . a well-proportioned medium-sized plaza is 600 feet long and 400 feet wide. The four principal streets are to leave the plaza at the middle of each of its sides and two side streets are to meet at each of its corners. The four corners of the plaza are to face the four points of the compass, so the streets leaving the plaza are not exposed to the four principal winds."

Obviously, there are vast differences between Havana today and the city before 1959. Many are completely apparent and even blatant. Others are subtle and will never be noticed by any except the most careful observer. Usually one quickly notices the absence of advertising billboards. All the old signs that used to promote the

Granma, the boat that brought Castro and his followers to Cuba in 1956, has been practically deified by a country searching for revolutionary symbols.

familiar American and Cuban products are now devoted to propaganda messages. New signs are constructed "Burma-Shave" fashion, giving the driver a message in depth about the glories of the First Party Congress, praising the Angola involvement, or honoring the twentieth anniversary of the landing of *Granma,* the boat that brought Castro and his followers back to Cuba in 1956. Individual billboards exhort Cubans to action with a vast array of admonitions: "Cleanliness and Beautification Are the Tasks of the C.D.R"; "C.I.A. Assassins"; "The Sixth Grade—A Task for All"; "Men Die—The Party Is Immortal."

Billboards are but one means of getting out the government message. Freedom of the press is a concept that was quickly consumed by the Revolution. The official position now is that the press, including Cuba's two television channels and its many radio stations, is an arm of the government and must disseminate information as the government decides. Jorge Lopez, editor of the afternoon newspaper *Juventud Rebelde,* explains, "The press is established to promote the history and culture of the people, but we never think the press is the judge of society, as you do. It is a reflection of what people think." A typical radio break, when U.S. listeners would expect a commercial and station identification, has a Cuban announcer saying, "From Havana, Cuba, [pause] first free territory in America." There are two countrywide newspapers: *Granma,* the morning paper and official organ of the Communist Party of Cuba, and the just mentioned evening newspaper, which is associated with the Union of Young Communists, *Juventud Rebelde* (Rebel Youth). In all cases, the newspapers and broadcast stations give the official position on domestic news, present the Cuban government's view of world news, censor information they want to keep from the people, and have for years presented a constant one-sided attack on the Yankee imperialism of the United States. As a convenience to guests, the government distributes free copies of the weekly English-language news in review at various Havana hotels. For a journalist, the omissions are as interesting as the inclusions.

Tourists who might have been in Havana before 1959 will also be surprised at the lack of slums, beggars, and prostitutes. The miserable housing was simply torn down after the Revolution. Naturally there was considerable difficulty afterward in relocating the residents. Anyone who has seen Caribbean slums knows how bad living can be. Cuba was no different. Great sections around Havana festered inside tin-walled, tin-roofed shacks with no electricity, water, or other utilities. Improving such conditions has been a constant problem for the government, one that is still unsolved and expected to remain so for another twenty years. Upgrading existing slum conditions to something better, having a population grow from 6 to 9½ million since 1959, and making only limited monies to pay for construction have been just some of the planners' plagues. There are still a few very small areas near Havana with substandard housing. Of course, there is a case to be made that most housing in Cuba is substandard. If the housing is compared to that of an industrialized Western nation, that is no doubt true. Rarely is there a home with a nuclear family. Most of the dwellings in house-poor Cuba are filled with aunts and uncles, married brothers and sisters, and some grand-parents. Conveniences are few, the rooms are small, and the waiting lists for new apartments are impossibly long.

Begging, pimping, prostitution, and gambling were about the first activities to disappear after the Revolution. Strict laws forbidding all of them remain in effect today. Industrial training classes were set up for any prostitutes who decided to stay and learn a new line of work. A very mild form of begging is just now beginning to surface. Around the tourist hotels it is increasingly common to see a few school-age boys shyly walking up to foreigners and asking for a ball-point pen, cigarettes, or a souvenir. In the same areas later at night a new development in the last year has been the appearance of a few girls looking for dates. The fee is more often goods than money—in a society where consumer products are very hard to obtain and a small transistor radio costs 180 pesos ($225 U.S.). The authorities do crack

Birthplace of the Revolution is how Cubans describe Santiago's Moncada Barracks. Fidel's abortive attack on July 26, 1953, was the first act by his followers that finally led in 1959 to Batista's ouster. Bullet holes were plastered over after the fight and uncovered when Castro gained power and converted the army barracks into a museum and school.

down and some of the girls have been seen in the early hours sitting around police stations.

One aspect of Cuban life recognizes the housing shortage and sexual realities. In a culture with little privacy, no automobiles for young people, no apartments for singles, and little mobility, the problem of dating creates some severe strains. One solution, which has been employed increasingly since the Revolution, is the *posada*. Operated by the government throughout Cuba, these motel-like enterprises charge couples about one peso an hour for a room, food and drinks extra, no questions asked. Saturday night is so popular that posada lines often go around the nearby corners.

Many other developments are common throughout Cuba, the result of central planning. New construction is practically universal. A central eight-lane freeway that will link Santiago in easternmost

Oriente to Pinar del Río in the west is in various stages of completion. For the first time it will be possible to make high-speed, reasonably safe motor trips between major cities. In every region, schools, industries and apartment buildings are under construction. A massive amount of money, for Cuba, is allocated for these basic improvements. In 1974, DESA, the construction ministry, spent 1¼ million pesos on new projects. That is only a fraction of the actual value of these projects because so much work is done by unpaid volunteers, and those workers who are paid receive minimal wages. Cuba is now in the midst of her first Five-Year Plan, which calls for rapid development, expansion, and industrialization in practically all areas. The 1976 plunge in world sugar prices drastically affected the country's income and severely curtailed some of the programs. The present government is committed to reducing the island's dependency on sugar by turning Cuba into a Caribbean industrial center.

Schools are going up at a feverish pace. Already over 300 secondary schools in the countryside are in use and 800 more are planned. Much of this construction is aimed at coping with the explosive increase in young people. Over half of the people in Cuba were born since the Revolution. School attendance is now mandatory through the sixth grade, and the Ministry of Education is adding years to that requirement on a regular basis. By 1980, compulsory attendance will increase to the ninth grade and will later be expanded to high school. The reason for this deliberate approach to education is that the Revolution took over a country where about a fourth of the population was illiterate and many *campesinos* dropped out of school by the third grade.

The countryside in Cuba remains beautiful, even with the construction and activity. Sugarcane dominates the roadsides, but there is much more to see. Unlike other Caribbean islands, which are either low outcroppings of coral, or which feature rugged volcanic peaks, Cuba is geographically varied. Surprisingly flat for such a large island, most of its terrain consists either of gently rolling agricultural land or level plains that make sugar harvesting ideal. Three principal mountain ranges break up this view. To the west, in Pinar del Río, the Organos are in the center of a tobacco-growing and tourist region. The little town of Viñales rests on a valley floor surrounded by such a strange collection of peaks that they appear to have been dropped down, one at a time, by some gigantic hand. The mountains here are composed of porous limestone that has eroded over the centuries, leaving sharp, sheer, jagged cliffs filled with caves. Palm trees grow from craggy openings hundreds of feet up.

Near the center of the country, along the southern coast, lie the Escambray Mountains. A beautiful grouping of tropical peaks, the Escambray are generally remembered in Cuba today as the center of counterrevolutionaries in the 1960s who tried to duplicate Castro's successful rebellion from other mountain strongholds. Finally, all the way to the eastern tip of the island, in Oriente, are the impressive Sierra Maestra, which, with sister ranges, make up the most inaccessible areas remaining in Cuba. Pico Turquino, the country's highest point reaches 6,560 feet. The Sierra Maestra hold a special place in Cubans' hearts, partly because of their size, the mystery that accompanies the unknown, and their beauty. Since 1959 they have attained added romantic appeal through a generation of propaganda as the cradle of the Revolution.

Fidel Castro and his Revolution both began near the Sierra Maestra, in the easternmost province of Oriente. In 1976, the government divided Cuba's six old provinces into fourteen new ones. Now Oriente is only the area around Cuba's second city, Santiago. The Sierra Maestra mountains are mainly in the newly named

Isabel Martinez guides guests through the Colonial Museum of Santiago, one of the oldest buildings in the Americas. Built between 1516 and 1520, the elegant old structure on the city's main square has had various commercial and residential functions over the centuries, and now houses period furniture in the style of a Spanish gentleman's family.

To casual observers, little will appear changed in Cuba. Enramada Street in Santiago is still the city's main shopping area, with neon signs, miniskirts and heavy traffic. However, the articles for sale have changed vastly.

Guarding the entry to Santiago harbor, El Morro fortress stands as a reminder of the Spanish presence in the New World.

Granma Province, and the far east is now Guantánamo Province.

Santiago, with over 300,000 people, is an important port and commercial center. The country's second oil refinery, seized from Texaco, is located in the area, as are a large cement factory, the old Bacardi rum plant, a major brewery, and many other enterprises. It has remained an important city from the earliest days of Spanish settlement in the beginning of the 1500s. Santiago was the second site chosen by the colonists. They had previously left a few people at Baracoa, around a harbor on Oriente's north coast.

Diego Velázquez and his 300 or so followers served two purposes for Spain: they could look for gold, and, by their presence, tend to legitimize Spain's claim to sovereignty over the area. Soon after arriving in Cuba, Velázquez chose as his second location one of the island's great natural harbors, at Santiago. A dramatically rising rock cliff stands over the narrow ocean entry. Then, just inside the harbor mouth, a large secluded bay unfolds. Offering perfect anchorages from storms and a defensible vantage point atop the bluff, Santiago became the center of Spain's early Cuban settlements. Work began immediately to build a massive stone fort, El Morro, at the peak of the hill. Observation and gun positions would look out to sea, across the narrow strait, and inland to the bay. Now a tourist attraction, the fort attests to the Spaniards' ingenuity, stamina, bit of madness, and determination to make their place in the New World.

Of course, Cuba looks considerably different today from what it did on October 28, 1492, when Columbus and his men gazed out on the largest, and to him the most beautiful, island in the Caribbean. Only a few days earlier, the Spanish crew had been at the point of turning back and giving up their quest for a short sea route to the Orient. Columbus had told them they should sail for three more days, and if land was not sighted, they would return. On the second night after that, at about 2 A.M., a lookout scanning the horizon by moonlight saw in the distance the shimmering silhouette of San Salvador, one of the Bahama Islands. After a brief exploration, the Europeans encountered the natives, whom Columbus called Indians, so sure was he that he had found the way to the Indies, Japan, and China. The Indians, placid Arawaks who had once inhabited all the Caribbean islands and who now held only the northern ones against encroachment by the fierce, cannibalistic Caribs, received the Spaniards in reverence and called them "men from heaven." After a few days, the three small ships set sail to the southwest and soon found Cuba towering above them. Mountains could easily be seen from the boats and lush wooded vegetation was spread in a green tableau behind the glistening white beaches. Over forty different kinds of building woods pushed their way upward through the leaf-carpeted forest—mahogany, ebony, rosewood, cedar, and Spanish elm. One early observer suggested that an agile climber could make his way from one end of Cuba to the other and never have to touch ground.

Time and steady occupation by growing numbers of settlers altered the richness of the scene. It took about 200 years to significantly change the impression of a basically uninhabited island, so small and concentrated were the towns. Virgin forests pushed in closely to the tiny Spanish villages. Then sugar became important and great clearing efforts finally denuded Cuba of her lush forest growth. Sugar production needed vast areas cleared to the ground for planting. Then trees had to be felled to provide lumber for the houses of the masters and slaves, timber for the sugar mill buildings, and, most of all, logs for the fires that burned constantly during harvest to distill the syrup into sugar crystals. The trees went, row upon row, until there were none left. So rapid and so complete was the work that islands to the east of Cuba actually had their climates permanently affected. St. John and St. Croix in the U.S. Virgin Islands are now basically deserts, with no appreciable rainfall. Apparently the forests that were eliminated had provided a surface cool enough to cause clouds to form and water to fall. Such a severe alteration did not occur in Cuba, which has a far greater land mass to heat and cool and assist in cloud formation. However, Oriente has experienced recurring dry spells in recent history. A tragic drought, now in its fifth year, continues to reduce sugar production. In eastern Cuba today, instead of hardwood forests, the scene is filled with miles of swaying sugarcane plants, often twice head height. Mills dot the landscape, the spindly chimneys announcing their presence on the horizon.

Visitors to Cuba will notice limited physical changes. Few new buildings have altered Havana's basic look. Certainly there is a vast amount of additional construction going on in the countryside, but the overall appearance of Cuba is much the same. There are differences between 1959 and now, more social and ideological than physical. The following chapters will examine those various areas of change.

Working and Living Conditions

2

> I am convinced that in no other Latin American
> country is there the austerity that we have here. That is an
> elemental principle. Here all the people know is
> work. They know nothing but work.
>
> —*Fidel Castro*

Work is a fundamental obligation of the people for themselves and the state under the system that Fidel Castro and his supporters have instituted. So vital is that obligation, according to the government, that a recent anti-vagrancy law requires all able-bodied males under sixty-five not in school or in the military service to be employed. Failure to comply with a warning results in a sentence to an agricultural work farm.

The reasoning behind these seemingly harsh rules is that a small, threatened, poor, industrializing country requires every hour of production it can get. And it is a violation of the socialist principles for an able person to live from the efforts of another. The Cuban Revolution is firmly on record as favoring the old Communist precept "From each according to his ability, to each according to his needs." Reality has brought about some modifications to other Communist teachings. At first, it was believed that moral incentives would suffice for workers to do the best job possible, perform to the fullest, accept only what was needed, and volunteer for extra jobs freely. A few years of that experiment taught the Cuban planners that people are still people, even when they are imbued with patriotism in an ongoing revolution. Monetary incentives, smacking of the castoff capitalistic principles the country was so anxious to discard, were found necessary to keep people producing at reasonable levels.

As the Revolution gained control of all aspects of Cuban life, the nature of the economic consequences became apparent. The Soviet model was followed in setting up government ownership of all income-producing enterprises. Cubans can own anything they can buy or anything they already had—homes, automobiles, appliances, clothes, etc.—but cannot own a business that makes money. Income production is a monopoly of the state. Every person who works in Cuba works for the state and receives a salary from the government. Fidel's hard-working, cattle-raising brother Ramón summarized the present attitude in Cuba by saying, "We are not living for a sweet life—living to be drunk, to smoke marijuana, to use cocaine—we live for work."

It would be good to pause here and recognize a fundamental difference between a Cuban's view of government and the attitude a typical American citizen holds of his state, local, and federal governments. For many complex reasons, Americans view government with skepticism and disdain. Politician jokes abound in our culture. Thomas Jefferson may have started us on that track by suggesting that the best government is the least government. As all levels of U.S. government have mushroomed, the gap between governors and the governed has fostered increasing distrust. A great many Americans, fearing their government and the secretive things it does, try to keep more than an arm's length from it whenever possible.

In a socialist or Communist country, the propaganda apparatus works daily to convince the citizens that they *are* the government. The concept is one of ownership. Since all the industries, apartments, agriculture, retail stores, and other businesses are owned and operated by the government, the people own the country and its wealth cooperatively. In Cuba the bureaucrats who run the country are managers—no more—and can never own any more than any other citizen.

The problem in Cuba is the same as that in all the other Marxist countries. Since the government has not reached the ideal of everyone working fully and producing enough to supply consumer goods to satisfy everyone (their explanation is that so much wealth has to be diverted to the military to protect the country from imperialism), there is a constant struggle between bureaucrats and citizens who want more goods at cheaper prices. Cubans do not live in a vacuum, without memory. Older people remember the capitalist days and what was available. Anyone can observe the streets recalling that once they were filled with autos and now there are few. Cubans are also exposed to outside publications, radio, and foreign visitors, all revealing conditions in the international marketplace.

For the contemporary Cuban worker, life is not necessarily overly hard, as it might be in a truly undeveloped country (which Cuba is not), but the days are full. The country is on a 5½-day workweek. Absenteeism is frowned upon. Not normally a problem, it is slightly on the rise now as a symbol of protest against the years of shortages. Under a system where so few avenues of public protest are available, work slow-downs or absenteeism are possible as a mild show of displeasure. Any overt act against work is an act against the state, and is illegal. In addition to the 5½ days, a Cuban with the proper revolutionary spirit also volunteers for unpaid weekend work, usually in construction projects.

Pay for regular work is handled differently from the method in the vast majority of countries. All transactions are in cash. After the Revolution, banking practically ceased to exist, and banks are now used simply as safe places to hold money. Now, every two weeks, on payday, cash is taken to each work center by a paymaster carrying a box or bag, often accompanied by an armed guard.

As one would expect in a regulated economy, the government sets the salaries. The peso is officially valued at $1.25 U.S. (In reality, it has virtually no value on the world market, but the unofficial or black market rate, when available, centers around 5 pesos per U.S. dollars.) Wages start at a low 85 pesos a month for unskilled labor. Typically, sugarcane cutters begin at this wage. More often, manual laborers make 100–125 pesos monthly. From there, salaries rise in relation to education, job, and skills. A factory worker can make 200 pesos while a manager may reach 250, and a few make 300. The highest wages for regular work go to medical doctors who are heads of departments and also teach at the University of Havana medical school. They get both salaries and can make up to 750 pesos a month. In Cuba, that is a very, very high payment. Cuba has perhaps 60,000 professionals who stayed after the Revolution in a labor force of 3 million who receive "historical salaries" as a reward. If a worker remained in his old job, he was allowed to keep his old wage, unless he had over the years asked for a job transfer or voluntarily renounced part of his high pay as an "un-revolutionary" amount. Entertainers, sugar mill foremen, and factory technicians are just some of the workers who still get up to 700-1,000 pesos monthly. The system is dying as laborers retire or change jobs. With rents fixed at no more than 10 percent of the household head's salary, and food costs fixed at about 25 pesos a month per couple, there is usually money left over from most wages.

No matter how much money a family has, it finds itself equal before the Cuban rationing system, which includes practically all food and consumer goods. The result of this rationing is a new "queue culture"—agonizingly long lines for everything. Government officials, doctors, housewives, and street cleaners all stand together waiting for their turn to buy the same amounts of everything for sale—and they all hate it.

Rationing is the most often criticized aspect of Cuban life, condemned from the outside as tangible evidence of the government's failure to support its people and from within as an annoyance, a waste of time, and a serious limitation on the ability to "get ahead in life." Whenever a country resorts to rationing basic products in peacetime, it has to expect serious questioning and criticism.

Cuba's rationing is one of the most pervasive in the world. Not only are food items controlled, but also a considerable list of hard goods, gasoline, and the limited-shopping group items that include appliances such as TVs, washing machines, and refrigerators. Every Cuban has a packet of ration books, one for each category. The most important, and most used, is for food. An elaborate list of foods and amounts is published periodically, informing the people what they can buy at the various shops and supermarkets. Since prices are tightly controlled by the government, there is little risk that inflation will alter a family's annual food budget.

The following table contains a group of rationed food items, the amounts available to each person, the recent price, and the frequency with which the product can be purchased:

Item	Per Capita	Price in Centavos			Frequency
Beef	¾ pound	45¢ per pound			each ninth day
Chicken	1 pound	65¢ " "			monthly
Rice	5 pounds	20¢ " "			monthly
Sugar	4 pounds	7¢ " "			monthly
Coffee	1½ ounces	6¢ per ounce			weekly
Beans	20 ounces	18¢ per pound			monthly
Lard or vegetable oil	1½ pounds	24¢ " "	(lard)		monthly
		33¢ " "	(oil)		monthly
Canned milk	3 cans	20¢ per can			monthly *

* Children under seven and adults over sixty are entitled to one liter of fresh milk a day at 20¢ a liter. Every family of five members or more can buy half a liter of fresh milk daily.

The shopkeeper (center) passes a liter of milk to a boy as he takes his ration card to mark off the purchase. Only children under six years and the elderly over sixty are allowed fresh milk daily.

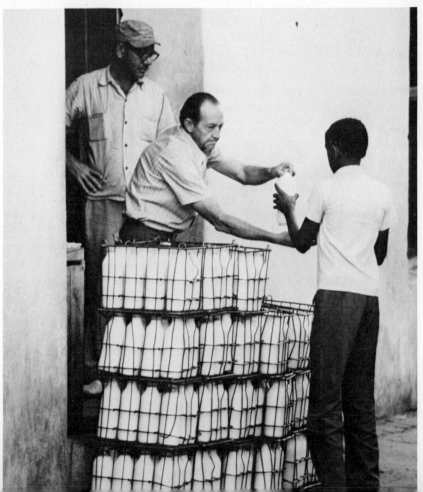

WARREN CENTRAL HIGH SCHOOL LIBRARY

Then there is a list of food items that can be purchased without frequency limitation. Those include root vegetables, catsup, mayonnaise, and canned goods such as beans, vegetables, fruits, etc. Finally, a list of nonrationed foods includes those that are more plentiful and those that Cubans do not like, such as fish. These free-purchase foods

Cubans complain that their best products from the sea are exported and they have to eat poorer quality fish. These packaged Soviet fish, destined for Cuban markets, are part of the reason for that complaint.

are eggs, seafood, flour, green vegetables, bread, fruits, crackers, butter, cream cheese, salt, vinegar, spices, and yogurt.

The safety valve on food rationing is restaurants. Any Cuban can eat out whenever he can afford it and order whatever the restaurant has that day. With more than one family member usually earning a salary, sufficient excess money is available for one or two restaurant meals a month.

Since rents and food prices are fixed and low, accumulating extra money is common. This is also facilitated by the absence of other consumer items to buy. So pent up is the anxiety to buy that the day a new, not previously seen product is displayed on a store's shelves, it

Refined white flour from the Soviet Union is unloaded at Havana harbor. Cuba imports its grains from various countries, and there is speculation that some U.S. grains sold to the Soviets might have been processed and shipped back to our southern neighbor.

San Rafael in downtown Havana, recently closed to automobile traffic, has been transformed into a "walking street." The limited shop choices do not deter customers who will stand in line to buy any new product.

is sold out. Buying seems unrelated to need or quality; the important thing is that it is there and for sale and there is money in hand to buy it. Recently some Soviet cuckoo clocks were set out at a formerly elegant jewelry shop in Havana that now features relatively cheap and unstylish rings and pins. Suddenly a line developed before the single salesgirl to pay forty-seven pesos for the overpriced plastic decoration. For the past two years the government has been taking advantage of this demand by systematically introducing some high-priced items into the economy. That way it siphons off some consumer tension and recoups excess pesos that were simply being held.

The quickest way to regain the extra money people are holding, and provide some happiness in the process, is with restaurants and entertainment. Cubans have always liked to eat out. Now they use the restaurants to indulge any craving they might have for such items as milk or beef. As with all other businesses, restaurants are operated by the government, formerly by INIT, the National Institute of Tourist Industries, and increasingly now under *Poder Popular,* the new representative government system. Quality varies as it always did, from stand-up counters along the highways to truly elegant Havana establishments featuring black-suited staff, china and crystal service, several entree choices, and a bill to match. Naturally, most habaneros choose something in between, with a variety of restaurants offering good-quality meals at reasonable prices. Placemats display the two INIT slogans "My work is you" and "Your right is to enjoy; our duty is to serve." After a few forty-five-minute waits, most customers wish the waiters would read the placemats.

An additional activity significantly altered by rationing is home entertaining. Since the amount of food is strictly limited to each person, rationing has almost ended home invitations except when everyone brings his own supplies. Being a gracious and generous host used to be the mark of a well-bred Cuban. Now it is practically impossible to invite anyone for dinner, very difficult to offer coffee, and quite expensive to serve drinks. Rum, still made in the Bacardi factory (now called Caney) and at a new Havana Club plant outside Havana, costs tourists $4-7 a bottle in duty-free shops but is $15-30 for Cubans. Beer is 60-80¢ in returnable bottles. The result is that people socialize at restaurants.

Food is only one of many rationed items. Most clothes, shoes, yard goods, and household products are available on a limited schedule. Each Cuban has a shopping letter, A through F. For industrial products, there is one day each six weeks when such purchases may be made, if the prospective buyer has the right coupon in his book. Working women, *trabajadoras,* are given one additional day of shopping during that period on a Monday or Thursday, and the best new products are displayed on those days. Each month, shops display calendars in their windows showing the shopping days for each shopping letter.

Rationing in Cuba is, without a doubt, one of the most complicated systems in the world. In March, 1977, the entire process was once again changed and new ration books distributed to each citizen. Under the revised rules, which even Cuban participants are finding difficult to comprehend, a woman gets sixteen yearly coupons and sixty-six trimonthly ones. With them she can buy one pair of good shoes a year and one pair of everyday or tennis-type shoes, one meter of good fabric or 1½ meters of average fabric, one blouse, and one skirt, or she can combine two of the above coupons to make one purchase of a ready-made dress or pair of slacks. She can use one of the trimonthly coupons to purchase a bra, panties, lipstick, compact, or cosmetics (when—rarely—they are available), or a pair of hose.

A Cuban man has yearly coupons to buy three of the following that cost over four pesos: a sports shirt, dress shirt, polo shirt, *guayabera* (Cuban dress shirt), or an item of exterior apparel. He can combine two of these coupons to purchase a pair of pants costing over twelve pesos. He also has coupons for a pair of pants worth under twelve pesos, one pair of shoes, a shirt for under four pesos, and a pair of work boots. The sixty-six trimonthly coupons for men will be used for underwear, handkerchiefs, pajamas, bathing suits, and such. As the head of a household, a man can also buy each year one replacement arm for a sewing machine, a blender, an espresso coffee maker, one bedspread, new upholstery for a piece of furniture, and a fan. His children have the right to buy two new school uniforms each year.

Large family purchases are even more complicated since they are controlled by the work centers. These items include apartment-size washing machines (the only size available), refrigerators, TVs, motorcycles, and sewing machines. To be able to get on the buying list for these appliances, a Cuban must appear at a monthly "Electrical Effects Assembly" where he works. There he, and others, state their need for such an appliance. After considering need, work attitude, revolutionary spirit, etc., the group votes for one worker for each appliance. Those winners then go on to a meeting of three or four work centers where the participants once again state their needs. The final winner is placed on a list at the store where he takes his money and gets his product.

Automobiles are in a special category, since the government decides who can purchase them. They are now limited to professionals, who either have to have the cash or borrow from the government the approximate $5,000 cost.

Yet another innovation is a rule requiring a buyer to be physically present "to mark in the queue" for major purchases. Roll calls are taken at noon and 9 P.M. To retain a place in line, someone must answer when a name is called. One recent example had a man waiting for fifteen straight days, by appearing at the two appointed daily hours, to pay 160 pesos in advance for a suit that would be ready in four months. A slight bit of capitalism is creeping back into the system with people hiring others to attend the roll calls and "mark" for them.

One of the most interesting rationing quirks is the set of rules concerning married couples. To encourage marriage and in recognition that couples need extra rationing considerations for setting up a new household, special rights go to newlyweds. For instance, the couple gets to buy one new men's suit without standing in line, an alarm clock, two sheets, two pillowcases, and a bedspread (practically impossible outside marriage), nail polish (nonexistent otherwise), one pair of men's pajamas, and one "baby-doll" nightgown, four towels, ten cases of beer for $7.90 each, and five bottles of rum for nine pesos each. These incentives for marriage were so great that what some Cubans began to call their "National Reno" developed—getting married just to get the products, and then getting a divorce three months later for forty pesos. The government realized what was happening and kept the mandatory three-month wait but raised the divorce fee to a hundred pesos to discourage the practice.

To discourage an old Cuban custom of common-law marriages, the government grants those couples living together first and later getting married only the cheap liquor purchases. All the other products are denied. Additionally, if a Cuban's work or study effort wins a trip abroad, the winner can take his legal mate free, but not his common-law partner.

Lines are the most visible feature of Cuban life. At the old Woolworth's store in downtown Havana, renamed Galiano's, prospective customers wait for the afternoon counter diners to finish.

Everyone resents rationing. One friend commented, "Of course we hate to stand in lines. It is a waste of everyone's time. Generally, a shortage doesn't cause the wait, but inefficiency and inadequate numbers of salespeople." It is also a matter of organization. In Galiano's, the old Woolworth store in Havana, yard goods and pizza counters are always packed, with lines winding around half a dozen departments. Simultaneously, nearby counters will often have two salesgirls standing for hours without any business.

Service is faster at gas stations because there are too few cars to cause delays. If a Cuban is fortunate enough to get on the buying list for an automobile, his choice will be limited to about three models—a Soviet-built Fiat called a "Jubilee" or a Peugeot or Fiat made in Argentina. Each costs about $5,000. Depending on engine size, a new car receives a monthly gas ration which accompanies the car for its life. Generally, it amounts to about sixty gallons a month priced at 60¢ a gallon. Additional gas is available at $2 a gallon.

Rationing permeates Cuban society and is the object of almost universal criticism abroad. The government has an explanation for its need beyond the obvious problems of insufficient funds and distribution facilities to provide all the goods that the country seeks. Ilidio Sabatier, an INRA (National Institute of Agrarian Reform) economics official, says, "Rationing does not necessarily mean shortages; rather, it is our way of guaranteeing equality. With more money around now, there is more demand, and our rationing system assures everyone the same access to goods, no matter how much money he has."

That equality is a reality. The doctor who makes 750 pesos a month can buy exactly the same as the poorest 85-peso cane-cutter. If hunger does exist, it is more a craving for particular items that are not on the shopping list than a calorie deficiency. Starvation is not a problem in Cuba as it still is in other Latin American countries. There is malnutrition, but it results principally from ignorance instead of any lack of food. At the Polyclinic in Alamar, of each 1,000 children examined, 33 suffer from malnutrition and 44 from overweight. The two conditions are really two sides of the same coin. The Cuban diet is almost entirely contrary to good health and the Cuban climate. Fruits and fresh vegetables are disdained; fish is looked down upon as something to be eaten when beef, pork, and chicken are not available; refined sugar (the mainstay of the Cuban economy) is dumped on everything to such an extent that it is probably slowly sapping the people of their energy and their health. If a Cuban has sweetened canned orange juice for breakfast, he typically adds two to five spoons of sugar. Yogurt, in itself a beneficial food popularized after Cuba's association with East Europeans, has much of its value cancelled out by the addition of half a dozen helpings of sugar. Rice, which has nourished Orientals for centuries, is almost worthless when polished, as it is in Cuba. And so it goes. By tradition, culture, and the absence of propaganda to the contrary, Cubans continue a detrimental diet that, coupled with almost universal cigarette smoking, is causing cancer, rotting teeth, diabetes, and numerous other diseases that a controlled system has the power to stop.

Although food items are limited, they are available. Other products are simply not to be had. If a homeowner wants to paint an aging home, he may wait two years for the material. Toilet seats are among the most elusive items in the country. Upon leaving a major hotel, the visitor is unlikely to see one until he reaches another hotel. It seems Cubans have stood on them for years and broken the old ones, and since the toilets were originally from the United States and the embargo prohibits any trade, no replacements ever came. Similarly, toilet paper and napkins are usually seen only in good hotels and restaurants. Sometimes supermarkets are without toilet tissue for months. No one can ever explain its absence.

Such a system of shortages makes a ripe condition for black-

Reminders of Soviet-Cuban cooperation are ever present on the island. This billboard says: "Long live the 25th Congress of the Soviet Communists." Cubans appreciate Soviet aid, but show little warmth for their benefactors.

Soviet publications fill Cuban newsstands, as this policeman knows. The materials offer low-cost steady propaganda on the benefits of socialism and the evils of capitalistic exploitation.

marketing. When one friend was asked if such practices existed, he leaned over and whispered, "I can tell you that it not only exists, but it is *intense*. If you had the money and wanted it, I am sure that in a few days I could produce for you on the Cuban black market a pink elephant with spots. Not only can you specify items that you want, but you can even get the right brand name. Name the brand of Scotch or tape recorder and it is available. Currently the most popular thing is Lee blue jeans. They are bringing eighty pesos a pair on the black market." The items find their way into Cuba via a variety of routes. Tourists provide some and diplomats and sailors others. Even the East European technicians who have "diplomatic store" privileges have been known to sell a few items here and there. Trading in currency seems less common, but there is a brisk business in goods.

Grand larceny has occurred, but it is extremely rare, if court records can be believed. Where would a truck hijacker sell a load of television sets when all the neighbors know who is on the factory buying lists for TVs? More common is the petty thievery resulting from people trying to get more than their share of existing goods. For instance, a Cuban might go into a shop operated by a friend, select his purchases, hand over his ration card, and have the friend only pretend to mark off the item. Then he could legally buy the products again. Another store might receive 1,000 liters of milk, sell only 950 legally with ration books, and black-market the rest, keeping the difference between the legal and illegal price. These instances have happened, and the government, through the Commercial Ministry of the Interior, has people making the rounds of stores, checking for thefts. First penalties are often mild, but a second offense is almost a sure trip to prison.

As high as feelings often run against rationing, even they are superseded by the frustrations Cubans have in seeking a few basic services. Americans complain, justifiably, about the general demise of quality and pride among craftsmen, but they can still pick up the yellow pages and choose from columns of plumbers or electricians anxious for the work. A Cuban with a small problem suddenly has an even larger one in trying to get it solved. The entire service field is a serious weakness in the Cuban economy.

Since the government is the only employer, all the craftsmen work for the various ministries. If a Havana apartment dweller has a plumbing problem and reports it, even a simple repair will usually take several months. That is how long the waiting list is for service appointments. When parts are needed, the situation becomes critical. Most of the pre-1959 fixtures, appliances, elevators, generators, etc., are vintage U.S., and, again, the trade embargo prohibits selling replacements. The solution has been to fabricate needed parts, buy similar new ones from Japan, Canada, or Europe, or get them from the U.S.S.R. or the other bloc countries. In the end, it is the consumer who suffers. Owners anxious to maintain aging homes face similar exasperation. No replacements are available for broken parts, no materials available for building or renovation, no help available to assist with the work. People are not supposed to work for other people in a Communist state . . . people work only for the state.

Typically, things get done the way they always do under stress, with ingenuity. If one man knows plumbing, he trades some of his time and knowledge for those of a person whose talent he needs. However, the barter system is inefficient and was replaced thousands of years ago by another kind of exchange—money—that is also used in Cuba. Anywhere else it would be called capitalism, but that is not a word to be lightly tossed around in Cuba. It is in these personal areas that people are victimized most by the collective system. Without the competition and pressure of free enterprise, the craftsmen do what people with security have done for years—they work slowly, keep regular hours, and do only what they have to, and the country's services degenerate daily.

The government has recognized the problem here and has inaugurated a rather remarkable solution. A new law was announced in October, 1976, legalizing private enterprise in limited sectors. It is still illegal to buy a product and resell it at a profit, but individual operation of certain service businesses is allowed. Some examples of the new service categories are hairdressers, gardeners, automobile mechanics, shoeshine boys, and seamstresses. All pay a monthly tax to be licensed, the only people in Cuba who are taxed besides foreign enterprises. A manicurist is taxed fifteen pesos a month, while an auto mechanic pays twenty-five. Whatever they make on their own, they keep. One worker recently charged a friend ten pesos to wire a fish tank light, which shows how rapidly capitalism returns when it is allowed.

Enrique Oltuski, a pre-Revolution fighter who has held several ministerial posts, discussed the new system. "We've made plenty of economic mistakes and everyone has had to pay for them with

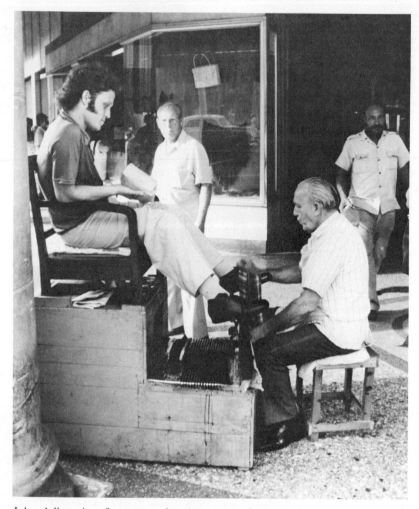

John Adlar, sixty-four, pays the government five pesos a month for a shoeshine license, charges forty centavos a shine, and clears about eight pesos daily. He is happy in his role as an independent vendor, saying it helps supplement his pension.

shortages and delays. One segment of the economy has to wait for another to catch up to schedule. We knew people were waiting for two to three months after contacting a government agency for repairs. So, we returned to a little capitalism to solve the problem. People may work harder when they can keep the money. This doesn't mean that we aren't still dedicated to communism. It simply means we are trying to ease the shortage by trying to meet a need for the

On the first day street-vendor licenses were sold, thousands of applicants lined up in Havana. This return to one-man business is viewed by the government not so much as returning to capitalism as serving some unmet needs.

people." In the first month of operation, 2,000 people took out licenses to be street peddlers in Havana.

Retirement is an interesting problem for Cuba. It is a concept that a Marxist government has to deal with because of the humanitarian aspects of providing full social services to its people and rewarding workers for the years of labor. Yet Cuba is hard-pressed to afford retirees at this time. They take up living space, require food and other commodities, and receive money though they are no longer working. These total up as a deficit in a country struggling to make monthly ends meet. But a retirement system is in operation. Men retire at sixty and women at fifty-five, each allocated a pension based on earnings while employed. Payments begin at about 100 pesos monthly and can reach 400 a month for doctors. Retirement is not mandatory and a person can continue working until death. Most often, retirees live with other family members and add their pensions to the family income. The idea of retirement homes is repugnant to Cubans. Cynics say the government lets retirees leave the country so they won't have to be supported. The number of émigrés does not fully justify this charge, although it is true that working-age Cubans are prohibited from leaving the country, while retirees sometimes receive permission to join their families abroad.

People who look for a one-sentence description of Cuba will be disappointed. The country is complicated and ever-changing. Work and constant talk about the Revolution are certainly common denominators, even to the point of being tiresome. One often gets the impression that Cubans continue the incessant dialogue and propaganda barrage about the virtues of revolutionary life for fear that if they stopped the talk, the Revolution might vanish. It would be unkind and inaccurate to characterize life as dreary, but the work hours are long, shortages are real, and the many activities, freedoms, and possessions that Americans consider necessary to happiness are either limited or unavailable. And still, the typical Cuban, brimming with confidence and a healthy dose of propaganda, stands convinced that he is contributing those long hours as his part of building the "New Society" and the "New Man."

In discussing this one warm afternoon at the Experimental Graphics Workshop just off Cathedral Square in Old Havana, a young artist, Diana Balboa, listened attentively to the charges that work, life, conversation, and art all seemed so somber these days. After only a short pause, she explained it all. "You see, in Cuba, happiness is very serious."

The Home Life

3

> Man doesn't need much to live. We have some
> facilities here: fishing, hunting, movies, if necessary. The
> clothing we use is usually a uniform. There is no
> need to change suits all day if we go out. We are all
> uniformed. We have all we need.
>
> —*Fidel Castro*

The "Maximum Leader"'s idealism and the reality of rising expectations may, in this case, be at odds. Cubans do not feel they have all they need, and the pressures for more consumer products continue to increase and cause friction between the government and the people. Private grumbling about the country's constant shortages equates the shortages with the heavy military expense drain and the new African experiments. Cubans do support the government and trust Fidel to lead them wherever he thinks is needed, but they are beginning to question a poor country's ability to support overseas military operations. If these excursions become regular, it will be fascinating to see whether Cubans resent the costs, or whether pride in the sudden world reputation as a military power offsets any negative reactions.

The whole area of costs, prices, and the availability of goods and services is considerably different in a tightly controlled socialist economy. As mentioned, money is generally slightly in excess in most families, since there are more people earning salaries than there are things to buy. In a strange turnabout, money becomes almost

33

worthless. The paper and coins are there, but the things a person might like to spend them on are not. Society has provided the means for earning a medium of exchange, while the fruits of any exchange are at the end of years-long waiting lists. Such, then, are the frustrations of a Cuban couple, trying to get started in life, to buy the things they want, and to get an adequate place to live and begin a family.

Although working couples generally have the money they need to move ahead, as a group, teen-agers seem to suffer from a lack of funds. While capitalistic systems have part-time jobs that fill the period between being old enough to need money and leaving school to begin a career, Cuba has only full-time employment. So young people are usually short of cash for dating and small purchases. Some things are inexpensive—movies in Havana are one peso or under and less in the country, but rides five centavos—but some, like restaurants and bars, are expensive. Because of the amount of pressure and emphasis on education today, the required military service, and the anxiety concerning getting the first right job, young Cubans are delaying marriage up into their twenties. Some of the sexual revolution has arrived, but to a far less extent than in Western countries. Young men often confide that it is indeed possible to proceed past kissing with an unmarried girl, but usually only if going steady. Extramarital sex seems at least as common as elsewhere with many married men having in-town girl friends. In typical Latin-American fashion, such activity gets high marks among male friends, but the suggestion that wives might also have affairs is met with complete condemnation. In order to foster a better family life, the government has expressed disapproval of all such activities. This prompted a recent letter to the editor of a Jamaican newspaper suggesting that the writer could dispel any fears about Cuba exporting communism to his island. He said if Communists didn't like extramarital affairs, they had no chance of taking over in Jamaica.

When the time does arrive for marriage, it is performed at a civil service conducted before a government notary. In Santiago, the Palace of Matrimony is located in a former social club for Spanish-heritage residents, a fine old building located just across from the cathedral on the city's principal square. Weddings are held in the baroque ballroom, slightly seedy with plaster falling and paint peeling. If a couple wants a church wedding, it is certainly allowed, but the civil service must follow to make the marriage legal. In

Havana's Palace of Matrimony specializes in Saturday afternoon "assembly-line" weddings. One just-married couple waits with the government-supplied photographer for the taxi that will carry them away, while another couple climbs the stairs for their brief civil ceremony.

Havana the services are held in the elegant Palace of Matrimony on the formerly fashionable Prado. Every Saturday people gather outside to watch the steady line of taxis bring up to forty couples, in rented finery, to go through the assembly-line ceremony. One couple is often arriving as another, leaving, struggles to get into a small cab.

Upstairs, a tape recorder plays the "Wedding March," family and friends assemble to one side, a notary reads the appropriate section from the new Family Code, books are signed, and the five-minute service is complete. Afterward, the couple takes a brief honeymoon somewhere on the island, and then moves in with one set of parents while the long search for an apartment begins.

Looking for housing is serious business in Cuba. Every aspect of life is interlocked within the system. The work centers control apartment allocation. If a person is working, doing so satisfactorily and with enthusiasm, and if he has the right revolutionary spirit, he will usually get serious consideration for housing. His peer group of workers meets to assess the availability of units and needs of families before voting to determine who lives there. Similar votes are made to distribute buying rights for hard-to-get appliances such as refrigerators, televisions, and washing machines. Getting a house is practically out of the question, since they seldom change hands and are never sold. When a family with a home needs to move, it has to find a family in the same situation and trade.

The new look in Cuban housing is the growing number of mass apartment complexes being built on the fringes of major cities. Outside Santiago, the largest one so far was constructed by the Soviets to replace large areas of slum housing washed away by a hurricane. Just to the east of Havana, located directly on the ocean, is the second largest project. Called Alamar, it was actually begun before the Revolution. In 1971, the government started a massive expansion to make it a showplace. Already more than 25,000 people live there; it has been designed to accommodate 150,000 by 1982.

Alamar was planned as a city in itself, with shopping, social services, a polyclinic, schools, day-care centers, a factory complex, and recreational facilities. Blocks are filled with the uniformly shaped five-story apartments, differentiated by brightly colored wall motifs. The unique aspect of postrevolutionary Alamar is that it is being built by volunteer "micro-brigades." The idea is that each apartment building is operated by a work center, e.g., the Partagas cigar factory. At the factory, when construction is about to begin, the workers meet and elect thirty-three men and women to leave their factory jobs and labor for two years or more on the apartment. They still receive their factory salaries and will come back to their old jobs. Skilled professionals do difficult electrical and plumbing jobs and whatever

The old and new looks in Cuban housing are found in Santiago, where the Marimon slum is being replaced by the José Martí housing project, Cuba's largest single-apartment development. A 1960s hurricane demolished much of the huge slum and prompted the government to begin replacing it with new housing.

Sometimes modernization dreams exceed reality. At La Yaya in Villa Clara, the new apartment buildings are up and occupied, but services such as the rustic barber shop are still housed in makeshift wooden structures.

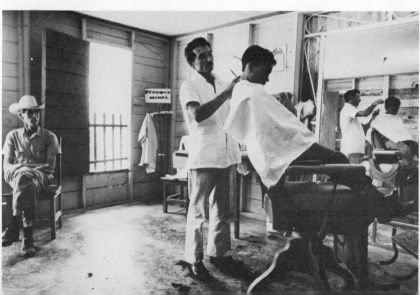

Construction architect Humberto Ramírez oversees the vast microbrigade-built project of Alamar, thirteen miles east of Havana. Already housing some 25,000 factory workers and their families, the ambitious complex is planned for a total population of 150,000.

the volunteers cannot manage. When the apartment building is completed, the workers meet to assess the housing needs of the factory. Requests are made, followed by a discussion and vote. Possibly the workers on the project will get preferential treatment in the voting, but not necessarily. The apartments are thus allocated and the new residents move in. They will then begin to pay 6 percent of the household head's salary. The unit will always belong to the government and always be managed by the work center. Utilities are cheap, but extra, except water, which is free up to one hundred liters a month a person. All the men and 60 percent of the women of the 5,000 Alamar families work. Two new twelve-story apartments are almost finished in an experiment to determine whether they or the standard five-story units are more efficient to build.

Alamar apartments, like others in Cuba, are small by U.S. standards, totaling only about 570 square feet, with either two-, three- or four-bedroom models. Floors, sink, shower stall, and laundry tub are terrazzo, and a counter-top gas burner is the only appliance supplied.

As in other large cities, apartments also house most Havana residents. The skyline is dotted with the slender buildings, most of them built before the Revolution. Apartments with a view were always more popular, and many of the most desirable ones were situated so the owners could sit on balconies and watch the ocean. When thousands of apartments became available as their occupants fled, lists were kept of all the units. (A source of unassuaged bitterness is that exiles were forced to leave all their property to the state, without compensation.) Cubans in need of housing were invited to come in and apply for one of the apartments. Some attempts were made to match the number in the family to the number of bedrooms, but the usual bureaucratic muddle created considerable confusion. A few lucky recipients picked up keys and opened fully furnished luxury apartments high above the city. After urban reform laws, rents were fixed at no more than 10 percent of one occupant's salary, no matter what it was, so anyone with an apartment could easily afford to keep it. Some people who had been paying rent all their lives were given free title to the property. Others were told they could pay rent for a fixed period, about ten years, depending on the amount, and would then receive title.

The city is now experiencing some new high-rise construction brought about by East European and Soviet technology. Yugoslav

Campesinos who gave up their land around the La Yaya community in Villa Clara have been relocated in new four-story apartment buildings. Clara Falcon is typical of many who received the apartments and furnishings free and live without rent.

expertise is responsible for a pair of twenty-story units just completed near the Plaza de la Revolución. No steel was used in the framework. Instead, prefabricated concrete slabs were made in a nearby field and pieced together on the job. An entire twenty-story superstructure went up in only thirty days. Next to them, three buildings have been joined together to make one gigantic 702 foot-long apartment with over 400 units.

Most of the new construction is of concrete and relatively plain and unadorned, but in no way like the long lines of gray buildings so common in East Europe. Often the slabs forming a balcony wall feature exposed aggregate stones in the concrete, and the Caribbean preference for bright paint gives the area visual flair. Maria and Manuel Muñoz and their three-year-old son, Erlan, live in a typical apartment in a twenty-story building. Too excited to wait longer, they moved in the day their unit was finished, although many other apartments were still under construction for several weeks. With only three in the family, they were allocated a two-bedroom unit. Manuel is a Communist Party member and also works for the Party on the regional level. His office is within walking distance. He is lucky, because most Cubans ride to work in buses, often crowded beyond belief, paying only five centavos for the service.

The elevator in the new building stops only at every third floor. That way the tenants never have to walk more than one floor in either direction. As usual, Manuel got the apartment through his work center, his Communist Party office. Available apartments and homes are placed with offices which then have committees to determine the housing needs of the employees. In theory, peers allocate housing to the neediest first, down to the childless newly married couple, who have the last priority for homes. The apartment in which the Muñoz family lives looks a great deal like all other new Cuban apartments. Design uniformity saves construction time and money. The entry is into the living room, which is about ten by twelve feet. Floors are terrazzo and walls plaster. Just to the right, through the doorless opening, is the kitchen, a narrow area open at both ends. The same terrazzo material comes up one wall and forms a concrete sink and counter top. Stained wooden cabinets hang over the sink. Around the far end, in a small cubicle, there is room for a refrigerator when the Muñozes get high enough on the list to buy one. Concrete laundry tub and shelves for canned food complete the area. Down the hall from the living room are two bedrooms and a bath. Terrazzo forms the shower stall. Each bedroom has a wooden bed, chest of drawers, and clothes closet, all locally made at the Alamar factory. Manuel will pay 6 percent of his salary as rent, about $17. The furnishings, which include a wooden couch, a table, and four chairs in the living room, cost 600 pesos, which he will pay off in a small monthly sum. When the interest-free loan for the furniture is repaid, the items will belong to the Muñoz family, even though this new apartment will always belong to the state, no matter how long they pay on it.

Two basic service problems will plague the Muñoz family in their new apartment, as they do families all over the island. Water and electricity, which are normally taken for granted, are always in short supply and often disrupted in contemporary Cuba. Typically, most urban Cubans live with water service only two hours a day. Essential amounts must be stored in bottles or cans until the following day. Certain faucets or hydrants on the street are operable for anyone who wants to go out with a bucket. Children can be seen every afternoon pulling wagons of water containers (garbage cans, fruit juice bottles, metal buckets, etc.) through the streets.

The water shortage is caused by several problems. First of all, there is the increase in population with the subsequent water demands of more people and more industry. Also, Cuba is a long but thin island, over 750 miles long, narrowing near Havana to a width of 30 miles. With only three main mountain ranges, the terrain is predominantly low and relatively flat. Consequently, rain that falls one day flows out to sea by the next. There is only one hydroelectric dam in the country and few locations suitable for the construction of others. The average yearly rainfall is forty to sixty inches in most areas, but it is lost in runoff. Additionally, the past five years have been atypical. Cuba's eastern region, Oriente, continues to suffer from a drought which seriously affects the sugar crop and leaves little water for the cities. No doubt the ultimate answer must be found in the sea which surrounds Cuba. Desalination, although expensive, is the only long-range prospect for providing fresh water to meet the ever-increasing needs.

Electrical disruptions are man-made. Here the basic problems lie in aging generating plants and how the people operate them. Many of the installations were built and equipped by U.S. firms before the Revolution. Since the Revolution, no U.S. spare parts have come into the country, nor have new generators. The trick until now has been for Cuban and Soviet engineers to keep the old General Electric gear operating. But the hour has come, and the generators are simply worn out. Every night a different area of Havana is selectively blacked out to conserve electricity; one duty of CDR representatives is to walk through neighborhoods asking that excess lights be turned off. Many dinners are candlelit by necessity. A driving tour of Cuba also has its dark moments. The blackouts seem diabolically to precede the car, arriving at motels just before the tourists. Inside unfamiliar buildings, they grope their way single file through obscure corridors, and like Diogenes follow a single candle flame.

There remain a large number of Cubans untouched by such problems because they live where electricity has still to be installed. For many of Cuba's rural residents deep in the countryside, life has barely changed. In the Sierra Maestra, the Victor Fernández family goes through each day much as campesinos always have. The Fernández family live in their *bohío,* the traditional country home, on the mountain slopes to the west of Santiago, overlooking the Caribbean. Before the Revolution, Victor, aged fifty, worked at the cement factory in Santiago. He and his wife, Delia, left the city to live on a small piece of mountain property owned by her family. Without a farm, Victor soon had to take a job. He found employment with the new National Institute of Agrarian Reform, INRA, doing odd manual labor jobs. Soon INRA gave him a small piece of land, forty by forty meters, just large enough for a bohio.

Victor built his home in the same manner taught to the Spanish settlers by Cuba's Indians. Small trees were cut and stripped to form the basic framework, including a pitched roof. The Indians used strips of palm, but Victor made the sides of his bohio with planks and

Blending the new with the old, Delia Fernández places her Cuban-made pressure cooker filled with the day's rice meal atop an open, wood fire in the cooking shed behind her bohio.

In this thatched-roof bohio in the Sierra Maestra foothills, Victor and Delia Fernández live with their seven children. Lacking all utilities, the family lives without heat, running water, or electricity. Twenty-three other people live in the two nearest bohios, almost making a community in themselves.

poured a concrete slab floor. Then he carefully thatched the roof with palm fronds, which insulate from the heat and serve to waterproof as well. Behind this basic structure of two bedrooms divided by a central hall, Victor built a separate thatched cooking-eating area, with a dirt floor.

Victor gets up early and leaves on horseback for his work. Often his day is occupied with the digging of fencepost holes for a new INRA cattle operation up the road. There are seven Fernández children, newborn to teen-age. In two other nearby bohios there are nine and ten children, making a total of thirty-two people within earshot. Most of the children are old enough to attend the nearby country school, but occasionally one or two choose to stay at home. The children walk down the hill and up one road to the bus stop. Considering the lack of electricity, running water, or any utility, the kids look amazingly clean and neat on their way out.

Delia spends her mornings taking care of the children who remain at home and doing chores around the small house. Some mornings she mops the floor because nine pairs of feet tracking in mud and dust keep it constantly dirty. Then she begins lunch. After carrying water from the well about 200 feet down the path, she stokes the wood fire to cook rice and beans, which are a daily staple.

Victor comes back before noon and wants coffee. He starts a separate wood fire outside by the outhouse, where he roasts some coffee beans in a skillet. Then they are ground and steeped into the rich, black, ultra-sweet syrupy brew that Cubans love. Everyone grabs some rice and beans and is off again. Delia will visit with her neighbors in the afternoon. The children will come home from school. One of the boys brings water for the evening and the girls wash a few clothes.

Five-year-old Domingo Fernández draws water for his mother. The fruits of the Revolution have yet to reach many bohio residents in the Sierra Maestra.

Delia Fernández calms her youngest child as neighbors look in on her open-air bedroom. Spartan conditions are still common in Cuba's rural areas.

Victor returns from work, often in the company of a friend, with whom he will smoke and talk. They sit in chairs on the ground at the front door while Delia makes supper, usually beans and rice again. After dark, the seven children pile into five beds in the two rooms, leaving space on one for Delia and Victor. With no lights and no radio or other diversion, the couple may choose to sit and talk for a while outside. A single wick stuffed into a kerosene-filled can provides the only illumination. It is a simple life and they appear to be happy with it.

The furthest thing from the Fernándezes' consciousness is a day-care center. For thousands of other Cubans, it is a pressingly important issue. Day care was a deliberate tool that the Revolution used to help achieve a stronger economic position. Established through the Cuban Women's Federation, day care is one of the primary mechanisms by which women can be used in the labor force. Cuba was similar to other Latin American countries in 1959. Most women who worked, worked as teachers, nurses, or domestics. After the U.S. embargo, all means were explored to strengthen the severely damaged economy. Men were already working to capacity, so the planners looked to the large untapped labor force, women at home. A new step-by-step program was implemented to use them. Factories were constructed, the women convinced that working was patriotic, incentives given in shopping and housing, and nursery schools established to care for the children who would be left by their mothers. So it was that day care came to Cuba. Beginning slowly in some of the old abandoned homes of the rich, the centers have proliferated to the point where they now have their own buildings designed to their specifications. Over 80,000 children are cared for daily, with an estimated need ten times that. Babies as young as forty-five days are accepted into the carefully controlled environment of the nursery section. As they grow, they are placed into classrooms by age until they reach primary school. To accommodate diverse schedules, the centers open at 6 A.M. for mothers who must bring children in before taking a bus a long way to work and remain open until 6 P.M. for parents who pick up children after office hours.

A child's day at one of the centers is full and active. No matter what hour he arrives, the youngster changes into a freshly washed and ironed school uniform and little issue shoes. This makes everyone look the same and saves the scarce street clothes from the inevitable

Day care is a reality for over 80,000 Cuban youngsters. The controversial system accepts children forty-five days old and keeps them until school age. Working mothers applaud the program, but sociologists worry that constant separation of parent and child creates problems.

Attention to grooming is taught and practiced in day-care centers. Female students studying to become teachers provide most of the care.

toll of play. Depending on age, the children play or attend morning classes, including political instruction. Cleaned up for lunch, all sit down to a hot meal prepared on the premises. Although touted as being nutritionally sound, like a meal at home, it is heavy on starches, with white bread, polished rice, and dessert usually included.

After lunch there is more play or classes until time for most of the children to leave. Showers for all follow and a change back into street clothes. Children leave as their parents' schedules dictate, with a few still waiting at 6 P.M. High school girls in teacher training assist the professionals at each center, and play with the children throughout the day, both in and outdoors.

Accepting the premise of day care, the Cubans seem to have paid careful attention to the needs of their small charges. One procedure requires a mother to stay at the center with her child until that child adapts to the others and gets through the day quietly. This also limits the disruption of the group by new children.

As expected, the system gets mixed reviews. Working women and women's liberation groups generally praise it as a great service to mothers. Critics point out that children are away from their parents, some from the age of forty-five days on, inside the system, and subject to the government line of indoctrination all their lives.

There is another Cuban institution flamboyant and die-hard enough to challenge the most ardent of American women's lib groups. It is the idea of *macho* and the street compliment, or *piropo,* both of which are practiced as a fine art along the roads of every Cuban town. Individual bravado is honed to perfection by boys and then replayed for years to the relative satisfaction of all concerned. If an automobile is involved, so much the better. Up ahead, the driver

Dolls are an important substitute for girls who spend years at day-care centers.

At Abdala Day-Care Center in Havana, a young boy models his play on the military. One of the problems with honoring a revolutionary military past is that it becomes a desirable model for future generations.

sees a female (age and attractiveness are not vitally important to the game, but refinements are, of course, allowed). A few honks on the horn accompany the decreasing car speed. Leaning way out, with admiring glances that seemingly envelop the girl, the driver delivers his well-rehearsed lines: "With skin as delicate as yours, you should be walking on the shady side of the street," or "I'm from Havana and new here and have never seen such beautiful girls as there are in ———." Playing the game without a car becomes more personal, since the boys and girls are closer and on relatively equal terms. Usually, it is good fun for all. The girls seem flattered by the attention and passers-by find it all entertaining. And, who knows, sometimes it works.

Macho as a concept is considerably more serious in Cuban society than elsewhere because the historical male notion of self and the new socialistic definitions are incompatible. Coping with these inconsistencies causes psychological strains. For example, Cuba has a Latin heritage and traditional roles are persistent. Women used to stay at home, tend children, seldom seek careers, and take a distinctly secondary position in all matters. For a number of reasons, the Revolution changed the legality of that condition. Now equality has been formalized by the government and the very fabric of Cuban domestic life has changed. As the state needed laborers and systematically encouraged women to go into the labor force, women left their hearths during office hours and entrusted their children to day-care centers. Education became open and mandatory for all, and women rapidly moved into fields once basically limited to men— medicine, law, engineering, etc. Then a new Family Code, part of the law of the land, stated that men were responsible for half the housework and care of children. The women began questioning men's rights to strut around acting as if they were in charge when the ladies were bringing in salaries and were equally active as revolutionaries. Obviously, domestic tranquillity has been jolted by such activities.

At the same time that so much was being said about the new equality for women, some serious examinations brought about new questions. Is encouraging women to leave their homes and children really liberating? Is working 5½ days a week in a dirty, loud factory an improvement in life-style? Further inquiries uncovered yet additional areas of contention. Of the 117 members of the all-important Political Bureau and Central Committee of the Communist Party, only 6 are women. Men continue to hold almost all high-responsibility jobs, such as factory manager and department head, and to exercise the leadership roles. When women do work, they are sometimes paid lower salaries. They are beginning to ask why they left home. Perhaps macho only changed its colors.

One area of men-women complicity brightens all of Cuba's streets. The miniskirt, a forgotten child of the Western fashion world, is still a great favorite throughout the island. So universal was the short skirt that it practically became the symbol and badge of the Revolution. One street-wise habanero explained its popularity. "Men like them for obvious reasons. Women like them because men look. And so little material is used to make them that the government likes them too."

One evening in a small town in western Cuba, two Cubans stood with the American photographer waiting for the sun to drop lower. Rapidly bored with the slow progress, they soon turned their attention to the female pedestrians, only to be disappointed that the first three literally spilled over their tiny black minis. With obvious disdain, one looked over and observed, "Cuban women are like lobsters; everything they eat goes to their tails."

The women in general are sensitive about their appearance and have had to deal with cosmetic shortages over the years. Other

Mini-skirted Elsa Cabrera washes clothes behind her Villa Clara bohio. Although she lives beneath electric wires, her home has no electricity and no running water. She would like to move to Havana, where she thinks her life would be better and more exciting.

imports have had higher priorities, although now the government is buying large quantities of Canadian lipstick. In harder times when there was little trade in "soft wear," the women had to make do with homemade substitutes. Their hair turned out in rainbow hues as various chemicals were tried as bleaches and dyes, and they experimented with every conceivable material for eye shadow and rouge. Currently, commercial eye shadow is the Cuban rage, and lines form early at counters where it is available. For some reason, red hair is also popular, and the type of dye currently sold reacts unfortunately with Cubans' hair color to produce an unattractive shade normally associated with mid-winter Miami Beach.

Discussing these changes with women brings the sudden realization that the Revolution has altered basic words in Spanish conversations. No longer are single girls addressed as *Señorita* and married women as *Señora*. Either is simply called *Compañera*, an interesting cross between companion and comrade. Only a very old man or a foreigner might be called *Señor*. The proper revolutionary salutation is *Compañero*, and looks will be exchanged if it is not used. Similarly, the universal Spanish farewell, *Adiós*, with its religious connotation "Go with God," is seldom heard anymore unless a more permanent "good-bye" is intended, and has been replaced by a simpler *Hasta luego*, "until later."

The farewell is not the only connection between Cuba and God that has been lost. Religion as a venerable institution is struggling for survival. As is typical of countries that have moved into communism, it is the older population who patronize the surviving remnant of the church, in this case Roman Catholic. Cubans who were staunchly religious before the Revolution remain the active but dwindling congregation in the crumbling old buildings. Like every other nation in Latin America, Cuba was called a Catholic country in 1959. Everyone was baptized, married, and buried within the framework of the church, yet estimates are that 5–6 percent of the people were active participants in church life and attended mass regularly. Such is the peculiarity of Catholicism in this hemisphere. For reasons best known to Communist theoreticians, that system and the church are mutually exclusive, even though stated aims of both for their members are similar. Fidel's brother Ramón Castro offers one view that illustrates the extent of the rift and how deeply contemporary Cuban thought has moved away from the church. He told the author, "If Jesus existed now, then he would have to be a member of the Communist Party. He said to the rich, 'Give up your property and follow me.' Fidel said, 'Give your property to the Revolution and follow me.' "

Since the Revolution, organized religion has markedly lost power. The greatest change was the takeover of the schools, always a large part of the Catholic Church's activities. Although payment was promised, none came. Only church buildings themselves and the property they occupied were left intact. The government claims to guarantee freedom of religion, as it did in the recently ratified constitution. However, these guarantees are somewhat specious. When the Communist Party of Cuba was formed, it repeated the rules of the Communist Parties of other nations, stating that no one

Santiago's ornate cathedral is normally empty, or nearly so, as few Cubans choose to overtly demonstrate their religion in a system that denies full participation in society to church members.

could be a member of the Party who was a member of any organized religion. Other pressures naturally grew from that. Churchgoers are passed over in many ways. The definition of a good revolutionary excludes church attendance, and to be anything less than a good revolutionary in Cuba is a cardinal sin. Benefits of society, cars, homes, apartments, promotions, etc., go to those who shun the church. The message is clear. Parents who take their children to mass know it might jeopardize their opportunities in the Young Pioneers, which influences membership in the Union of Young Communists, which is the vehicle for getting into the Communist Party. School success might be affected, and certainly social life is. Every religious parent faces a terrible dilemma.

In a society that discourages dissent and prohibits protest, religion does play one minor and pressure-venting role. Poet Roberto Fernandez Retamar says being active in religion is a legitimate form of protest against the system: "Religious beliefs are an honorable way of saying you are against socialism. You can say, 'I want to defend Christianity, the beliefs of my parents.'"

Stories of wrenching inter-family strife surface as the young and old try to juxtapose any deeply held religious feelings with the reality of communism. While a parent lies on his deathbed, children argue whether or not to send for a priest as the old man asks. It will cause comment at the CDR to have a priest coming to the house.

The reality is that religion in Communist Cuba is still alive but seriously weakened. More than half the island has grown up under a system that tolerates religion but excludes its members from the benefits of life. One long discussion revolved around the premise that atheism is taught in Cuba's schools. A Cuban official explained that the proper description of religion and the schools is that nothing is taught on the subject—neither religion nor atheism. That may indeed be the official position, but the reality is an implicit stigma on people who choose to attend church.

In 1959 Cuba had 800 Catholic priests and 3,000 nuns, the women mainly occupied in teaching. When schools and hospitals were nationalized in 1961, most of the nuns left the country. In 1976 there were only 200 priests and 300 nuns. They are now mainly in caretaker

Twin worries of keeping religion alive in a Communist society and requesting funds from the government to repair his church's leaking roof and deteriorating interior occupy much of Father Carlos Manuel Céspedes's time.

roles, since church attendance is down to about 1 percent of the population. The critical problem is that such a tiny group is trying to support the church, buildings, and people without government or outside income. As a result, the church personnel are living meagerly and the buildings are crumbling. They are, however, open and meeting their mass schedules, even though many services are conducted for one or two members.

Father Carlos Manuel de Céspedes, a forty-year-old priest, is the great-grandson and namesake of one of Cuba's first independence fighters. He is pastor of the Jesús del Monte Church and professor at the Seminary of Holy Scripture. In a private interview at his church, he discussed the relative state of religion in Cuba today. "Freedom of religion is certainly guaranteed by the Constitution and by the First Party Congress, which also quickly added that religion cannot be used to work against the Revolution." As he walked through the leaky old building, deteriorating from neglect, he observed, "This is the largest parish in Havana, serving over 200,000 people with 10 priests and 5 churches. We might have a total of 2,500 people attending Sunday mass, or about 1½ percent. That's probably high over the country. Our most serious problem is not persecution, but the atheism encouraged onto the people. We have the national seminary here in Havana, with only 60 students. In all, we graduate about 8 priests a year, barely enough to keep the system operating. A smaller seminary in Santiago teaches a combined church-state curriculum. A family has to really be committed to the church to bring the children. Each of our 5 churches has only about 30 to 40 kids in catechism classes, not very many. But think about the pressures on the families. It is a major decision to include a child in the church because it limits him in society. He can be a Pioneer but not in the Union of Young Communists or in the Communist Party. What worries me are the conflicts that must torment children's minds as friends, schools, and all the government propaganda have their positions on religion, and the kids are then studying religion.

"We used to have all the weddings at the church. Now I suppose it is down to twenty or thirty a year. People are allowed to come here for a service, but must still have the civil ceremony and sign the book at the government office to make it legal. All in all, I am optimistic that religion will not be completely eliminated in Cuba. I believe some will survive this. It may be small, but it will still be here."

The Mass Organizations and the Communist Party

4

> The highest responsibilities are in the hands of the
> Political Bureau of the Party, the Central Committee of the
> Party, and the Congress of the Party. They lay down
> the line, and against that line, no one can go.
>
> *—Fidel Castro*

In an all-pervasive revolutionary experience such as Cuba's, it is practically impossible to be a loner. The system demands active participation. Indeed, if a Cuban is not enthusiastically engaged in some of the many approved activities, he is viewed with some suspicion by his neighbors because, as noted, passivity is one of the few dissent mechanisms.

At any given time, almost all Cubans are members of one or more of the mass organizations. Childhood is spent in the Pioneers. For many, that experience is followed by membership in the Union of Young Communists, the UJC. Open to all are the truly mass organizations, the Committees for the Defense of the Revolution and the Cuban Women's Federation. Of the many who begin the journey, only relatively few are chosen to become members of the powerful Communist Party of Cuba.

The Pioneers, patterned after other Communist country organizations, were formed in 1961 by Fidel Castro. Under the supervision of the Union of Young Communists, the Pioneer organization admits youngsters between five and thirteen. As described by Hector Paz in the activities section of the José Martí camp outside Havana,

"Pioneers are the political organization that supervises and controls Cuba's youth."

It would be a mistake to compare the Pioneers to the Boy Scouts, as is often done. The Pioneers are far more politicized. Students and parents have to ask to join and, typically, a boy or girl enters the first grade and the Pioneers during the same year. Compañero Paz explains, "The children can meet in or after school. There are several goals: to be good students, to be patriotic, and to know what is useful social work. These will help them try to make the New Man."

In their blue-and-white uniforms, the children are formed into detachments of ten. All the detachments comprise a school congress and elect a chief. Each classroom at school has a board that is kept by Pioneer members with up-to-date national and international news. After school, there is social work with adult volunteers on projects chosen by the organization.

In addition to the various local activities, two national camps are already in operation and one is planned for each province. Pioneers come to the existing camps for two weeks each year. José Martí Camp can handle 10,000 children in these national gatherings. As with all

Young Pioneers march through Havana on their way to practice a precision-drill program for an upcoming parade.

other aspects of Cuban life, competition for success is encouraged. During each academic year, schools with the best grades are chosen to reward all their Pioneers by sending them to camp for fifteen days. And in the summer, individual schools pick a few of their best students to come for an additional week.

The José Martí Camp, about fifteen miles east of Havana on the road to Matanzas, has a beach, a lagoon, dormitories, classrooms, athletic fields, a ceremonial square, and a series of staff houses. Pioneers who come here have class work for half of the day and other planned activities for the remainder. Currently, the camp is scheduled to be half full in winter and completely full each summer.

Brightly painted red and yellow rowboats line the lagoon dock across from the usually full beach. Just around a hill from the water, a new amphitheatre is under construction for outdoor meetings, theatrics, and entertainment. The program is obviously designed to be fun, and parents are prohibited. They leave their children at the front gate and retrieve them one or two weeks later. Except for day

Beach time is part of the recreational activity at the José Martí Pioneer Camp outside Havana. Children selected to come for a week spend part of each day in classes and part in physical activities.

care, this is the first exposure of children to the system, and once in, there is steady indoctrination.

Math is taught with the usual tables, plus an additional lesson in arithmetic: How many years since the beginning of the Revolution? How many years ago did *Granma* land? Reading is taught from books about revolutionary heroes. Whose picture is this? What did he do? When did the Yankee mercenaries kill him? It is all subtle. It is all done quietly. It is all so constant.

The other Pioneer camp, Circulo Camillo Cienfuegos, is in Camaguey. Built in 1974, it has 15,000 square meters of camp, recreational, and educational facilities, in addition to a just completed million-dollar Japanese amusement park. Pioneers enjoy it free during the week, and on weekends local residents can play for a nominal fee.

A standard Pioneer greeting is given each new visitor by a double line of children in neatly pressed uniforms. The short, memorized welcome is delivered in Spanish by the leader, followed by everyone shouting in unison the Pioneer slogan, "Pioneros para comunismo; seremos como El Ché" ("Pioneers for communism; we will all be like Ché"). (Ché Guevara, a major revolutionary leader with Castro, is idolized by the Pioneers. Ché, ever the activist, was unhappy in his various ministerial roles after the fighting, and was later killed in Bolivia leading a small group trying to organize the peasants.)

Each Pioneer in Camaguey comes to the camp for 2½-hour sessions, twice a week. The periods include a snack, sports or recreation, and a group assembly before class. Twenty-three subjects are available and each Pioneer chooses one field to study for a year. For example, classes are available in sugarcane operations, cattle raising, the military, folk dance, ham radio, civil defense, and others. Visitors to the civil defense class will find walls of war materials supposedly captured in Cuba from the C.I.A. operatives. There are radios, rubber boats, scuba gear, rifles, pistols, binoculars, and maps. On request, one of the young students will pick up a Soviet AK-47 automatic rifle, break it apart rapidly, put on a blindfold, and assemble it by feel in no more than one minute. It is a skill they learn early.

The Union of Young Communists is designed to be the training ground for Party members. It is the vehicle for social work, instruction, and Party activities at a formative age. Membership is

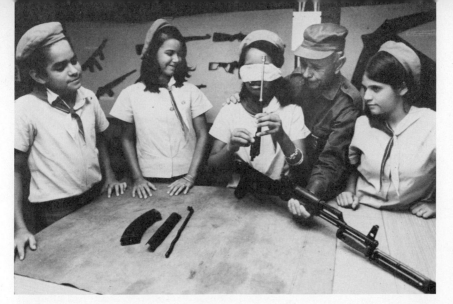

These young Cuban girls, all members of the Pioneers, are learning to strip and assemble a Soviet-made AK-47 automatic rifle in less than a minute, while blindfolded. Such weapons-training begins early for Cuban youth and will continue throughout their lives, in either active military duty or in the civilian reserves.

open at fourteen years, and by a new law, anyone reaching twenty-seven must begin the processing for Party membership, a procedure that takes about six months.

Participation in the first phases of mass organizations can be viewed as a layered pyramid, with a broad base made up of the masses and the pinnacle being Fidel Castro, the leader himself. The vast numbers of Pioneers are reduced to a more select membership in the Union of Young Communists. That smaller group is further diminished to the restricted rolls of the Communist Party of Cuba, the PCC.

Over a hundred thousand marchers assemble for the annual May Day Parade down the Paseo and before Fidel and the government hierarchy. Basically a labor celebration, the function features union groups with signs, banners, and slogans honoring the causes of the moment.

The first Communist Party in Cuba was formed in the 1920s, when a worldwide effort brought the movement to many nations. In a constant struggle for survival over the years, the Party vacillated in its support of various existing Cuban governments. The Party held on until the Revolution, but with a very spotty record. Although the fact is now often denied, the old Communist Party made numerous statements against Castro when he and his small rebel band were fighting in the Sierra Maestra. At that time, the Party opposed armed rebellion as a means of gaining power. (Jealousy probably figures as another motive.) There is ample evidence, both in the record of those days and in actions taken by the Castro government, to show that the present regime in Cuba wanted little to do with the old Communists and has actively kept them from power even today. The only exceptions to this policy are Carlos Rafael Rodriguez, for years the Foreign Minister and member of the Political Bureau, and now a vice-president of both the Council of State and Council of Ministers, and Blas Roca, an old-line Communist from the 1940s, who headed the group to write the new Constitution and was just elected President of the National Assembly, a relatively powerless position.

By the time Castro's revolution was successful and Batista had fled the island on January 1, 1959, the rebels had achieved their principal goal—they had toppled the hated dictatorship. No one knows for sure what secret plans Castro may have had for a future government at that time, but it is relatively certain that many of his supporters were fighting to rid Cuba of Batista and his followers and had little forethought about forming a government in its place.

Fidel Castro had made some of his dreams public after his famous trial in 1953. Using his legal training for his own defense, he spoke to the court in a ringing denouncement of dictatorships and oppression of the people and listed some relatively mild socialistic goals that he said would have been followed if his rebellion at the Moncada Barracks had been successful. Although the judge forbade any publication of the remarks, one newspaper reporter copied most of the hours-long defense, and later, in prison, Castro reorganized it. Published as *History Will Absolve Me*, it has had a galvanizing impact on Cubans through the years.

The important point is that Castro never mentioned communism and never set Communistic goals as his own. He wanted some land reform, to give 55 percent of the profits of large businesses to their workers, and to take away property obtained by dishonest means. The 26 of July Movement, as the Castro rebels were called, worked to gain control of Cuba without the support of the old Communist Party. As we have seen, they even found the Party working against them at times.

It will be left to other writers to attempt an explanation of the many actions of the early days of the Revolution when the Cuban government moved toward socialism. Here it will suffice to report that Castro made a number of statements indicating that he expected to cooperate with the United States, asked for an early agrarian reform law, and visited New York, Washington, Harvard, and Princeton, in an attempt to explain his new government. Extremists in the Revolution disapproved of the trip, saying it would appear as if Castro were caving in to American pressure. Already, by April, 1959, numerous charges were being raised in the United States about Communist influence in the new government. It was increasingly apparent to the Cubans that the United States did not care what happened to their country, as long as it did not turn Communist.

Castro was under pressure from both sides. Obviously wanting to be his own man, he could only resent the constant questioning of his intentions. A group of Cuban economists drew up a plan prior to the trip that would ask for $500 million in U.S. aid for a variety of island projects. Castro did not mention the plan once during his April visit to America. Nor did he or any member of his party ask for any aid, even though they were prepared to, and would likely have accepted it if aid had been offered. The United States, on the other hand, expected to be asked, and was prepared to give aid, but did not offer any. The two countries faced a standoff—neither group could bring itself to make the first move, and, therefore, no move was made.

From a public relations standpoint, the trip was a great success. United States crowds followed all his appearances, the press was lavish in its coverage, and Castro was entertaining and popular. Yet a distinctly sour note surrounded his most publicized meeting.

Fidel Castro was not on a state visit. He had been invited by a group of newspaper editors, and right to the end his trip was conducted as a private visit. There was concern prior to the journey about a possible meeting with President Eisenhower, of whom Castro had been critical in speeches. Castro did not wish to see the President, anticipating that he would be embarrassed if he had to meet Ike.

Eisenhower later wrote that he was "more than irritated" over the visit and wished he could have denied Castro a visa.

Since the trip was private, Eisenhower found it possible to be playing golf away from Washington during Castro's stay. The responsibility for talking with the bearded leader fell to Vice-President Richard Nixon. For Cuba-U.S. relations, that two-hour chat in Nixon's office may have been one of the most important ever held. The two men talked alone in English. Apparently Nixon turned on Castro immediately when Fidel showed little interest in the Vice-President's file of Communists among his Cuban supporters. Nixon also complained that the executions (after highly publicized trials) of former officials were causing a very bad impression in the United States. Castro later said, "I simply confined myself to . . . explaining the realities of our country . . . and to demonstrating that the measures we were going to take, some of which affected North America, were just."

When Castro left, Richard Nixon wrote a memo suggesting that the Eisenhower administration arm a group of Cuban exiles to overthrow the Cuban government. He justified it by saying that either Castro was naive and did not understand communism or was under Communist control. The Bay of Pigs disaster thus had its birth.

Incredibly, before leaving the United States, Castro was asked to

At the Bay of Pigs Museum in the town of Giron, where the principal landing and fighting took place, Soviet-supplied equipment is displayed that was used against the U.S.-backed Cuban invaders. Along the far wall, photographs of the 160 Castro troops that admittedly were killed are shown with mementos carried with them into the battle.

meet with the C.I.A.'s Latin American expert, a man who was at the time called Mr. Droller and who would later be called Mr. Bender (when he was in charge of the Cuban exiles in their fight against Castro). After talking for three hours, Droller said, "Castro is not only not a Communist, he is a strong anti-Communist fighter." Moreover, in the final U.S. speeches, Castro was saying publicly that he was not a Communist, his brother was not a Communist, he knew of no Communists in his government, and if there were any, they were not influential.

As his journey continued to Canada and South America, Castro confided to a plane-mate that he was not a Communist because "Communism is a dictatorship of a single class and I . . . have fought all my life against dictatorship. Communism means hatred and class struggle, and I am opposed to any form of hatred." In his May 9 speech back in Havana he said the Revolution was "entirely democratic" and was not Communist because "not only do we offer people food, but we also offer them freedom."

But by summer, American newspapers were quoting what Cubans were saying, "The Revolution is like a watermelon; the more you slice it, the redder it gets." Upon this background, many things began to change inside Cuba. Some of the old Communist leaders did emerge in positions of power, and those voices who were calling for a purge of the Communist taint to the Revolution were silenced. On the day Castro had left for the United States, Hubert Matos, a commander (major) in the revolutionary army and military governor of the Camaguey Province, made an exceedingly strong anti-Communist speech. By autumn Matos was publicly saying the government was infiltrated with Communists. He resigned his commission and wrote Castro a mild denunciation of the "Communist problem." Fourteen other officers resigned with him. Castro was furious and ordered the city occupied by armed forces. He personally came to Camaguey to arrest his former comrade in the Sierra Maestra. Matos and the other officers calmly surrendered. The following day the whole 26 of July Movement executive in Camaguey resigned. As fate would have it, that night an exile officer from the air force, Diaz Lanz, flew an old B25 from Florida and dropped leaflets over Cuba calling Castro a Communist. In the confusion of firing at the plane from the ground and from an offshore frigate, forty-five Cubans were wounded and two killed. The government published a pamphlet called *Havana's*

Pearl Harbor and its newspaper headlined THE AIRPLANES CAME FROM THE U.S.A.

Hubert Matos was tried, and the government asked for the death sentence. He received a term of twenty years. The twenty-one officers who resigned with Matos received sentences of two, three, and seven years. Hubert Matos has not been seen since, and it is assumed that he is still in prison.

In the years 1959–1961, when the tone of the Revolution changed from mountain rebel to socialistic, a number of old Communist leaders played significant roles in guiding the country's new policies. They were there with organizational skills and experience and helped mold the character of the constantly changing government. Since 1962, those older Communists have been pushed more into the background, leaving only Blas Roca and Carlos Rafael Rodriguez to share the limelight with Castro's men. An attempt was made through the ORI (the Organizaciónes Revolucionarias Integradas) to blend the all-powerful 26 of July Movement with the old Communist Party. In 1963, the ORI faded away without an announcement. It was followed by the PURS (Partido Unificado de la Revolución Socialista), not quite a Communist party, but recognized by the Soviets as a "fraternal party." That too dissolved when in 1965 the people were told of a new Communist Party of Cuba, the PCC.

Last-minute painting is completed in the Paseo for the upcoming May Day Parade, where workers will carry signs and banners extolling the socialist work ethic.

Even though historical differences separated the old and new Communists, it is interesting to see how Castro worked his solution. Following the lead of other Communist governments, the PCC's initial organization had a Central Committee of a hundred that would oversee the Party, a Political Bureau (or politburo), and a Secretariat, both of which were superior to the Central Committee. The first Central Committee had sixty-eight of its one hundred members chosen from the military. Twenty-one were what the Cubans called "old" Communists. Significantly, not a single one of the old Communists enjoyed membership on the Political Bureau or Secretariat. Those powerful bodies were completely controlled by the two Castro brothers and their followers from the Sierra Maestra. Ten members of the Central Committee had either actually been present for the Moncada Barracks attack in 1953 or had arrived with Fidel on *Granma* in 1956. Over half the hundred served at one time or another in the Sierra. Even though these Party leaders were now calling themselves Communists, they were, first and foremost, *Fidelistas.*

Currently, PCC members number about 200,000 in a country of over 9 million. Although Communist states are notable for withholding information about themselves, it has been reported that Cuba's percentage of Party members to population is among the lowest in the world. The only official explanation is that only the best people who are nominated are selected. Carlos Rafael Rodriguez, a Vice-President of the Council of State and Council of Ministers and member of the Politburo, offered his explanation: "The number is small because we prefer to have a highly selective party. The workers have to know that the Party members are totally devoted to the cause of socialism. We need a stronger party with more members, but we don't want to sacrifice quality for quantity. We are trying to have more people in the Party now, mainly workers. We feel we have too many people coming from the middle strata, intellectuals, former Party officials, administrators."

Enrique Oltuski, a rebel leader in Santa Clara during the revolutionary fight and now Vice-Minister in the Fishing Ministry, explained the membership process. "It is difficult to get in and we intend to keep it that way. It takes about six months to process a person. For a Cuban to become a PCC member, he must have the desire, the Party must have the desire, and he must be recommended by his fellow workers as well as have a background check.

"It works like this. A person's fellow workers meet and vote to suggest to the Communist Party that this is a desirable person to include—a good worker with the right attitude. Then the Party makes a complete check of the person's whole life—his school record, his private life, his family life, his politics, his economic views, his friends—everything. If the Party agrees that this is a desirable person, it returns to the fellow workers, reviews the record with them, tells them it agrees, and asks them to vote a second time on recommending the person for membership. If that is done, the person can become a PCC member. However, if the Party does not agree to the person after the record check, it returns to the fellow workers to explain why and lays out the record. The fellow workers can agree with the denial, or they can vote again for the person, in which case the Party must go back and review the record. This is serious business and never taken lightly by the PCC. This procedure can continue as long as the work center presents new information for the Party to consider. There are two innovations concerning membership that the PCC instituted last year. Cubans can now recommend themselves for membership instead of waiting for their work centers to vote, but their cases must still be taken before the work centers for approval. Additionally, before becoming a full voting *militante,* as Party members are called, a one-year probation period is required after acceptance by the PCC."

In a country that calls itself a republic and has a new constitution with elaborate voting and legislative procedures, it is reasonable to assess the role of the Party in relation to the people and the real power structure of the country. The Cuban government is constantly stating through official publications that its kind of governing is the only democracy since it consistently represents the will of the people. It accuses Western democracies of violating the true meaning of the word because their governments represent only special interest groups at the expense of the people. Obviously, there is a severe problem in semantics here.

What better place to begin than at the source of policy determination. In a private interview, Fidel Castro discussed the Party's role with the author. "The new Constitution recognizes the leading role of the Communist Party. The Party lays down the state political line. It is then supposed that the state will carry out that line [program]. For instance, at the Party Congress, the Party presents goals and directions for the next five years, including economic and political directions. That Party line will be followed by the state and the mass organizations. If that did not happen, the Party would be discredited, and there would be a political crisis. Initiatives for laws may come from various sources—the Party, the National Assembly, or others— but no one can go against the program. When the Party line is being discussed in a Party Congress, it can be changed. Even the Constitution can be changed by the proper means. But no one can go against the Party line or against the Constitution."

After a decade of promises, the First Party Congress was finally held in December, 1975. It laid out the first Five-Year Plan, which included considerable economic and industrial expansion. Unfortunately, the projections were based on sugar prices at the time, about 17¢ a pound. By the autumn of 1976, prices had fallen to 7¢ and the projects had to be curtailed.

The Party, preeminent among Cuban organizations, sets policy and offers leadership in all aspects of island life. Its spokesmen have chafed when the PCC has been called elitist by foreign journalists. The PCC's position is that elitism is impossible in a socialist society and that PCC members are chosen from every walk of life and always begin by a worker's recommendation, giving its ranks a distinctive labor-oriented look. The term *elite*, in this case, may have confused the Communists, who relate it to upper-class capitalists oppressing

The goose step, not seen by most Americans since Hitler's downfall, is the parade form used by Cuban troops. Obviously a carry-over from Soviet influence, it seems oddly out of place in the Caribbean.

the workers, a view commonly held throughout Cuba. Expanding the definition to mean a small group setting policy for a nation, dispensing favors and privileges in jobs, housing, and even daily necessities, and choosing its own members, just might make the "elitist" appellation acceptable.

One thing is clear: Words take on entirely different meanings when used in revolutionary socialism. Talking with scores of Cubans about their government is enough to convince any semanticist that black really is white. It also points up the disparity between Americans' views of the people living in a Communist system and the view those same peoples have of themselves. If there is a typical American view, it is that communism takes everything away from the people, suppresses, enslaves, and keeps them economically depressed—in short, that the government controls every aspect of their lives.

Fidel Castro says, "The disappearance of private property makes miracles." He explains that the people are not controlled by the government, but the people *are* the government. Since a country should be made up of one people working for the common good, the production facilities of the country are jointly held by all the people to be used to benefit everyone. (Such a theory probably will work better on a small island than anywhere else, since the feeling of being united is stronger than on a land mass where languages and cultures overlap.) When asked directly about the absence of human rights in Cuba, Castro said, "We have guaranteed many rights which are essential to our people. We have not set up a liberal system. These are things that concern the people of the United States. Ask Cubans and you will find they are troubled about many things, but the absence of those rights is not what troubles them."

The ideal of communism as described by Marx and others is certainly appealing to small, poor countries either just becoming free or struggling to break away from an oppressive system. It does appear to be idealistic, fair, working always for the common good. As more and more nations slip into its influence, one might reasonably ask, is anyone choosing free-enterprise capitalism any more? A few are, but for reasons more complicated than an open vote of the electorate. Communists are currently more effective in selling their system by being available to aid independence movements and colonists against dictatorships, without any apparent long-range exploitative goals. The rebel groups in Africa, for instance, need help and can find only two potential sources, capitalism and socialism. Looking at past capitalist exploitation of their country and wishing to have the least foreign influence, they are apt today to choose the socialist assistance. They are also more likely to see a desirable master plan in socialism, by which a new government's leaders can control the country's destiny rather completely, instead of dispersing such control among numerous business interests.

It all sounds so logical, but the Cubans and others who work daily under the system know better. They are dedicated Communists and have been told it is the best and most honest system. But the bureaucracy is top-heavy, and the economy is always lagging. As one Western diplomat in Havana observed, "The difference is incentive. Capitalism rewards people who succeed. If you work hard and get ahead, you make money, can buy the things your family wants, and feel accomplishment. Here you work hard and see little for it. The promises are marvelous, but the delivery never seems to arrive." There are some tangible accomplishments, some of which will be covered in later chapters, but the question remains, at what price have they been achieved? No one asked by the author in Cuba could answer the basic concern of any student of communism: If the system is so successful and desirable, why won't it work without the massive restrictions on individual liberty?

If the PCC can be considered a general in Cuba, making policy from on high, then the sergeants to carry out the programs are the Committees for the Defense of the Revolution. The CDRs are the mass activists, omnipresent and committed to "revolutionary vigilance." Each block in Cuba has one, 78,000 in all, meaning that it is truly a neighborhood organization. There is nothing quite like the CDR in other Communist countries, because it is far more extensive than the "cell" and involves practically the whole country. Since there is a CDR on every street, there is no escaping a formal reporting system that knows everything about everyone in the country. Since anyone can join, membership rolls are long—4,800,000 total, about half of Cuba. This represents 81 percent of all the people above fourteen years old.

The CDR's origin was as dramatic as its growth. On September 28, 1960, Fidel Castro was giving one of his famous orations in the Plaza de la Revolución. His still-new government was under attack from a small group of counterrevolutionaries, and, during the speech, some

This type of sign identifies the home that operates as the CDR office on each block throughout Cuba. Names of "martyrs" or revolutionary dates or events are chosen to personalize each office.

bombs went off in the distance. (No one ever proved the claims at the time that Castro's men set the blasts.) Fidel looked over in the direction of the noise and said that Cuba needed a neighborhood organization that could watch every street so that such things could not happen again. So the Committee for the Defense of the Revolution was formed. Now, each September twenty-eighth is a special day, with houses all over the island filled with decorations, parties, dances, and drinking, and a mass rally in the Plaza, where Castro gives an important policy address.

On that September 1976 evening, half a million people filled the great plaza in front of the José Martí statue to listen attentively as Castro spoke to them like a favorite teacher. Formalities aside, he approached his subject without notes, and with a deliberate speed and quiet that captivated the crowd. Straining to hear, the people were lead through the economic maze of supply and demand, world sugar prices, and surplus crops to the crux of the message. Castro was using the forum, as only he can, to tell his country that things were going poorly, sugar prices had plummeted, more belt-tightening would be necessary, some consumer goods would not be available, and coffee rations would be cut immediately. The applause was polite, but not enthusiastic. They had hoped for a better message.

Now that the counterrevolutionary bombers are gone, the CDRs spend their time performing more than 300 separate tasks for the

Fidel and Raúl Castro, Cuban military leaders and governmental officials review their troops from a platform at the base of the José Martí monument in the Plaza of the Revolution. All the important mass rallys, parades, and special revolutionary days are celebrated at this Havana landmark.

state. Since they cover the entire country, their work supports all the ministries of government. They administer over a million oral doses of polio vaccine to children; organize 150,000 blood donors annually; mobilize women for Pap smears and breast cancer checks, keep academic records of every child on the block and organize parents for volunteer work at schools; get people out for volunteer work in agriculture, construction, and sugarcane harvesting; collect old bottles, cans, glass, paper, and cardboard for recycling; save used postage stamps for sale to foreign collectors; guard their block from 11 P.M. to 5 A.M. in street patrols; conduct political and ideological meetings; hold chess matches between CDRs and military personnel "to stimulate patriotism and maintain the links between the military and the people."

David Duran, chief of the CDR's Latin American section, proudly explained, "With almost 5 million members, we only have a paid staff of 2,200 throughout Cuba. All the rest are volunteers. Membership is also voluntary and open to anyone fourteen or more years old. The requirements are that the person agrees with the Revolution and is ready to defend the Revolution. That does not mean to defend with arms but to carry out the Revolution's tasks. Dues are 25¢ a month, also voluntary, and there is no requirement that the person be either an atheist or a Communist. On my block we have religious believers and even some people who attend church."

Compañero Duran spoke in his office at the CDR's national headquarters in Havana, formerly a home. His plain room seems empty with a few pieces of wooden revolutionary furniture, a brilliant yellow curtain from marble floor to ceiling, and one large photograph of the Castro brothers. His discussion of the CDR's early days explained some of the reputation that still clouds its work today. "At the time of the Giron [the Bay of Pigs], Fidel asked the military and the CDRs for help. The CDRs knew the bad people on their blocks. Those people were reported. On April 15, 1961, when the bombings of the airfields began, the bad elements in the communities were rounded up. By the time the attack by the mercenaries came on April 17, those people were no longer in circulation and in the seventy-two hours of the Giron fight, there were no incidents around the country to support it." It is just this role of neighbors observing and reporting on neighbors that troubles many critics.

Another controversial task is vigilance, originally manifested in twenty-four-hour daily patrols of every block in Cuba. Now that the invasion threat is gone, vigilance is more a preventive function to "reduce anti-social activity"—which means to watch for crime. This guard duty is organized on the "zone CDR" level, which is a collection of eight to fifteen block units. That way the vigilance can include shops, hospitals, and commercial areas in addition to homes.

The CDR-organized Sunday morning cleanup is a standard feature on every block in Cuba. In the once fashionable Miramar section of Havana, leaf-raking and burning is done by the current occupants of the old mansions, vacated by exiles who fled Cuba in the early 1960s. The large homes are now used as multiple family dwellings, schools, dormitories, or offices.

Women CDRs take the 11 P.M. to 2 A.M. shifts and men get the 2 A.M. to 5 A.M. duty. Frequency of an individual's guard responsibility depends on the number of CDR members in his zone, but the average is about one night every two months. On any given night in Cuba, there are about 34,000 CDRs out on the streets.

This nighttime activity has not been lost on the criminal element. They have switched their schedules and now do breaking and entering in the daytime. One European diplomat returned to his home to find it burgled and every pair of pants he owned stolen. The poor man had to fly out to Mexico to replace them. Items that have great value on the black market are taken—cameras, TVs, radios, and hard-to-get clothes. In Varadero there has been a problem with thefts of clothes, sunglasses, and towels. Surprisingly, the crimes continue even with the very stiff sentences of twenty to thirty years. Stealing in the face of such penalties seems to indicate a real desperation.

The CDR's watching and reporting roles are at the point where Cubans can joke about them. One current Havana favorite has the president of a local CDR in Oriente, who was also a veteran of Giron and the counterrevolutionary fight in the Escambray, finding that there was a meat black marketeer on his block. He got dressed up with his uniform and gun and went to the man's house. At the door he said he understood the man sold meat on the black market. The poor seller pleaded for mercy because he had a family, needed the money, and had never before done anything wrong. The CDR veteran quieted him by saying, "You don't understand—sell to me, sell to me!"

It is the CDR's political activities that many critics resent. Study groups on communism are held on every street and propaganda materials are distributed. One of the CDR's campaigns is to "counteract all behavior detrimental to the social system." Over-zealous CDRs report innocent activity which then has to be explained by the unfortunate victim. Once while looking at a painting of a bug-eyed fish, a Cuban remarked, "Just like a CDR, ever vigilant, he never sleeps." Although it is a system that serves the government well, it also creates neighborhood problems since it violates privacy, causes suspicion, and generates difficulties among residents.

The CDRs are really at the heart of the Revolution. Since relatively few Cubans are in the PCC and not all work in factories or

Civilian militia is a regular, but seldom seen, part of adult life. Carrying Soviet automatic rifles, this Saturday group was training near the Bay of Pigs until the photograph was made. Its leader argued for half an hour before being convinced the photograph was not a security violation.

are in labor unions, it is the CDR that connects the people to the system. And the CDRs are incessantly busy creating the new Cuban culture, filled with its Party line, its propaganda messages, its uniformity, and conformity of the masses to what the government image is of the New Man.

The New Man is having to alter some of his basic Latin macho biases to include the new Cuban woman. At the vanguard of this movement is the Cuban Women's Federation, or FMC, one of the multimillion-member mass organizations. Headed by Wilma Espin, wife of Raúl Castro, the FMC is housed in a beautiful pink palace in the once fashionable Vedado section of Havana. Fresh flowers, a statue of Venus, and mural-sized photographs of Ché Guevara and Tania, a revolutionary who died with Ché in Bolivia, decorate the mansion walls. Monica Krause, an FMC official, explains the organization's background. "We were founded in 1960 as a direct result of Fidel Castro's concern for the female forces in the country. The general cultural level of women and their literacy were low. There was a lack of political awareness and we knew if we were going to create a new society, the masses had to understand what we were setting out to do. In 1959, if women worked at all, they were employed as teachers, nurses, or domestics. We first incorporated women into the work force in 1964 at the height of the hemisphere's economic blockade, which caused great scarcities here. In time, we began to coordinate our work with industry so that when a new factory was planned, we would set up a training program for women.

By the day the factory opened, we would have women trained in the skills needed to work there."

Monica, an attractive East German, came to Cuba sixteen years ago to work in the Revolution, married, and stayed. Her enthusiasm bubbled over as she described the Federation's work. "Our goals here are to raise the political and cultural levels of Cuban women to those of men. We are into all areas of women's lives. We work to see that women get all their vaccinations and their Pap smears. The Federation formed the day-care system so women could safely leave their children and work. We saw a need and solved it and now care for 80,000 children daily. Women volunteers, organized by the FMC, pick two-thirds of Oriente's coffee crop. We work with women prisoners to train them in trade skills and to prepare them for acceptance by society. [Most of the women in jail are there for theft and corruption, a holdover heritage from capitalist days, according to Monica.] Cuba has the highest percentage of working women in Latin America—over 25 percent—and these are skilled laborers, not domestics. The FMC is proud that over 60 percent of Cuba's medical students are now women. Over 80 percent of the island's women between fourteen and sixty-five are FMC members—more than 2 million—and they each pay 25¢ a month to finance our programs."

Obviously the real picture is not quite as bright as the one the FMC would like to paint. The editor of *Casa de las Americas* magazine, poet Roberto Fernandez Retamar, offers a more realistic evaluation. "It is impossible to erase by law racial and sexual prejudice. It is forbidden by law, and you can go to jail if you do not let a person enter a place or give him or her a job without prejudice. Many Cubans are very good revolutionaries, but they cannot accept this. There still is the man who will not let his wife go out in the evening or the father who doesn't like his daughter going out with a Negro boy. The very existence of the Cuban Federation of Women admits there is a problem."

The one thing that should be clear is that Cubans are enveloped by their Revolution. It consumes their time and thoughts, and fills their weeks with socially oriented activities. It also restricts their movements and freedom of choices. Many outsiders rebel at the thought of the curtailment of rights.

How do Cubans accept all the restrictions? To a large extent, they are enthusiastic supporters of the government. Undoubtedly many

Flip-card demonstrators, such as these depicting the Cuban flag, practice for weeks to perform precision tricks for the May Day Parade. As with other activities, participation is considered a social obligation.

wish for more freedom. They would follow Fidel anywhere, having already supported him throughout a total social revolution. Although there is no propaganda against the American people, for whom there is widespread regard, they are told repeatedly that the American government is the enemy of Cuba. In the early days of the Revolution, when Castro was moving more and more toward socialism, a considerable opposition grew, supported somewhat by the C.I.A., and sabotage became common. Counterrevolutionaries fought in the 1960s from the Escambray Mountains until the military eradicated them. As the ill-fated Bay of Pigs attack grew near, Castro used the tension as an excuse to round up dissidents inside Cuba. Exiles claim that the C.I.A.'s lack of notification allowed agents to be caught in the web that effectively wiped out organized opposition to the government.

Of more immediate concern now is whether the Cuban people will continue in their passive acceptance of the island's new international role while consumer scarcities exist and even become more numerous. It is, on the one hand, quite understandable to expect Castro to become a bit bored with his position after eighteen years and search for wider horizons. It is quite difficult to find a similar interest in overseas adventures by a Cuban family standing in line for food and clothes when they realize it costs money and lives to send an army to Africa. A massive propaganda program whipped up enthusiasm for

Angola for months, but when the news of deaths and injuries spread (by rumor and word of mouth, since there have been no official announcements), the questioning began. Cubans, who at the core are just like other people, can be expected to live on promises for only so long. They know what they once had and what the rest of the world now can buy, and they are becoming disenchanted with a system that always seems to produce less than its leaders promise. With the U.S. embargo and constant threats of invasion, enthusiasm was high. Now that U.S. tourists are walking around Havana, U.S. subsidiary trade is brisk and normal trade may soon be coming, no one seriously talks of invading Cuba, and there is no one on whom to blame the deficiencies. Castro will have to produce or stop talking. It is probably no longer possible in this more sophisticated world to keep people's patriotism peaked for long with little wars. In another era, the Nazis did it. Now people are weary of such games, and war is too dangerous to play with, even for a small country.

The initial result of this attitudinal change is the presence of dissent. Formerly none was allowed and none surfaced. Now Cubans are talking somewhat more openly about the problems their country faces. CDR and union meetings air grievances, but with careful reservations. Since groups vote to put citizens on buying lists, etc., people are reluctant to voice serious complaints for fear they will be passed over for new appliances. In private, almost any Cuban will freely disclose all the ills of his Communist economic system and talk about personal freedom losses. Whenever a second Cuban is near, the talk suddenly goes bland. It may not seem important, but voicing any complaint to a foreigner is a significant step toward more open dissent. Cubans are grumbling more and are critical of their system. Just such activities brought some of the consumer and personnel changes in the Soviet Union and Eastern Europe. Although dissent is weak and unorganized, there is some, and ultimately it must be considered by the government. When large numbers of citizens are unhappy and without proper procedures to vent their emotions and complaints, the system must bend, or face work slowdowns or open protest.

Today almost all observers agree that there is no organized resistance inside Cuba. One long-time resident says it is probably impossible now with so many CDRs around to watch. Dissent is manifested by simply withdrawing from the system, working slowly, and doing nothing more than is required. Another resident notes that

Secondary school students march through the Plaza of the Revolution in the annual May Day celebration. In a reference to Angola, the background mural says: "Long live solidarity with the African people."

many may be unhappy but can do little to protest. In 1958, Castro could fight against an army of 30,000 when most soldiers quit at five, few had the stomach for a guerrilla war, and the arms available to both sides were rather primitive. Now, any armed resistance would challenge a force of perhaps 200,000 equipped with Soviet MIGs, missiles, and an entire array of modern weapons of destruction.

One Cuban, in a risky moment of confidence, expressed his displeasure with the system. "Cuba is not for Cubans now. It is only for the Russians. Look around, they are everywhere. It was a lot better when the Americans were here. The government talks about liberty. What liberty? There is the liberty to work without getting paid. If you want to drive to Santiago, you had better have the right paper showing you're either working or on vacation. Otherwise, you will be arrested. What kind of freedom is that? Before the Revolution, I worked for a U.S. firm here. I got five pesos a day. If I worked at night or on weekends, I got paid overtime. On those twenty-five pesos I could support a family, have a house and a car. Now I make over five times as much and cannot have a home or a car of my own. You notice that your drivers never speak English. If they learn, they are transferred. Then they could speak to foreigners. No one is supposed to tell what's going on here. If you do speak English, as I do, any contact you have with a foreigner is watched."

Another Cuban asked to come sit in my hotel lobby to discuss new developments in photography. He looked worried and said, "I'm taking some risk by coming here. You may not notice it, but we are being watched. Someone will later ask me what I was doing with an American, what did we talk about, and why did I come?"

It is this kind of fear that is one of the most troublesome aspects of Cuba. One young man on the street volunteered the suggestion that anyone who spoke out against the government might get twenty years behind bars. At the Revolutionary Museum, formerly the Presidential Palace, a collection of Soviet, Cuban, and U.S. military hardware used to rest on the public street in front. A translator thought photographing the items might be prohibited, even though they were in full view of everyone. There is a fear of approaching any Soviets on the street, of going into any building unless all the necessary advance work has cleared it, of expressing displeasure with the system, of publicly criticizing anything, or of getting too close to the military.

Some of the government's fears are well founded. In 1976 an Air Cubana flight was blown from the skies as it left Barbados, killing all aboard. The two men apprehended were Cuban exiles who lived in Venezuela. Castro charged the C.I.A. was behind the bombing, but the only links between the agency and the suspects occurred many years before, about the time of the Bay of Pigs invasion. Another bomb exploded in a luggage cart in Jamaica, awaiting an overdue Cubana plane. Fishermen have been attacked and killed, sugar fields set aflame from airplanes, and infiltrators put ashore in small boats. Such events receive maximum media play in the government press, aiming to keep revolutionary fervor at a high pitch.

Fear does not grip the island now as it did in the early 1960s when the threat of invasion was high. But the Cubans keep their readiness high and their militia in constant training, and their CDRs walking the streets nightly looking for signs of trouble. Workers take turns guarding their factories, hotels, restaurants, and offices for possible nighttime attack. It is anxiety-producing, and the Cuban temperament shows it. The "Happy Latin" image prior to 1959 is gone. Cuba's tone is more serious now, with fewer smiles and a bit more suspicion. As one woman assembly-line worker said, "I don't have time now to be happy. Maybe later, but I'm too busy now."

The Economy

5

> The Revolution is going to solve in twenty-five years
> the problems it would have taken us a hundred years to solve
> without success under a capitalist system. Private
> property engenders egotism. The absence of private property
> makes miracles.
>
> —*Fidel Castro*

Studying the economy is easier in Cuba than in most other countries. People talk about it the way Americans discuss the weather. Since everyone has an up-to-the-minute opinion on the best way to run the country's economic programs, economic research becomes mainly a matter of editing. Naturally, most of the discussions center around rationing and shortages, but there are many other intriguing aspects of turning an economy from capitalism toward communism in just a few years.

Whenever public opinion polls are conducted in the United States, the same three basic areas of concern always top the lists as most troublesome. Inflation, unemployment, and street crime are major problems in contemporary Western cultures. Cubans, who are eager to show off their system and make favorable comparisons whenever possible, are quick to point out that their government has solved all of these ills. In the economic realm, their centrally controlled fiscal system, at whatever expense, has stabilized prices at near 1962 levels and kept everyone working. Each area bears closer examination.

Inflation is the result of constant pressure from workers demanding higher wages, by manufacturers asking higher prices, by producers increasing the value of goods and services that a country needs, and by international businessmen raising the costs of imports. In a free-enterprise capitalist system with only moderate market restraints, inflation is normal. People do want to make more money. Rising expectations are an acceptable part of growing older and gaining more experience. A person is worth more in his job as he learns more, and he therefore expects to be paid more. The history of the world is one of inflation. Of course, setbacks (commonly called depressions before some governments decided that the psychological impact of the word was too much for the people to accept), when they periodically occurred, did bring prices and wages back down. But inflationary pressures traditionally started again with recovery.

A revolutionary socialist government has many of the means at its disposal to greatly curtail inflation. Since inflation was viewed as a monstrous ill of capitalism by early Communist writers, later practitioners have usually sought to eliminate price rises. (Such a view is contradictory to one commonly held by capitalist planners who feel that some inflation is not bad but actually stimulates the economy. If wealth is considered a paper commodity, only relatively valuable in one's short lifetime, once a person's basic needs are met, any additional money is superfluous. The idea is that it simply does not matter what things cost because marketplace pressures will drive wages up at about the same pace, and, relatively, buying power will remain about equal.) The Communists charge that capitalists push the prices for their products higher and higher to make great profits, but that wages remain low and the people suffer. Any serious student of capitalism will quickly point out that products can sell only when there are people with money to buy them and when the price is attractive. It would be foolish to increase prices in the hopes of inflating profits, and watch the items go unsold. Ah, the Communist says, but capitalism encourages monopolies which then produce goods and services which the people must buy no matter what the cost, and so the poor suffer even more.

Once again the problem of semantics emerges. Young Cubans study Marx and Lenin and quote the nineteenth- and early-twentieth-century works as if the great railroad and oil monopolies still operated. No amount of argument will convince them there is any difference between the "robber barons" who ruthlessly gathered power and wealth in the last century and General Motors, Standard Oil, or A.T.&T. today. From their purist viewpoint, the very essence of capitalism is acquisition, control of the market, and then price increases to gouge the consumer. It is certainly a quaint view of our system—and of the United States in particular—that might have a few proponents in the Ralph Nader groups. It completely overlooks any ability of the marketplace to stabilize itself or the government to oversee.

One day, while we drove through irrigated farmlands in Pinar del Río, an INRA official explained the roles of the government and the farmer. INRA controls the supplies to the farmer, fixes the prices of any seeds, fertilizers, help, etc., and is the sole market for finished products, once again setting the price. It is a closed system where INRA controls the entire marketplace. Such control is repeated in every phase of life. But isn't that a monopoly? "Oh, no," the indignant official shot back, "INRA could never be called a monopoly. It is operated by the state, by the people."

Any 1880s monopolist would lick his chops at the thought of countrywide control of complete industries. What right do Cubans have to question prices, go to an alternate source for goods, or strike for higher wages? There is a certain arrogance in an approach that allows one-source supply at fixed prices with no complaints permitted when it is offered under one name, and damnation of similar actions when done under another name.

After spending the day among tobacco farmers, the author noted he felt he had been let loose among a group of "petty bourgeois." Two shocked government officials insisted that this was not the case. And why not, they were asked. These small farmers, who are responsible for 60 percent of Cuba's tobacco, own their own land, own their homes, own their animals, grow the tobacco on their land, sell it to the government, and keep the money. They certainly appear to be capitalists. "No, no," said one official, "they cannot be capitalists because they have a socialistic outlook. They think like socialists. It doesn't matter what they own or what they keep—if they think like socialists, they are socialists."

There are two ways to view employment in a totally socialist state. Since the government is the only employer, everyone can be employed. On the one hand, by the simple mechanism of giving every citizen a job and a salary, full employment is reached. Then the question arises, is there work for everyone to do? Until recently, full employment was a reality of Cuba's economy. So many projects were under way simultaneously, especially in basic construction of apartments, schools, industries, agriculture, and roads, that there was actually a labor shortage. One of the stated reasons for luring women into the work force was just that condition. Now there seems to be a slackening of demand. When the *Poder Popular* (Popular Power) provincial and municipal assemblies were elected in the fall of 1976, they were given most of the functions formerly controlled by the central government, i.e., supervision of hotels, restaurants, schools, construction, etc. The national bureaucrats who managed those programs are no longer needed and, even though they continue to draw their regular salaries, many are without duties half a year after their jobs ended. Periodic reports mention short work weeks in some areas. (Although the government still officially insists Cuba enjoys full employment, many unemployed can be seen. One young man was in technical training when a distant relative fled to Florida. The student was told to seek another area and has been unemployed for three years. Others suffer from joblessness when no work exists near their homes and no housing exists near possible work centers. Two-hour bus commutes are common to fill low-paying positions.) In many areas of manufacturing and retailing there appears to be a tendency to pad the personnel rolls with more people than can be efficiently utilized, just to keep everyone working. For example, at the L'Aiglon Restaurant in the Hotel Riviera, two maîtres d'hôtel seat the few guests when one would be more than sufficient. Often at the downstairs Primavera cafeteria, three black-suited people fill the function of seating customers while twenty-one personnel stumble over one another to serve a single room, and it still takes five minutes or more to place an order. More money can be printed to pay these salaries, since the peso has relatively little international value and only circulates internally. The government's problem is to keep enough food and consumer items available to soak up the money it is paying out. Cuba found, as other nations did earlier, that consumer tension builds when currency savings increase without adequate sales outlets.

The government's solution has been to import expensive products systematically to relieve that tension and also return the excess pesos to the treasury. Black-and-white TV sets from the Soviet Union cost 600 pesos ($732 U.S.); a small Japanese stereo unit commonly selling in the $100 to $170 range around the world costs Cubans 450 pesos. Hand-sized portable transistor radios assembled in Cuba from

Japanese components (of the type Americans casually buy for $5 to $15) are 180 pesos. This overcharge is deliberate. With food and rents kept so low and everyone working, the government knows there is spare cash. Expensive imports make people want to work and save, and they also provide the state with a mechanism for creating a profit without really having to expend any money or production facilities.

All Cuban workers are paid in cash twice a month. The paymaster picks up the money at the bank, often accompanied by an armed guard, and returns to the work center with a box of new bills. Banking as we know it does not exist in Cuba. There are no checking accounts and no checks. Since wages are paid in cash, so too are debts and retail transactions. A Cuban is allowed by law to keep up to 1,000 pesos at his home. Any above that has to be placed in a bank for safekeeping, interest-free. Western-style banking was abandoned as being exploitative, since the Communists believe paying lower interest on savings than is charged on loans takes advantage of the people. Interestingly, it is not considered exploitative to insist on holding a nation's savings and paying no interest whatsoever.

The peso, like several other Communist currencies, is not fully accepted on the world market. "Hard" currencies are traded interchangeably, with minor daily fluctuations, so that goods can be freely purchased between nations and paid for in any negotiable money. Cuban officials call this a capitalistic conspiracy to keep her poor and without proper credits. Western bankers feel that the peso is backed by inadequate reserves, have little faith in the Cuban economy, note that money can be printed at will, and calculate that its value is artificially inflated. (Cuba places the peso as worth $1.25 U.S. dollars.) The fact is that the country does suffer from the problem. She must barter or obtain hard currencies in order to buy products from non-Communist nations. Sugar is the means for accomplishing this. She sells about half her annual output on the world market and uses the funds for international purchases.

A complete revolution changes the reality of an economy as well as the aspirations of its planners. Alfredo Lopez was a private accountant in 1959, with his own business. Now an economist with the University of Havana, he can explain what has been happening and what the government hopes will happen inside Cuba's fiscal system. "First, you have to look at an economy from a different viewpoint when you have state ownership. We feel that complete services can be

As a move designed to help poor people and to contrast present government policy with that of prerevolutionary, United States–controlled utility companies, public telephones were free in Cuba until 1977. The service became too expensive to maintain, and calls are now five centavos.

maintained and new free services offered, such as health care and education, from money that would normally be siphoned off as profits in a capitalistic society." (Such a notion completely overlooks the fact that capitalistic profits are distributed to people—stockholders—who then spend them, thereby creating more jobs, wages, and products. Profits are not removed from society by some amorphous company, never to be seen again.)

Lopez continued, "By centralized control of the economy, we can become more efficient. We are also trying to change attitudes, to alter desires so people no longer want things from the past, like the same foods Europeans eat. We do this by starting with children and changing their attitudes." Compañero Lopez most likely realizes that efficiency of the sort he mentions is also a dream, since most writers on Cuba agree that the economic planning to date has been a series of disasters. For years, Cuba has been a government by trial and error, conducted by people who had more experience in guerrilla fighting than in agency management. The pattern was to plunge ahead in one direction until the program either succeeded or failed, and then proceed in a different way. The long heralded "Ten-Million-Ton Harvest" of 1970 turned out to be a fiasco that set back sugar and all other industries for years as workers and resources were diverted helter-skelter to make the unworkable successful. The military as well as every segment of society turned out in the disastrous mass program, and the country paid for the mistake with new shortages. On another front, realizing the expense and scarcity of leather, Cuba bought two shoe factories at considerable expense to the struggling economy. The products were designed to be cheap and plentiful, but they were made of plastic. Anyone trying to wear plastic shoes in a hot climate would rather go barefoot. Even faced with deprivation, the Cuban consumers turned their backs on the output. There are many other examples of trying to move the system forward, despite crippling handicaps such as the U.S. trade embargo, a lack of international credits, and sugar harvest problems, to expand goods and services and keep the people happy.

Simply stated, the economy suffers mainly because its leaders have chosen to live beyond Cuba's means. The island cannot pay for all it is doing. As Cuba hopes to leap ahead in industrialization to achieve in one generation what might more logically be expected to take several, certain economic laws inexorably continue. A small system is under severe strain if it expects to have everyone receive a salary even when not producing fully, provide universal free education and health care, maintain a huge military complex, fight wars in Africa, and engage in vast construction projects. One depressant has been that the people remain low-paid and have few of the consumer benefits that Western countries accept as normal. This helps, but the economy needs still other assets. Cuba's benefactor has been the Soviet Union. With estimates of aid running from $1 million to $3 million a day, much of the slack of the economy is being covered by the foreign grants. Additionally, there are long-term loans with low or no interest and the real prospect that they will never be recalled and so will become aid also. The Soviets gave Cuba its military hardware, free, and they update it periodically. They also supply all of Cuba's petroleum needs at about one half of the world price, buy sugar at 30¢ a pound when the world price has moved to 7-10¢ a pound, and reportedly buy nickel at $6,000 a ton, considerably above the world price of $4,800 a ton. In addition, Russians give technical assistance, sell complete factories at attractive sums, offer replacement parts and favorable terms for car and tractor purchases, and are involved in many areas of aid that make it impossible to calculate the complete worth to Cuba. The country is almost totally dependent on the Soviets' help now and would probably fail economically should their support stop. Americans who think that reestablishing relations with Cuba will simply switch the Soviet trade to the United States are sadly misinformed. Neither the U.S. government nor private concerns are about to give Castro the terms he has been receiving from his ally.

Alfredo Lopez commented on the question of assistance by saying, "No one knows how long it will take to become self-sufficient. It is our goal, but it will be years. We receive aid and we aid other countries. We couldn't call ourselves Communists if we did otherwise. We are aiding Angola, which is our duty and privilege."

To clear up some of the confusion about ownership in Cuba, Lopez discussed its role and property compensation. "A Cuban can own everything except the means of production, such as stores, taxis, apartments, factories, etc. Private automobiles, homes, and all personal possessions are, naturally, the person's. When the government nationalized businesses and land, a system of compensation was established to pay people up to 600 pesos a month for their former property. The rate was determined according to the value of what was taken. For instance, a small store might bring only 50 pesos a month, an apartment building 200, and a big factory 600. Sometimes the payments were scheduled to go for life, although most had a time period attached. In reality, almost all the property owners left the country for Florida and abandoned their buildings and factories, so no compensation was paid. Anyone who owned a home prior to 1959 and stayed here still owns the home, with no taxes."

Although the government denies it, there is evidence of favoritism toward professionals who remained after the Revolution. They have good jobs, with salaries that are often higher than newer people in similar positions. With the entire middle, technical, and professional

Signs of Soviet-Cuban cooperation are seen everywhere, as with this massive Soviet scientific exhibition held in the old capitol building. Rockets, sputniks, satellites, holograms, industrial equipment, and consumer products were all featured.

Photographer Alberto Korda documented Castro's early days for U.S. and Cuban publications. After his business was nationalized, he held various governmental photographic positions before joining the new Institute of Oceanography as its underwater photographer. He had a plush Vedado apartment and a beach house and had to relinquish one, so he kept the apartment, which he ultimately traded for this home in Cubanacan.

classes virtually wiped out when the half million exiles fled, the country seems anxious to help those who stayed. One propertied friend was given his choice to keep one of his three residences (two apartments and a beach house) and was permitted to retain both his cars. After having his business nationalized, he received a government salary at management instead of employee level. Another acquaintance had a sports car left over from before the Revolution. Since transactions for automobiles are strictly monitored, she was quietly approached and offered 20,000 pesos for a car worth no more than $2,000, but completely unavailable in Cuba. The lady refused the offer because she had a salary and some spare money and knew if she sold the car, she could never replace it.

Thus far, the Cuban economy would have to be rated as a failure, if one considers as a criterion successful service to the Cuban people. The current generation is suffering from the economy, with long workweeks under fairly primitive conditions for low salaries, and with few consumer goods available. The dream is that this is a transitional generation and that the workers today are building a New Society for tomorrow. The question is how long the present generation will tolerate such deprivation.

One foreign diplomat in Havana observes that Cuba is building an industrial complex beyond its means and beyond its needs. The assumption is that the country sees itself as the industrial supplier to Latin America, to the Caribbean, and to the Angolas and Guyanas of the future. Various officials confirmed part of this view by asking why the United States should always be considered the hemisphere's producer. With no raw materials except nickel, plus energetic workers and a basic sugar economy, why, they ask, shouldn't Cuba be like Japan, an industrial giant important beyond its size? There is a definite feeling that long-range Cuban planning is based on the island's ability to import raw materials and transform them into the products that a future socialistic hemisphere needs.

There is a disturbing aspect to this kind of projection that Cuban officials ignore or gloss over. The paper dream of communism is an absence of government and a near-perfect state of cooperation among people, who will then work to produce according to their ability and consume according to their needs. There should be no exploitation, no imperialism, and no private ownership of production. However, the long-range goals of the Cubans look remarkably like those of the imperialists of the 1880s: planning to set up an industrial power base, speaking of helping their neighbors in their fight for freedom from oppression, willing to send in troops to foreign countries to achieve this goal, and dreaming of a "sphere of influence." Perhaps the Cuban explanation that this is not imperialism is the same as the tobacco farmer who is not a capitalist—if it is done in the spirit of socialism, then it is socialism.

For the foreseeable future, the Cuban economy will remain vitally linked to sugar. It is ironic that the Revolution began by placing the blame for Cuba's backwardness on the U.S. exploiters who kept Cuba to a one-crop system. Charges were made that sugar dependency was the root of Cuba's distress and the Revolution would change that. After eighteen years, Cuba is still just as dependent on sugar. The

Revolution's planners found what the prior capitalists knew: certain economic laws continue to work no matter what kind of government is in control. As long-time ministry official Enrique Oltuski says, "Remember, we hated sugar. It symbolized the enemy. We were sure our troubles would be over as soon as we eliminated it from our island. But we learned, sometimes bitterly, that sugar is Cuba's most efficient agricultural crop." Without factories, raw materials, skilled labor, and an industrial infrastructure, Cuba has been hard put to switch suddenly from sugar to anything else. There were not only land for cane, mills in place, expertise, and the proper soil and climate, but also a reasonable world market for the output. Even though prices have sometimes fluctuated wildly, the demand has been relatively steady. Other agricultural products have been tried, but Cubans have learned from long experience that sugar can bring fifteen times as much money per acre as corn, rice, and beans. The hard reality of the marketplace shows it is better to grow and sell sugar and import other foods. Facing this tough lesson, the government continues to be at the mercy of the world market price for the sweet.

Fluctuations in the sugar price have been critical to a country that depends on international sales for over 80 percent of its foreign exchange. At the beginning of the Revolution, sugar was selling at 1–2¢ a pound. A series of dizzying rises escalated Cuba's fortunes along with the prices until sugar futures once sold for 65¢ a pound. The country's first Five-Year Plan was formulated when sugar was bringing 15–17¢ and the Soviets were buying half the crop at 30¢. Then the bottom fell out of the world market. At the CDR rally in

Pablo Romero is one of the new planners who hope to solve Cuba's chronic economic problems by more skillful use of limited resources. At INRA's headquarters, he plots countrywide agricultural development.

September, 1976, Castro said Cuba was spending more to raise and process sugar than the current world price of 7¢. The Soviets continue to take half the crop, but the price is negotiable and may well fall below the now greatly inflated 30¢ figure.

All economic planning had to be reevaluated in light of the diminished foreign exchange expected from sugar sales. Trading partners found that firm orders were no longer quite so firm. Companies that had manufactured, packaged, and shipped goods ordered by Cuba, discovered that the freight was turned back on the docks. Various ministries tried to get long-term credit from the countries where goods were purchased or asked to string out payments over years. One Canadian firm with a large government order in hand was asked to send a delegation to discuss it. The Cubans wanted either to cancel the order or to stretch out payment. The Canadians, impatient at events and having already spent considerable funds on securing and beginning work on the contract, were in no mood to alter an in-hand order. When the Cuban leader began by saying, "I suppose you've heard we're having some shipping difficulties ..." the Canadian businessman roared back, "Bullshit, you're broke!"

Coffee has been chosen as the symbol of sacrifice. During the September 28 speech, Castro acknowledged that Cubans loved their coffee and that any limitation would be a hardship. However, he explained, the rising world prices for coffee meant that Cuba was paying more and more for its imports. So the already meager ration was further reduced to 1½ ounces per week per person. What had been selling for about 2 pesos a kilo soon jumped to 5 pesos in Oriente and word went around that coffee was available on the black market for 15 pesos per kilogram. Compared to basic materials, coffee is a small item in the annual budget. But hard currency has to be found for the foreign purchases, and hard currency is in very short supply in Cuba this year. During Castro's December 2, 1976, speech inaugurating the new National Assembly, he observed that Angola had noted Cuba's coffee shortage and, in thanks, offered 15,000 tons worth $40 million, on any terms. Great applause filled Karl Marx Theatre. Castro continued by saying that it was a generous offer but one that obviously could not be accepted. Very slight applause followed.

There are certainly positive aspects of the Cuban economic experiment. To understand them fully, it is necessary to remember life before the Revolution. Although Cuba was more industrialized and enjoyed a higher standard of living than many of its Latin neighbors, it was still basically similar in social structure to other South American countries. The rich lived very well indeed. Corruption was rampant and a considerable number of people in the country operated in concert with it. Political violence was common, killings and beatings routine, and fear of authority accepted. Mafia figures, whose names are only distant memories in the United States, ran Cuba's gambling casinos and paid off Batista's men for the privilege. Prostitution and sex shows were explicit enough to gain Havana the title of "Sin Capital of the World." Massive blocks of land were owned by U.S. companies. One firm was said to have holdings in Oriente that stretched all the way from the Atlantic to the Caribbean. Of course, some Cubans were also great landowners, sugar mill operators, and coconspirators in the crime rings. But it is the U.S. participation that revolutionaries remember. Additionally, U.S. firms either controlled or had large interests in Cuba's communication systems, her utilities, oil refineries, transportation companies, and many basic industries. When nationalization was complete, the U.S. State Department estimated that over $2 billion worth of U.S. property had been seized.

For the Cubans who worked within the system in 1959, living was easy. There was plenty of money, tourism was heavy, the big spenders came for the gambling tables, sugar was king, and the United States was always there with needed expertise. But most Cubans did not work within that system. Most were poor—not in the same sense that Haitians are poor, but poor nevertheless. Over a fourth were illiterate and had no hope for anything but manual labor. Unemployment usually ran about 30 percent. Hundreds of thousands of cane cutters worked for minimal wages for up to five months a year, and then went without work for the rest of the year. High school graduates were rare in rural areas, and college education was only for the wealthy. Half the island's doctors lived and worked in Havana, and health care was, at best, unreliable outside the larger cities. The tragic aspect of it all was that hope was gone. As long as anyone could remember there had only been the Spanish rulers, and then a long series of dictatorships. Being a Cuban and being anything except upper middle class or wealthy meant living without any great prospect for the future.

Fidel Castro changed that. By the strength of his personality and his convictions and his uncanny ability to lead the Cuban people wherever he wanted, he gave the average man hope for the first time in his life. He told the people they were all equal, that racial discrimination would not be allowed, that they could be anything they wanted to be, that they should be proud to be Cubans, and that if they worked hard, they could pay for it all. Believing, Cubans rallied around their Maximum Leader.

The professionals, technocrats, wealthy, and crooked felt betrayed. Most fled to Florida. The Cubans who stayed have, by and large, seen their lives bettered. Obviously, not every single Cuban is living better than he did before the Revolution. But most are. The poor and deprived, the peasants and the factory workers now can feel they are working together for something they own. It is, after all *their* revolution. If they believe in the direction of their country—and most do approve—they can now relax knowing their children will be housed and educated, that medical care will be available and free as they get older, and that they can enjoy that strange intangible never allowed before, when all the tourists looked down at them as "sort-of-colored." Now they are Cubans, running their own show, leaders in the Third-World nations, a country to reckon with, a country that has gotten the best of the United States.

Beach homes either left by exiles or used as vacation homes by Cubans who stayed are now available to workers for one or two summer weeks as rewards for good work. This meatcutter-union member's family relaxes at Guanabo.

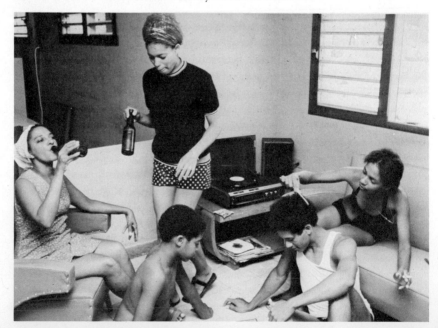

Education

6

> I have always had a great addiction to education.
> My plan, which was not original, was to universalize study
> as well as work. The alternative would be to have an
> intellectual elite and a group that does not study which
> would always perform hard manual labor. People
> talked about it and gave it attention, but Cuba was the first
> to put it into practice.
>
> —*Fidel Castro*

Through the dawn mists, the first colors of sunrise glinted across a light dew. Already the air was moist and becoming warm. It would be another hot day. In the distance, a moving column of figures cut across the arrow-straight rows of head-high trees. A little laughter and the rapid chatter of teen-agers mingled with the sounds of birds out for breakfast. Another school day had begun, and thousands of students on the Isle of Pines were starting their morning routine, tending millions of grapefruit trees, whose fruit the Revolution needs for foreign exchange.

Activities began at 6 A.M. with exercises and cleanup. Breakfast preceded a 7:10 A.M. assembly between buildings, where the flag was raised, announcements were made, and a patriotic program created by the students was presented. Half the students at assembly were dressed in school uniforms and half in work clothes. At 7:30 the first half went off for four hours of classroom instruction (in such subjects as Spanish, history, math, geography, English, Russian, chemistry, physics, biology, and Communist morality) while the remainder

Outdoor morning assembly at seven o'clock begins the day at each secondary school. Flag-raising ceremonies are followed by patriotic readings and programs.

Regimentation comes early in a system with standard buildings, classrooms, uniforms, textbooks, and teaching procedures and approaches.

worked in the fields for three hours. At 11:30 the morning program ended and there was half an hour for cleanup and rest. Some preferred a quick swim. Lunch was from noon to 1:10, when an afternoon assembly met and the two groups changed, going from classroom to fields and vice versa. A two-hour individual study period from 5:30 to 7:30 was followed by dinner at 8:30. Evening free time included TV, films, library, sports, study, or just talking. Lights were out at 10:00. Daily school routines are the same throughout Cuba.

Students are at their schools from 10 P.M. Sundays until 9 A.M. Saturdays, when buses take them home for the weekend. Parents do visit periodically, helping to clean dorms and kitchens and working around the buildings.

Before the Revolution, normal school days for primary-age children in Cuba ranged between two and four hours. Very few buildings used as schools throughout the country had been designed for the purpose. So poor was the quality of teaching that even campesinos were scrimping to keep their children enrolled in the growing number of private classes. In one area of Camaguey in the 1950s, there were forty-eight public institutions and forty-five private schools. Over 20 percent of the annual national education budget went for central administration. The amount of graft was overwhelming in a ministry required by the Constitution of 1940 to be the largest in government. Teachers were appointed for life and received full salaries whether they taught or not, or knew their subjects.

The most visible and controversial innovation in the Castro educational system was the introduction, in 1968, of secondary schools in the countryside like the one on the Isle of Pines. These are large boarding schools for about 500 seventh- to tenth-grade boys and girls. The idea is to fulfill Castro's vision of combining work and study in a positive way that would benefit both the children and society. Immediately the charges arose inside and outside Cuba that the government was taking the children away from parents and forcing them to work for the state. Max Figueroa, General Director of Educational Development in the Ministry of Education, described the government's actions. "We knew there might be problems with the new idea, so we tried it out first in our most provincial area, Camaguey. The students presented no difficulties. For them it was a holiday, with recreational facilities, being away like at a camp, and lots of fun. For the parents, it was hard. Our program calls for the

Under the watchful eyes of Fidel and Brezhnev, two students at the First of May School in Santa Clara find a moment alone. Parents worry that, at the very time children are likely to need a mother or father most, the youngsters are boarding away from home in secondary schools.

children going home each Saturday noon and returning to school Sunday night. So, we had to work to gain parents' confidence. They began to see their children coming home stronger and happy. Gradually, parents saw our program as a good idea and accepted it. Now, they struggle to make sure their kids get admitted to the schools."

Long, low concrete secondary schools have become Cuba's new landmarks. On numerous roads, particularly in Matanzas and on the Isle of Pines, they stand like sentinels in the fields, a new one coming into view before the last disappears in the distance. Consisting of three parallel buildings, each of a standardized shape, three or four stories high, the schools are designed with classrooms, dormitories for 250 girls and 250 boys, a cafeteria, and surrounding recreational facilities, usually including a very popular swimming pool. Already 305 of the innovative complexes dot Cuba's landscape. By 1980 an additional 800 are planned to house and teach the more than 400,000 secondary students the country will have then.

Each school is located near the center of a plot of agricultural land covering about 500 hectares (1,250 acres). The idea is that by splitting the day between classes and field work, the students will learn academic subjects, gain experience and an appreciation for agriculture, and help produce food for Cuba's markets. The system works.

To ensure greater yields, research is done in each school region to determine the most productive crops. For instance, at the First of May Secondary School in Santa Clara, located near Cuba's center in the new Villa Clara Province, bananas, malanga, tomatoes, and corn are produced. Southwest of Havana at the General Simón Bolívar school, the specialty is strawberries, along with smaller plantings of guavas and citrus. On the Isle of Pines, almost all effort is put into cultivating grapefruit.

The students receive help in their work. Machinery and expertise are provided by adults employed to supervise and teach proper agricultural techniques. Much of the three-hour periods is spent weeding, a never-ending process. The students also harvest the crops and do whatever work is needed throughout the year.

Eva Maria Valdés, a trim sixteen-year-old student teacher, is in her second year of teacher training. Every day she has classes from 7:30 A.M. until noon and teaches eighth-grade physics at the General Simón Bolívar School between 1:00 and 5:00 P.M. Once a week she has field work for three hours, sponsors a seventh-grade girls' dormitory, and is an organizer in the Union of Young Communists. Although her schedule is full, she is an ardent supporter of the study-

After spending three morning hours weeding strawberries, these girls at General Simón Bolívar Secondary School near Ceiba del Agua march back to change their clothes, have lunch, and attend a full afternoon of classes.

Agricultural fieldwork is half of each secondary-school student's day. Weeding malanga plants (a root vegetable) is a regular chore for these First of May youngsters in Villa Clara.

work program. She says, "These schools are the best educational facilities in the country. As you can see in the fields, the students work with enthusiasm and happiness. We know that large efforts have been made to provide us with free education. There is no questioning whether or not to work. Everyone must work. We have the examples of our parents and heroes. We want to upgrade ourselves, our future, and our culture."

Obviously, when children as young as twelve are taken to schools away from home, there are some problems. Eva acknowledged this in

Only slightly older than the students, Mirma Montesdeoca, sixteen, teaches seventh-grade physics at General Simón Bolívar Secondary School. To ease a constant teacher shortage, students studying to become teachers are used as instructors for younger grades.

recalling, "It is often hard at first. Naturally, they miss their families. Some cry a lot and there is unhappiness. But there are so many things to do, they soon get over that. There is class work to keep them busy, music, art, plays, recordings, and soon the students forget about missing parents. They get involved here. Occasionally someone just cannot adapt and goes home, but it is rare because there is so much pressure to get into these schools."

Field work is not the only labor the students perform. The secondary schools have no janitors or caretakers. Each day a few students rotate in the cleanup duties, sweeping the corridors, picking up around the grounds, to make sure the school is neat. Each dormitory group is responsible for its sleeping room and bath. Other children assist in the kitchen so that everyone does each job throughout the year.

Such a program is extraordinarily expensive for a small country. All students receive free tuition, books, food, housing, and transportation, and some even get money. Max Figueroa elaborated on the financing. "Cuba can afford this because the secondary students are dedicated to work. The average school costs us 1,350,000 pesos to build. The annual expense to keep it operating is 350,000 pesos. In such a school, the 500 working students spend three hours a day doing work that is valued at 2,100,000 pesos annually. This means that we can build all the schools we need because the students actually earn more money than their costs and expenses."

Undoubtedly, there is truth to the statement that the students' work has value. However, any but the most casual observer will note incredible inefficiency as students spend hours playing and talking in the fields. Anyone who has grown a garden knows that there are insufficient tasks for 500 people on the plot every day. To produce 2,100,000 pesos per school annually would mean that each child's work is worth 4,200 pesos a year—420 pesos for each of the ten months in a school year, or 19.38 pesos a day for his three hours. For unskilled manual labor, that is highly unlikely.

The principal value of the student work for Cuba may be in a direction other than peso totals. The agricultural program creates an awareness in the children about the land and its meaning. It ties them together in a common purpose and gives them pride in working for a goal beyond themselves. Digging teaches that there is no shame in getting hands soiled to help grow food for one's countrymen. In one generation, the stigma of being a campesino tilling the land has been dispelled, since Cuba's brightest youngsters are out in that same dirt every day. Fidel Castro has underscored the importance of these lessons by saying, "Working together builds character. Cuba will keep the work program even after its economic need passes."

A fresh new assembly line signals a different kind of work in a breezy, brightly lit installation outside Havana. Colorful plastic cases move beneath a bank of fluorescent fixtures as busy hands place circuit boards, speakers, and candy-striped copper wires inside ever-growing component packages. This, too, is part of the overall study-work program; here technically minded students perform industrial jobs for their half days instead of agricultural field work. The radio and television assembly lines are part of the Lenin Vocational School, the first of a proposed new series of scientific institutions for high-schoolers. In Camaguey, the Máximo Gómez School opened recently as part of a plan to give each province its own technical school.

Originally, the pilot Lenin School brought students from all over Cuba, but as other provinces open local schools, Lenin will serve Havana Province only. Twenty-eight-year-old Tatiana Perovani, in charge of visitors there, explained the school's purpose. "Our mission here is to produce good technicians for Cuba. We have 4,500 students living here in grades seven to thirteen. After completing this work, they can go on to universities. Beginning in grade seven, incoming

At the dedication of the new Máximo Gómez Military Academy east of Havana (locally called the West Point of Cuba), Raúl and Fidel Castro listen to the principal speech being given by General Vickor Kulikov, First Vice-Minister of Defense of the Soviet Union. An enshrouded bust of Lenin was unveiled as the Soviet Union's present to Cuba.

Cuba is willing to expend an enormous amount for students. Lenin Vocational School, the first school of its kind, was designed to house the country's best technically minded youngsters. Two Olympic-size swimming pools and a competition-size diving pool are only part of its elaborate facilities.

students spend two years exposed to various disciplines of study and come in contact with different jobs. By the time they enter the ninth grade, they choose one area of specialization."

Tatiana's tour of Lenin School includes a look at the scale model of the area and a walk-through to see the airy classrooms, dormitory wings, two Olympic-sized swimming pools plus diving pool with platforms, gymnasium, basketball and baseball facilities, cafeterias, and surrounding vegetable gardens. The school and grounds have seventy-five acres. Obviously that is not enough for the typical secondary school field work, and Tatiana explained the difference between regular secondary schools and the new vocational-technical schools like Lenin. "To enter, a person's academic average from grade four must be 85 percent or higher. We have the very best students in the country here. We have designed work that is more in line with their interests and lessons than the agricultural work done by other students. The school is still divided with classes and work for half the student body in the morning and a reversed schedule in the afternoon. But our work is in factories attached to our school. There the students make radios, televisions, TV antennas, mini-calculators,

In a new enterprise, black and white Soviet television sets are being assembled by Lenin Vocational School students. The parts are imported, but the labor is done by youngsters who work part of the day to pay for their education.

Students at Lenin Vocational School, considered to be the best school in Cuba, perform technical tasks instead of agricultural work for their half-day for the state. Portable transistor radios are assembled from Japanese parts.

batteries, computers, and sports equipment. Some work has to be done in the gardens, on the grounds, in cleanup, and in the cafeterias, but most is in the factories."

TV manufacture is the newest assembly line addition. Cuba had a countrywide television network prior to 1959 with all U.S. equipment. (Interestingly, it was just that system that allowed Castro to reach all the people in his hours-long speeches explaining the Revolution and its plans.) With the U.S. embargo and Cuba's new ties with the Soviet Union, television imports switched from U.S. brands to the large old-fashioned Soviet black-and-white models. Now, components are being imported from the U.S.S.R. for assembly by the students. The price is still high, about 600 pesos for a black-and-white twenty-one-inch screen set.

Small hands reach out and pick up the brown perforated circuit boards as acrid solder smoke curls upward before the scrubbed faces. A wire here, a knob there, and all the pieces are slowly joined together to form two models of portable radios to be sold on the domestic market. Little black-and-white plastic cases are placed over the Japanese components in sixty "Taino" hand-size sets daily. At the end of the bright, long assembly belt, adults use Soviet testing equipment to ensure proper operation of each set. The government pays about 12 pesos for the radio parts and sells finished units for 180 pesos.

On the opposite side of the moving belt, an equal number of students work on a larger model radio, the "Agricola," finished in a light blue plastic case. With space for more and larger batteries, the "Agricola" is designed for rural areas without electricity. Techniques are faster on the big unit and production reaches 180 radios a day. At the end of the warehouse-style room, sets that pass all tests are cleaned and boxed to be sold by the trade ministry.

Tedium is more of a problem in the factory-type work conditions. Kids in the fields change jobs often and are out in the open, moving about. Three hours on the assembly line brings yawns and boredom and seems more like a genuine job.

In a nearby building a new industry is taking form. Mini-calculators destined to be used by various government offices are assembled from components sold by the Sharp Company in Japan. About sixty of the large desk model A.C. units are assembled daily. Cuba has no plans for introducing the pocket calculators that are so popular elsewhere.

The prize for a few select students at the end of each academic year is a free one-month group tour to the Soviet Union. The Lenin School Faculty chooses fifty outstanding students to receive this honor on the basis of grades, production work, attitudes, and the recommendations of their worker groups. Photographs and souvenirs from past trips are displayed in a small museum near the main entrance of the school. Beside them are photographs, text, and paintings re-creating events in the life of Lenin.

While Lenin School provides a unique solution to educating new technicians, a much larger and more comprehensive secondary school system is rapidly expanding on the Isle of Pines, located sixty-five

Relaxing is a part of school life too. On the Isle of Pines, once a month, students are bussed to the beach for a Sunday outing.

miles off Cuba, almost due south of Havana. Long feared as the country's "prison island," the area was renamed the "Island of Youth" by the Revolution in 1966. (The old federal prison, composed of five circular buildings patterned after the jail in Joliet, Illinois, is kept open now as a museum to highlight past abuses and to show where Castro spent his twenty months of confinement.) Over 11,000 students are busy transforming the once sparsely populated island into a citrus center.

Columbus discovered the 850-square-mile island on his second voyage in 1494. Siboney Indians lived along its shores in a peaceful existence that the Spanish soon ruined. Now protected in a cave at Punta del Este on the island's southeast corner are drawings predating the arrival of the Europeans. One particularly beautiful and astronomically important design has fifty-six large circles; twenty-eight red ones indicating the number of monthly lunar days are separated by twenty-eight black circles for the lunar nights. An arrow crosses them and points to the summer solstice, the place the sun rises on June 21, the longest day of the year. Thirteen smaller black circles beside the larger ones mark the thirteen lunar months to a year. Another figure looks like a comet, while many additional drawings have unresolved meanings.

Because of its isolation, the Isle of Pines was always underpopulated and undeveloped. Mountains of marble were responsible for some industry, but few people were needed to work the stone. A strange and confused period followed Cuba's independence from Spain in 1898. Since the United States got embroiled in that fight and considered it had a moral right to determine Cuba's future, the 1902 Platt Amendment, passed by the U.S. Congress, specifically eliminated the Isle of Pines from the rest of Cuba and said the island's status would be determined at a later date. Cuba, naturally, considered the smaller island to be a part of Cuba, but was in no position to argue.

Following this declaration, during the island's legal limbo, Americans came to colonize a new land, apparently with the full blessing of the U.S. government. William Jennings Bryan came as Secretary of State in 1913 and spoke of annexing the land as part of the United States. Local island publications openly called for annexation as Americans numbered over 600. Then in 1925, the Hay-Quesada Treaty between Cuba and the U.S. established ownership for Cuba of

Student labor has made the citrus operation possible on the Isle of Pines. Weeding and picking are almost exclusively tasks for the seventh to tenth graders, who provide most of the island's population.

an island she had always felt was hers. The Americans slowly drifted away, and the only excitement after that was in 1930 when the local American newspaper headlined a story that Charles Lindbergh, working for Pan American Airways, was visiting in search of a landing-refueling site for a newly proposed Miami-Panama flight route. Another spot was chosen, and the Isle of Pines slumbered again.

After the Revolution, the government found that one of Batista's relatives had acquired much of the island's acreage and built a resort for wealthy yachtsmen on the south coast. Aside from that, the prison, a little fishing, and marble mining were about the only activities. Only 11,000 permanent residents called it home, and most of them lived in the single town, Nueva Gerona. INRA was looking for agricultural projects for the Revolution and investigated citrus prospects on the Isle of Pines. Soil and climate seemed ideal for grapefruit in particular, and the decision was made to renovate the island.

Now, mile after mile of cleared land is planted in grapefruit trees, all tended by the students. Over 3 million trees surround the schools and another million are being prepared. In one field outside town, volunteers and INRA employees are transplanting 250,000 seedlings to develop them for final planting. Production is already up to 20,000 metric tons annually, 90 percent of which is shipped as fresh fruit, mainly to Canada. In 1959 only 1,500 acres of Isle of Pines land yielded citrus crops. Clearing is under way to have 112,500 acres planted by 1980.

After the 7:30 A.M. school assemblies, half of each student body marches off into the citrus trees for the morning's work. Bearing their hoes as arms, they attack grass and weeds to give neat rows of new plants room to grow. One busy group greeted the author with friendliness and curiosity, asking immediately about nationality. A slight recoil and looks of disbelief met the answer, *"Norteamericano."* Struggling to find some reason why an American would be on the Isle of Pines, one bold student ventured, "Are you a member of a political organization?" Back came the answer, "Yes, I'm a Democrat." Quizzical expressions were exchanged, then another asked, "Is that a secret organization?"

University students generally have a better grasp of U.S. politics than that, but their views are also distorted by the steady propaganda aimed at all Cubans. Higher education still, as in the past, is centered around the University of Havana, recently renamed the University of the Nation, but the education ministry is planning provincial universities, and already has three other universities and three higher education centers spread around Cuba.

As a center of learning, the University of Havana has had a notable history. Located principally on an attractive hill in mid-town Havana, it has enjoyed twin reputations for academic achievement and for student dissent against the dictators over the decades. Under communism, the dissent role is gone, and if freedom of thought is considered an integral part of academic excellence, then that achievement too has been subordinated.

Prior to the Revolution, only relatively few Cubans actually made it to the university. Wealthy citizens often sent their children abroad to college. In March of 1957, after a student uprising against Batista, the university was closed, not to reopen until several months after Castro took power. Then the enrollment was 11,000, with 65 percent of the students majoring in medicine and law. The university was considered anti-Marxist before the Revolution and, in the European tradition, was considered separate from the state, with policemen prohibited from entering the grounds.

Such independence was quickly ended by the new government.

Now the university is considered an intimate participant in the development of Cuba's "New Society." Completely Marxist in outlook, the institution includes Communist theory in all departments. No other theories are allowed, except as comparison to show their basic inferiority. Currently, the university is viewed as a tool for training the people who will fill Cuba's future job slots.

Alfredo Lopez, a professor in the economics department, explained the system. "We set out to find what the country needs and then how to get those people. We give countrywide tests to check interests and abilities. Then we send specialists to the various secondary schools to describe their jobs. Following that we take the students on field trips to show them the different work areas. After all that, the university preregisters students during their eleventh and twelfth grades. They choose a first, second, and third career. After that, we check with the Ministry of Education and get a five-year jobs list that shows how many of each specialty we expect to need. Then, going mainly by school grades, we pick the people to be admitted. For instance, if we needed a hundred doctors in five years, we would take the top one hundred students who chose medicine and enroll them. If a student feels he's been overlooked by this process, there is an appeal procedure. After receiving a free university education, the student is required to serve for up to three years wherever the Revolution says there's a need. Then, he's free to go to work where he wants."

Although that freedom to move sounds reasonable, the reality is somewhat less so. Since work itself is totally government controlled,

Long the center of student protests against government abuses, the main entrance to the University of Havana (recently renamed the University of the Nation) is quiet now, as only Marxism is taught in the classrooms—and protests are banned.

and apartments are allocated by work centers, the government must approve any move before a new job or location is possible. Additionally, new ration cards, and all the necessary papers to show that the move has official approval, must be issued. The government can and does assign people to work where it has need. There are two appeals from such a decision. If both are denied, the Cuban has to work where the state says.

Such problems did not exist before the Revolution, when hundreds of thousands of Cubans were unemployed for several months each year and an estimated one-fourth of the population in the 1950s was illiterate. Although alarming in itself, in Latin America during the same years, only Uruguay, Chile, and Argentina had more literate populations. Haiti was the worst off with over 90 percent illiterates. According to Cuba's 1953 census, only 56 percent of children between the ages of six and fourteen were attending schools (and the figure, particularly in the countryside, could have been much smaller). Of teen-agers between thirteen and eighteen, only a shocking 10 percent were in school. (In 1977, 98.3 percent of children between six and twelve are in school, and 82 percent of those between thirteen and sixteen.)

Fidel Castro's first public statements on education came after his initial revolutionary act, the unsuccessful attack on the Moncada army barracks in Santiago, July 26, 1953. On trial for his life, Fidel used his legal background in a brilliant courtroom defense speech, later published as *History Will Absolve Me*. In addition to outlining his plan for a revolutionary Cuba, he emphasized his concern for the state of education at that time. "In any small European country there are more than 200 technical and industrial arts schools; in Cuba there are only six such schools, and the boys who graduate have no place to use their skills. The little rural schools are attended by only half of the school age children—barefooted, half-naked and undernourished— and frequently the teacher must buy necessary materials from his own salary. Is this the way to make a nation great? Only death can liberate one from so much misery."

Castro's time in the Sierra Maestra brought him in daily contact with the poor campesinos, who were offering him aid, comfort, and support. As he learned more about them, he promised to benefit their lives if his revolution succeeded. When it did, they were among the first to receive help.

The first major effort was the Literacy Campaign. Castro said that people who could not read and write were ungovernable. The Ministry of Education rapidly worked out plans to assure children a fuller education. But what could be done with a fourth of the population past school age but still illiterate? In a massive program, 100,000 youngsters spread out over the island to teach their elders. Illiterates were told they were victims of the past dictatorship's cruelty and should learn now without derision or shame, in order to become fully functioning revolutionaries. The plan was ingenious. It reduced illiteracy to about 3 percent. Almost as important, it bound the country together. Young people were out working for the Revolution, helping old people, who in turn began to feel a part of the Revolution.

The new government's early aim was to universalize education and also end the pervasive corruption that had characterized its operation under Batista. School attendance was made compulsory for all.

Clinical uniformity marks the girls dormitory of the President Salvadore Allende Teacher-Training School outside Havana. Twelve-year-old Alina Alfonso folds her towel in the fashion distinctive to her floor. Each secondary-school girl brings a doll.

Sexist roles prevail at the President Salvadore Allende Teacher-Training School, where 83 percent of the students are girls.

Typical of the new look in Cuban schools is the President Salvadore Allende Teacher-Training School outside Havana. Bright colors and an open, airy design are common to the hundreds of secondary schools recently built or under construction.

Currently, children are required to stay through the sixth grade, but there is a strong "Revolution Moral" that pressures all able students to remain in school until they are fifteen or sixteen years old. The goal is slowly to raise the mandatory grade requirement until high school is a standard achievement.

A flexible education system is constantly being revised to meet changing conditions. Max Figueroa explained the current status of various programs. "Over one-third of our entire population is enrolled in some kind of organized education. To pay for such enormous involvement, we are spending 10 percent of Cuba's gross national product, over 700 million pesos now, and an estimated one billion pesos by 1980. The highest outlay before the Revolution was about 80 million pesos a year. We have two principal educational networks; youths are called student-workers, and adults are worker-students.

"Youths have two years of voluntary preschool and then compulsory primary school through the sixth grade. At the end of primary school a decision must be made to go into one of three directions: to a technical or polytechnical school for three years, to secondary school for four years, or to a school for primary teachers for five years. In making a choice, the student, teachers, and parents go over the student's permanent cumulative record, including all aspects of academic, social, and economic life. If technical or teacher training is chosen, that completes the education process. After secondary school, if that route is chosen, there are five areas of specialization: pre-university, language, technology, economics, and agriculture, that last for three additional years, to the equivalent of grade thirteen. Finally, those graduates can go on to a university and choose one of eight specialties."

The adult "worker-student" program is more direct. Realizing the relatively low status of education among the masses, the government set a goal that every Cuban would be literate and achieve a basic sixth-grade education. Currently, almost 400,000 adults are taking classes to accomplish the dream. Many aspects of education will change by 1980, the end of Cuba's first Five-Year Plan. By then, it is assumed that all adults will have finished their basic education and the program can be phased out. Adults will still be able and even encouraged to continue in school as long as they can. Secondary education will be reprogrammed to end at twelve years instead of going on to thirteen now, and compulsory attendance will be increased from the sixth to the ninth grade.

Unquestionably, education is one of the finest achievements of the Revolution. Universalizing it for the masses has forever altered Cuban society. That single act has brought the island together, creating much of the favorable public opinion and mass support the Revolution enjoys. It has opened Cuba to the world's achievements in science and technology. Unfortunately, because of the strictures of communism and its refusal to accept any conflicting thoughts, the educational process has closed Cuba to much of the world's thinking in the arts and humanities. Only music, which is by its nature nonpolitical, has survived relatively untouched. With modern science equipment imported from the U.S.S.R. and Japan, Cuban technical accomplishments should continue to increase as emphasis in the area persists.

Serious questions have to be asked about the quality of all this new education. By decree, students must be more than academicians. They must work, participate in sports, engage in social programs, and spend hours each week aside from class work. Although admirable in many ways, the system points out that intellectuals are not going to be prized as such. No one knows the long-term effects on a culture that values only well-rounded people to the exclusion of "thinkers." Time spent in the fields and on revolutionary or Marxist-Leninist courses means less time for regular studies. So many students are now registered that a teacher shortage forces schools to use other students for instructional purposes. For Lenin Vocational School's 4,500 students there are 250 regular adult teachers and 300 high school students in teacher training who instruct classes. At General Simón Bolívar Secondary School, only 11 adult teachers are available for 589 students, while 61 high school student teachers take up the slack. It seems that at least one full year has been eliminated from the total time needed to complete a medical degree.

All these shortcuts have to have an effect. Student teachers, political classes, half days, emphasis on science at the expense of the humanities—all of these play a role in shaping Cuba's "New Society." The numbers, and the achievements, have been impressive. The sum total has to be weighed in relation to where Cuba is today, and where her leaders want to take her.

Modern medical devices are being purchased to update Cuba's health-care system. Dr. Alberto Hernandez Cañero, director of the Institute of Cardiology and Cardiovascular Surgery, checks the automatic readout from Japanese equipment that performs constant monitoring for six intensive-care patients simultaneously.

Public Health

7

> Our physicians are very good. Before the Revolution
> we had about 6,000 doctors. Now there are 11,000 and by
> 1980 we plan for 15,000. Almost half our doctors
> went to the U.S. after 1959. Now we once again have all the
> physicians we need and are even able to lend them
> to other countries. We will soon be able to have a doctor in
> every school and on every merchant ship.
>
> *—Fidel Castro*

Little one-day-old Noralmis Vega Cordero snuggled up to her mother, comfortably propped up on the coverless metal-frame bed. Dalia Cordero beamed with her new loving, motherly smile and cradled the small black head in her work-callused hand. Noralmis nudged open the gown top to get at the soft breast she had learned to use only yesterday. No fewer than an even dozen women, their own pregnancies bulging against the loose white cotton pullover smocks, hovered over the scene, anxious to repeat it successfully through the following few days.

Outside the tiny hospital, steep slopes drop on all sides to the warm, clear Caribbean waters. One tiny road connects the small peninsula to the mainland and the hot, dry Oriente coastal town of Chivirico. Over the community's tin roofs, shimmering in the midday heat, the Sierra Maestra Mountains begin their immediate rise from the sea, forming a barrier that has always physically separated these mountain people from the rest of Cuba. Currently, this small fishing port, about forty-five miles west of Santiago, marks the end of the

115

All the expectant mothers at Chivirico's small maternity hospital gather around Dalia Cordero and her day-old daughter, Noralmis. Each in turn will deliver at the facility in the Sierra Maestra foothills, and then return to her mountain home.

road. Only jeeps and horses and feet go farther. Now the government has a road project under way to encompass the entire coastal perimeter of the Sierra Maestra, introducing to this remote section electricity, running water, and many of the other conveniences of modern society.

As Fidel Castro likes to say, that is what the Revolution is all about. This was the area he and his band of rebels chose when the *Granma* brought them from Mexico in 1956. He could use the isolation and lack of transportation and communication to his advantage as a guerrilla fighter. But what he saw as he lived among the mountain peasants for twenty-five months greatly affected his outlook for the Revolution. He called these poor, honest people the backbone of Cuba who had been abused the most by past governments. They had no education, no medical services, and no hope for the future. They had only been used by the people in Havana and had received nothing in return. As he lived in the Sierra, he said and wrote that, if he was successful, these peasants would be the first beneficiaries of his fight. Fidel Castro has kept those promises.

The story of the Literacy Campaign to teach everyone in the

country to read and write has been covered in the last chapter. Simultaneously, the government set about to decentralize public health from Havana and make services available and free to people who had never before seen a doctor or taken a prescribed drug. The little hilltop Giraldo Aponte Fonseca Hospital in Chivirico is one of the results of this effort.

Dr. Robert Gandarilla, an OB-GYN specialist from the University of Havana, is in charge of the small facility and typical of the new look in Cuban medicine. To repay the Revolution for his lifetime of free education, and to reinforce the commitment to the countryside, he and all other doctors agree to spend at least a year of their practice in rural areas. He is the only doctor on the staff of eleven. The ten women nurses handle most of the routine calls for the little general hospital and tend to the pregnant women and new mothers, who make up most of the patients. In less than a generation, the Revolution has coaxed the Sierra's women from their bohios for delivering in an institution. Since travel is difficult and distances can be quite far, the women are asked to come in during their thirty-seventh week of pregnancy to wait the final three weeks at Chivirico. Their days are spent chattering and gossiping and going from bed to bed to ogle the latest addition, while waiting for their own moment of attention.

Obviously, the relatively sparse conditions of the Chivirico hospital show only one aspect of Cuban medicine. As one of the principal goals and brightest accomplishments of the Revolution, public health progress has brought vast changes in every area of medical study and practice. The first change, which prompted half the doctors to leave for Florida in the early 1960s, was nationalization of businesses, including private practices, clinics, and private hospitals. Cuban doctors work for the state and receive regular salaries just like other employees.

There are a few historical exceptions to this. A small number of doctors and dentists who stayed after the Revolution remain in practice and, as in England, if a citizen wants to go to them and pay their fee rather than receive free government care, he may. The Public Health Ministry declined to make exact figures available, but it seems reasonable to say there are a few hundred such private-practice doctors at work. It seems to be mainly a Havana phenomenon. In order to reward doctors who were willing to stay after the

Revolution, the government ruled that they could not operate clinics or own buildings, but they could practice and keep their fees. Doctors graduated since the Revolution are not granted this privilege. With office visits averaging around 20 pesos, the doctors find their schedules filled by the diplomatic community and the many Cubans who would rather pay and receive an appointment and fast service (not to mention what many feel is better and more mature care) than wait in line at a polyclinic.

It has been relatively easy for doctors to remain in private practice because it does not require capital outlays by the government or the physicians. Patients are diagnosed and prescriptions written to be filled at the many public pharmacies (out-patient medicines prescribed to adults are paid for by the patient anyway). Hospitalization, surgery, or any complicated treatments are referred to state institutions. Dentistry is another matter, due to the equipment needed and replacement parts required for practice. Because of this, only a tiny number of dentists work in private practices.

In response to nationalization, the medical faculty at the University of Havana dropped from 110 to 14, creating a severe teaching strain which is now leveling off after sixteen years. In 1959 there was one Cuban doctor for every 1,000 people. That percentage was sorely affected by the physicians going into exile to Florida. Only in 1976 did Cuba once again reach the same proportion of doctors to patients.

The important thing to remember is that the Revolution took public health out of the hands of the doctors and made it into a cornerstone of government policy. No matter the cost or the difficulties, Fidel Castro said that every Cuban would have free medical care all his life, regardless of the person's background or position or salary, and regardless of the special care that might be entailed. Once that decision was made and central control of health became a reality, many other aspects of care were introduced into the system. With central planning and payment, medicine no longer had to concentrate on treatment but could expand into the far more exciting area of preventive care. Once the government had the means to manage the entire country, simultaneously eradication programs that are only dreams in other countries became a reality in Cuba.

Dr. Jorge Aldereguía, Vice-Minister of Hygiene and Epidemiology in the Ministry of Public Health, like every other contemporary government official, fanned out reams of statistics showing vast improvements his ministry has made from 1959 to today. Generally, the repetition of every sentence beginning with "Before the triumph of the Revolution," is tiresome, but in this ministry's case, the facts are truly significant. Dr. Aldereguía could be a doctor anywhere. Tall and thin, with a gray business suit (highly unusual in Cuba, where a guayabera shirt is formal enough for any occasion) and pleasant bedside manner, he relayed statistics with an ease and pride that indicate years of familiarization with the material. "At the triumph of the Revolution, public health in Cuba was similar to other undeveloped countries with common communicable diseases, high infant and maternal mortality rates, malnutrition, and general hygiene problems. Our most common communicable disease with workers was malaria. In 1962 we had 3,519 cases. With a mosquito-spraying program and constant treatment of all cases, we reduced the number to 7 in 1967 and then eradicated malaria."

More and more statistics detailing accomplishments were piled on by the Vice-Minister. Tuberculosis deaths dropped from 1,146 in 1959 to 309 in 1974. Maternal mortality decreased from 118 mothers' deaths per 100,000 births in 1962 to 56 in 1974, the lowest rate in Latin America. There were 46 new polio cases in 1962 and none in 1974 after a countrywide campaign to give all children the oral vaccine. Only 3 new cases of diphtheria have been recorded since 1971, after a high of over 900 cases in 1963.

While we drove to inspect an intensive care unit for heart patients, Dr. Aldereguía continued to recite facts. "We have constantly looked at health care as a current reality and compared it with what we would like it to be. In 1959 over half of Cuba's doctors and hospital beds were in Havana, a city with less than a fourth of the island's people. Obviously, facilities and physicians were where the money was. With socialism, we could look at care from a countrywide viewpoint. We started outside Havana and now have 50 hospitals and 150 dispensaries operated by the Rural Service. While increasing hospital beds from 28,000 in 1958 to 44,000 in 1974, we deliberately placed them in the country. Havana's share of hospital beds dropped from 62 percent in 1958 to 42 percent in 1974, which is much more in line with the population here.

"The Revolution has altered Cuba's health care in two significant ways. Before 1959 doctors only treated disease, since there was no

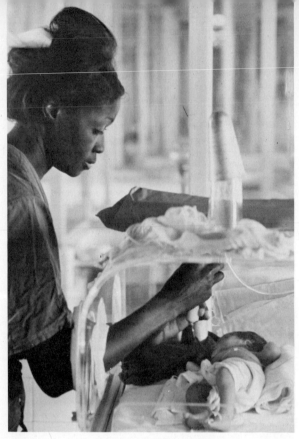

A premature baby is fed intravenously while in an
incubator at the Ramón Gonzales Maternity Hospital in
Havana. Such care and equipment have brought Cuban
infant-mortality rates to among the lowest in Latin
America.

Dr. Yolanda Santos is a beneficiary of equal opportunity in education and medicine
for women. She is in charge of bull-semen production at the Rosafe Signet Provincial
Insemination Center in San Jose.

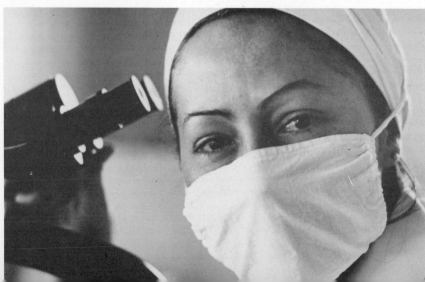

central program aimed at preventive medicine. Now we try to eradicate entire diseases before they can begin. Next, the Revolution has brought about a general awareness in the people about diseases and public health. When people were poor and seldom went to doctors, even if they were sick, no one thought about the large issues of good general health. Now, with free care and massive education programs to inform everyone about health, Cubans are more aware than ever what public health means."

Two of the mass organizations, the CDR and Cuban Women's Federation, discussed earlier, are responsible for carrying out many of the Ministry's programs. For instance, each April, for five days, the CDRs give oral polio vaccine to every child in Cuba. Prior to that time, the CDRs have made a census of the children in their areas and have received the necessary doses of vaccine and the sugar they will be put on. This saves doctors, nurses, and technicians the massive task of administering over a million doses annually. For diseases requiring injections, the CDRs are responsible for making a list of the people to receive shots and bringing them to the offices. There technicians are free of administrative details and can give injections and return to medical work.

The Cuban Women's Federation sponsors educational campaigns to get women to come in for Pap smears (uterine cancer tests) and breast examinations. Among Cuban women, breast cancers are the most frequent, followed by cancer of the cervix and lung. The programs are so well accepted that Cuba leads all Latin American countries in the percentage of its women to receive Pap smears.

At the center of the new health care system is the polyclinic, Cuba's basic medical unit. Now more than 340 of them are distributed throughout the country, each designed to serve about 25,000 people. It is to these polyclinics that Cubans usually go first for any medical care. The one closest to home keeps medical records on each family in its area, and it is normal for individual patients to see the same doctor over the years.

One such busy facility is the Plaza de la Revolución Polyclinic, named for the nearby Plaza in the heart of Havana. Its director, Dr. Cosme Ordoñez, is typical of other directors in that half his time is spent teaching medicine at the university. As is usual in most areas, the polyclinic is housed in a prerevolutionary building originally designed for other purposes, in this case for offices. Only a few new

Juan Caraballo is one of four doctors and twenty-two residents practicing medicine at the Plaza of the Revolution Polyclinic in Havana. He keeps records on the people he normally sees and is responsible for the health care of about a thousand people.

housing developments have polyclinics built to order.

Dr. Ordoñez, who began his explanation by saying that he and his co-workers were revolutionaries first, doctors second, and teachers third, described the functions of his clinic. "When a citizen gets sick, he makes a decision based on the seriousness of his problem. He can go to the emergency room of the nearest hospital or come to the polyclinic. If it is an accident, or a night sickness, he will likely go to the hospital. A normal sickness that can be treated during day office hours is usually done here. If he comes here, care is based on medical decisions, and we will either treat him or recommend a general or specialized hospital, for instance heart disease or cancer. We serve a large area here, 33,000 people, but our organization is the same as for any other polyclinic. We have 26 doctors and 26 nurses. We try always to assign one nurse to each doctor. There are 76 students of medicine who work here and 22 residents (9 in internal medicine, 5 in OB-GYN, and 8 in pediatrics). On the staff here we have one internist, one OB-GYN, and one pediatrician. The polyclinic system is planned to have one pediatrician for each 1,000 children, one internist for each 2,000 adults, and one OB-GYN for every 2,000 women up to 50 years."

To replace the 3,000 doctors who went into exile took time, effort, and some extra allowances. Since 1959 about 8,000 physicians have graduated. First they came from the University of Havana, the only medical school. Now there are three others. In the same time over

50,000 medical technicians have also been trained. Nursing schools were increased from six to thirty-four to fill vacancies and also to expand the personnel to meet the new interest and demands in health care. The typical curriculum for medical students has a one-year internship after graduation followed by up to three years in rural service wherever the Revolution may assign them. Recently, this service might be overseas in Angola or one of the other countries that Cuba is aiding. Following those years, the students have a three-year residency where they may specialize. It is this group of residents that is providing Cuba with its basic care in the polyclinics.

Regular patients get prescriptions and pay for any medicines they may need. Maternity patients, babies up to one year old, and TB patients get free medicine, as do admitted hospital patients. Appointments to see doctors are not usually made, so the nonemergency patient comes to the polyclinic during regular hours and waits his turn, creating yet another time-consuming line. Such waits may run into hours.

For many reasons, doctors have been singled out to be the "princes" in Cuban society. So much of the Revolution's prestige and health rests on so relatively few people. Following the Soviet example, women are now entering the field for the first time in large numbers. To keep the physicians happy, a special group of moral and material incentives apply. Doctors get the first priority to buy cars, the highest pay in the country, and the most vaunted place in the community. Medical students are paid an allowance based on years in school. It is usually 30–80 pesos monthly, with last-year students receiving 100 pesos a month. Postgraduates in rural service get 200 pesos, while residents are paid 220–250. A specialist will earn 350 pesos, while an experienced specialist who publishes, teaches, and works in research might get 680. Teaching in the university and heading a polyclinic or department will earn the maximum pay in Cuba, 750 pesos monthly ($937.50 U.S.).

At Alamar, the rapidly expanding housing project just east of Havana, one of the new polyclinics, named Docente Alamar (meaning *teaching polyclinic),* is housed in a new building designed for the purpose. Dr. Jesús Perea Corral is chief of its pediatrics department and a professor of medicine at the University of Havana. He guides his guests through the waiting parents and children into an air-conditioned conference room, where he explains the public health

The good life is still available for some in Cuba, especially for physicians. Dr. Jesus Perea teaches at the university and heads the pediatrics department at Alamar Polyclinic for a combined salary of 690 pesos monthly. By law, rent cannot exceed 10 percent of the household head's salary, so he pays 69 pesos for a modern house in Havana. The religious art pieces were collected on a recent business trip to Rumania.

Among several important perquisites for physicians is the ability to buy a new automobile. Dr. Jesus Perea recently bought this Argentinian Fiat.

goals in child care. "This polyclinic serves 22,000 people, of which 8,500 are children. There are thirty doctors and thirty nurses on the staff, including two psychiatrists, an orthopedic specialist, a dermatologist, and a specialist in circulation diseases. Most of the doctors here are postgraduates doing their residency. In pediatrics, my field, each doctor has a group of 1,000 children to treat and he always keeps the same group. Last year, 85 percent of the children who live here were in the clinic for some treatment. That doesn't necessarily mean they were sick, but they were here for injections, preventive care, or because of illness. Our treatment schedule calls for seven examinations annually for children under one, two examinations a year for one- to three-year-olds, one a year for three- to five-year-olds, and after five we see children when they are ill or are in need of routine preventive care."

It takes only a few meetings with Cuban medical residents to realize how young they are, often no more than twenty-three or twenty-four. These are the first-line medical personnel who are doing most of the routine treatments. Dr. Perea confirmed the observation. "Children start to school early here. One hundred percent of the kids under six in Alamar are already in school. It is also possible to skip grades along the way. After secondary school, the equivalent of tenth grade, premed students go to pre-university classes for two years (equal to eleventh and twelfth grades) and on to medical school directly for five years instead of going to a regular university first for four years and then on to med school for four more."

Obviously, Cuba is more interested now in getting people into the field quickly than in producing scholars and thinkers. Many of the secondary-school courses are taught by teacher-training students only one or two years older than the pupils. The school day is short to allow for work in the fields, and the total number of school years has been decreased for doctors to get them into polyclinics. Quality is bound to suffer under the system. It is Cuba's way to solve the critical medical shortage it has had since the early 1960s. It is to be hoped that once that void is completely filled, a little more attention can again be paid to scholarship.

One appreciated feature of medical treatment retained in Cuba and practically lost in the United States is the house call. Polyclinic doctors generally work about four hours in the mornings at the office seeing approximately twenty cases and then spend the afternoons making house calls and doing other work outside the clinic.

During those morning hours, a roomful of Alamar youngsters impatiently wait outside a corridor lined with small identical offices. Eddy Ruíz is only nine, but is a tall boy and not feeling well. He stayed home from school today, so his father brought him in to see what the problem is. As his name is called, Eddy leads the way into the all-white room sparsely furnished with a tiny desk and two chairs. He stands for a moment until white-smocked Odila Quirós asks him to be seated. Odila is only slightly larger than Eddy and considerably smaller than his father. The man is somewhat shy about sitting in a little room and discussing medical questions with a woman. Still, this is the new Cuba, and Eddy's father knows that this young woman is a doctor and a privileged member of society. Odila, who is twenty-three and in her first year of residency, has pulled the file and writes the details of this morning's sickness. Eddy goes into the next room to have his height, weight, and temperature taken by nurse Ana Chirino. As he climbs onto the scale, he seems not to notice that his socks have no toes. Odila does a quick examination and says it is only a cold and not to worry about it. She puts away the file and gets out another one. And so morning goes. She has fulfilled her dream from childhood. She studied hard, made the right decisions at the right times, and has become one of Cuba's chosen few. Her career in medicine has begun.

Across Havana, another medical drama is being played with an unlikely cast in an even more unlikely setting. Breakfast is over now and the athletic field of the fenced-in compound is filled with small groups of men following one another, walking in little circles. Their dull gray uniforms give no indications of their work. Soon, another group appears walking in a column, each man with his arm on the shoulder of the man in front. The line disappears into a new building, and another group comes into view. Who are these people and why are they parading around beside the main road between Havana and its airport?

The bizarre scene represents Cuba's innovative approach toward dealing with the mentally disturbed. Instead of being hidden away to languish in remote institutions, the patients and facilities at this, the principal psychiatric hospital in the country, are regularly on display to the public and especially during special tours for foreign dignitaries. Officials are justly proud of the advances made in mental care, and many of the patients actually seem to enjoy all the attention.

As always, every story begins with how bad it was before the Revolution. In this case, Havana's psychiatric hospital was the only one in Cuba and campesinos with problems usually received no treatment at all. Over 6,000 people were crowded into the compound, often naked and with minimal care. A photographic exhibit on the grounds today looks more like a German concentration camp than a hospital. More than 80 people died in some months, said to be partially because officials stole money intended for food and medicine.

Now the facility has been turned into a model hospital, shown to health groups and tourists as an example of the Revolution's concern for people. A staff of 83, of which 39 are psychiatrists, tend 3,590 patients, 72 percent of them suffering from schizophrenia. Seven other mental hospitals around the island bring the total committed to 5,000. Deaths are down in Havana now to about 80 a year, from natural causes.

The reason tours are brought through is that the entire hospital and grounds look more like a school dormitory and factory than a mental institution. Bars are gone from the windows and flower plantings accent the little green areas in front of dorms. Patients are not confined to traditional cells but may roam freely. In small buildings near the rear of the compound, men and women live in separate homelike atmospheres that completely eliminate the institutional feeling.

Cuba's innovation, however, is not the setting, but the program for patients. In Cuba today everyone works. The law that makes it illegal to be able-bodied and unemployed could as easily apply to the hospital. Everyone who can works here in an elaborate plan that combines occupational therapy and an output of usable products. Just like everyone else in Cuba, the mental patients march off after breakfast to one of several factory areas to begin the manufacture of rope, toys, hats, shoes, and furniture. For those able to manage the minimal responsibilities, the combination of activity and companionship seems to create quite a pleasant and open atmosphere. Some patients seem perfectly happy to do the same repetitive job all day, while others have to change tasks to compensate for short attention spans. Depending on hours and complexity of the jobs, patients are paid fifteen to seventy pesos a month. The value of the products they

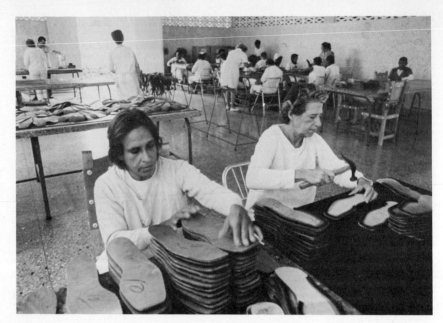

Occupational therapy is a substantial portion of the care at the psychiatric hospital outside Havana. The manufacturing of shoes is but one of several tasks the patients perform to help pay their way and occupy their minds.

make is estimated at over 2 million pesos annually. That output goes back to the state for distribution and sale.

Free public health care has moved from being a dream of all Cubans to being a birthright. It, along with free and universal education, has become a most visible and laudable achievement of the Castro Revolution. The Organization of American States, in a rare moment of praise for Cuba, called the country's public health facilities the only truly integrated system in Latin America. It has been remarkable to follow the struggle to implement Fidel's mountain promises to the formation of one of the hemisphere's largest and most comprehensive health programs. Healthier people should serve Cuba well over the coming decades.

The Arts, Entertainment, Cinema, and Sports

8

> Within the Revolution, everything is possible;
> outside the Revolution, nothing.
>
> —*Fidel Castro*

Fifteen thousand fans grew quiet as the tall, muscular figure strode across the red-rimmed mat. Stepping to the microphone, he lifted two typewritten pages and looked out over the crowd, glanced at the gigantic portrait of Ché, and adjusted his bright red shorts. He might have been a movie star, so even were his unmarred features. Bulges crowded the thin white athletic shirt as he began to read, his unchallenged muscles tensing only in response to the audience. The message was perfectly predictable but the people did not seem to care, for they had come to see him in action and not to hear him recite revolutionary greetings and accomplishments. This was Teófilo Stevenson, two-time gold medal winner in Olympic heavyweight boxing and the closest Cuba has come to having a superstar.

Stevenson is the epitome of a new sports system that Cuba has patterned after its Soviet and East European partners. Before the Revolution sports were for fun, even though there was a little professional baseball and a great deal of activity related to betting, including racing and jai alai. The Revolution ended all ownership of teams and making and charging money for events. The government took over the entire sports operation in the country with two goals in mind. One was the logical extension of universalizing education. By making sports activities and sports equipment available to all people, it would be reasonable to expect that the people would then be healthier and happier. From the early days in the 1960s, this has been the mission of INDER, the sports ministry.

A potentially more interesting ambition in Cuba is the use of sports to accomplish new goals in the international arena that might be impossible or too costly to achieve through other methods. If the competition being conducted throughout the world between capitalism and communism can be considered as a struggle for men's minds (now that all-out war is generally thought to be counterproductive or even unthinkable, depending on a civilian or military viewpoint), then international sports take on a role seemingly far beyond their inherent importance. Sports have become an acceptable means for countries to compete in a nonviolent or nonmilitary way with some of the old benefits of victory still going to the winners.

The Soviet Union should probably get credit for seeing the possibilities to further its global ambitions in the Olympics and other games. With centralized state control and planning, potential athletes could be screened early and developed in special schools for maximum competitive skills. Such activities would give youngsters incredible advantages over the participants in capitalist countries, such as the United States, where an amateur status is mandatory to compete and the last thing any child considers is letting the government or some equipment company take over to turn him into a "sports zombie." A few losing Olympics changed some of those attitudes when the results of fifteen years' training began to pay off for the socialist athlete.

The impetus to participate in sports activities permeates contemporary Cuban life. Children are encouraged to come to playing fields after school for instruction and fun.

In a well-disciplined program, youngsters with sports promise are encouraged to enter into specialized training. Sports are emphasized where there is a likelihood of winning international competitions.

As a small Third-World power with limited strength at the international bargaining tables, Cuba took this lesson to heart. Her leaders realized that strong showings at the Olympics, in the Pan American Games, and in other overseas meets would give her a reputation, respect, and importance far beyond her size. Patterning a new system after the Soviets, Cuba set about to make sports a national target and to produce winners. INDER, created in 1961, is a

Exercise and sports training are mandatory and designed to produce international competitors. At Lenin Vocational School, even the technically and scientifically oriented students participate in a full recreational program.

full ministry, with a budget of over $48 million a year, about 2 percent of Cuba's national outlay.

Selection starts in primary schools. Children with talent are singled out to play on the better teams. Local teams are pitted against one another to form provincial champions. All-star teams are organized in different sports and finally there are national play-offs. Only the fortunate few, the best, are filtered through this elaborate system to the national teams. This select group of athletes, as in the Soviet Union, achieve a new status and are cared for by the state. But, unlike Soviet athletes, Cuba's athletes are not isolated and pampered with extra care, services, and pay. Often they are given physical education teaching jobs and sometimes work in regular factories. But their pay is within the confines of other Cuban workers' salaries, 150–400 pesos monthly, depending on responsibilities. They do receive free travel expenses, food, transportation, sports instruction, and time off from their work for practice and training. And they are heroes in a culture that has no movie stars, rock singers, or pop idols. Only Fidel is more popular than the leading sports stars. Teófilo Stevenson, as a mark of his standing in the country, was elected as a representative of the first National Assembly, constituted in December, 1976. It would be like electing Muhammad Ali to the U.S. Senate.

To become an international competitor for Cuba means being subjected to observations and testing that would send chills through the average American footballer. Children with prospects take mental and physical tests to determine motivation, agility, I.Q., and the kind of sports at which they might excel. Computers are more and more used in this work with such incredible attention to detail that a printout on a single boxing match might show the precise number of left hooks a fighter executed in each round. As Teófilo Stevenson and Alberto Juantorena, the gold medal runner, attest, the system works.

Part of the infrastructure supporting the nationwide organization is the Superior School of Physical Education, located in the Sports City complex in Havana. There 1,200 students, 40 percent girls, at the university level to become Cuba's next generation of sports instructors. Cuban and foreign (mainly Soviet and East European) teachers work with the carefully selected students for four hours daily. The remaining half day is spent in work, at first in agriculture and construction, and then as physical education teachers. Only the best students make it to this school, since 90 percent averages are required as well as superior athletic ability. Upon graduation, the students are placed in the best sports jobs in the country, at the top' salaries, training students with the highest potential. It is a well-organized system, designed to produce international champions who will get the maximum amount of favorable publicity for Cuba, and it is proceeding on schedule.

The one place where all this super-Olympic planning fails to work is in dealing with the Cuban passion—baseball. As a legacy from prerevolutionary days, when all things U.S. were freely imported into Cuba, baseball was seized on as the number one sport. Elsewhere in the Caribbean, cricket is the rage on formerly British islands and soccer is almost a full-time activity on the French ones. But in Cuba, everybody seems to play or watch baseball. Ironically, it is considerably more popular in Cuba than in the United States. From the government's standpoint, baseball is an unfortunate choice for popularity because it is not an Olympic or generally accepted international competitive sport.

Still, throughout the hot spring months the sounds *beis-ball* and *stri-kee* are heard from one end of the island to the other. Sandlot play is

Winning at sports competitions is no accident for socialist countries. Rigorous gymnastics training begins in elementary school and for the talented continues in this elegant setting on Havana's formerly fashionable Prado. Once an elite Spanish heritage social club, the building now features gymnastic and fencing instruction areas.

As a legacy of decades of close U.S. ties, baseball remains the Cuban sports passion. In the National Series finals, Las Villas is batting against Oriente.

everywhere with sticks and rag-tag balls providing all the equipment needed. Practically every empty lot in Havana has an afternoon pick-up game in progress. For the older group, the provincial teams provide all the thrills and excitement that professional competition used to bring. When the play-offs occur, most nighttime activity stops as nationwide television coverage captures the fans' attention. Crowds of 55,000 commonly fill Latin American Stadium in Havana (until 1960 the home of the Havana Sugar Kings in the International League), and full houses are normal in all the other provinces. As with all other sports, admission to the events is free. Fidel himself is a big baseball fan and often shows up at games and usually bats a few for the people.

Basketball, which besides baseball is the only other sport invented in the United States, is fast becoming the number two sport in Cuba. Since it is a competitive game, it has received all the attention possible to produce championship teams. Interestingly, when Senators Abourezk and McGovern made the suggestion to the Cubans that a U.S.-Cuba competition would be a fine way to begin to break the diplomatic impasse that has marred relations for sixteen years, it was a basketball team composed of two South Dakota college squads that broke the ice. Cuba had originally asked the United States to send the Yankee baseball team as an opener, but the U.S. baseball commissioner refused, saying it would give the team unfair publicity. (Such is the kind of thinking that the Cubans find so vexing about the United States.) Now that the April, 1977, basketball games were so successful, with Cuba winning both games by fielding their best national players against the two small Midwestern schools, the next step in sports diplomacy will be the Cuban basketball players coming to the United States in the autumn of 1977 and the United States sending an all-star baseball team sometime during the year. For everyone present, it was a thrilling and moving experience to see the American teams marching onto the court below 15,000 yelling fans, holding the Star-Spangled Banner, and to feel the electricity in the air as the National Anthem was played in Communist Cuba for the first time since relations were broken in 1961. The Cubans loved it and yelled still more loudly while the young American players were literally bursting with pride.

A different kind of pride accompanies Ebemito Hernandez in his daily work, only a few steps away from the excitement of the coliseum. In a row of similarly shaped tin-roofed buildings, Cuba is building an industry to cope first with the loss of sports equipment

Cuba fielded its best national team against South Dakota's college boys, defeating the Americans roundly. The political significance was not lost to the standing-room crowd.

imports from the U.S. and then with the exploding demand within the country for more products. Compañero Hernandez reaches over to a stack of wood, each piece Canadian white ash, and holds one of the blanks. It's about three inches square and three feet long. This one is just like the hundreds of others he has picked up today and the same as thousands more stacked out back. By experience and his eye, he will lock the stick in a lathe and hand-form a baseball bat. Chips fill the air, covering his hair and the floor as he moves back and forth before the block, carving the graceful handle and thick hitting end in less than a minute. To a computer, no two of these bats could possibly be exactly alike, but as the stack grows during the afternoon, each one looks just like the last, and only the absence of the name "Louisville Slugger" gives away their origin.

No assembly line efficiency interferes with this work. Alfredo Garcia takes the new bats and hangs them upside down on a homemade rig suspended over a vat of varnish. Soon, the line is dipped and another 50 bats are completed. It is a "make-do" operation, but like so much else in Cuba, it works, and although it is costly in human labor, about 70,000 bats are made by the team of lathe workers each year.

With only his well-trained eye as a guide, Ebenito Hernandez turns a clear piece of white Canadian ash into a baseball bat. Since the U.S. embargo prohibited the sale of equipment, a new factory called Sports Industry now fills domestic needs.

At Sports Industries, baseball covers are sewn by hand. Production has improved sufficiently to allow Cuba to seek export markets for its surplus.

Things are considerably more automated in some of the other buildings. Ada Ortega sits in front of one of the most diabolical-looking contraptions ever designed. She inserts a small black rubber ball into its center and steps on a foot pedal as wheels whirl and hop, string whips through the air, and in a few seconds, the entire inner section of a baseball is ready for its cover. The manager proudly points out that much of the design work on the machine was done at the factory.

Cardboard boxes filled with the stringy balls go to the next building for yet another hand job. Workers sit at large circular tables, cooled by big electric fans in the open doors, and sew leather covers over the balls. Production is so high that in some weeks over 5,000 baseballs pass through their hands. This is enough to give Cuba a new export industry of selling baseballs to other Latin American countries. It is one of INDER's hopes that there will be a market in the United States when the embargo is lifted. Now, handmade baseballs are purchased from Haiti by American firms.

In the next building, a combination of assembly line and manual labor techniques turns out baseball gloves. Girls at sewing machines from Czechoslovakia and East Germany fit together the leather pieces and padding. After each step, a slowly moving belt carries the partially completed gloves to the next assembly procedure. Pretty Marisel Hernandez has five years' experience sewing gloves. She is nineteen.

Many other items are manufactured in the facility that employs about 1,100 people. About 500 pairs of baseball and soccer shoes are produced daily, some 50,000 uniforms a year, and varying numbers of fiberglass kayaks and rowboats, Olympic racing boats, canvas mats, volleyballs, basketballs, and miscellaneous other sports gear. The operation has even expanded to Lenin Vocational School, where some students fulfill their work obligation by making goods said to be worth over a million pesos annually.

In contrast to the large and visible public effort on behalf of sports, the arts in Cuba have suffered enormously since the Revolution. Simply because there is neither freedom of expression nor an outlet for the finished works, literature, poetry, and sculpture have been severely limited, and even painting has had some of its earlier license curtailed. The quantity of output has remained high, but the quality and subject matter have been altered considerably.

Fidel Castro recognized and acknowledged early that the censorship was present and even desirable to the government. In a 1961 speech he said, "The Revolution is first to lament that individual guarantees cannot be granted ... the Revolution explains that to concede those guarantees would serve the powerful enemy who has tried to destroy the Revolution and to drown it in the blood of the people." Many Cuban artists, who had been the creative leadership of the country, simply went into exile and continued their work in other countries. Fidel set the tone for all artistic development in Cuba when he told the artists, "Within the Revolution, everything is possible. Outside it, nothing." Today, Roberto Fernandez Retamar has brought the policy up to date by saying to the author, "You won't go to jail because of your beliefs, but because of activities based on your beliefs. There is no freedom of action—how could there be?"

Music would seem the least likely field to alter its methods to blend with a new government. But something has happened even here. Before the Revolution, Cuba was always giving the world a new dance or rhythm. Over the years the *cha-cha-chá, mambo, conga,* and *rumba* were delightful Cuban exports. Since the island imported the *Internationale,* the new songs and dances seem to have ended. The country still has new popular music, a small recording industry, and a few well-known performers (who are often seen at the Copa or Tropicana), but the old spark that ignited the imagination of dancers overseas seems to be gone. As incongruous as it may seem, most good restaurants in the country have pianists who entertain nightly with old standard 1950s U.S. tunes.

The performing arts are alive today, but not especially well. There is an opera company, but it is not very popular. Symphonies are played, but to rather small gatherings. Drama and musical groups perform regularly, utilizing some classical material and a great deal of new revolutionary writing. With the government controlling all aspects of employment, theatres, costuming, publication, etc., nothing can be produced without approval. The most popular music continues to be the lively music of the day, played on the radio and performed in nightclubs and on records. Dancing is still enjoyed, mainly among the young at the increasingly popular discos.

Painting has enjoyed more freedom than writing. It is difficult to explain precisely why because no one in power has ever clarified the issue. Perhaps the Revolution simply does not view painting as so large a threat as the printed word. There was a suggestion in 1963 that Cuba should ban abstract expressionism as Khrushchev had done in the Soviet Union. To that, Fidel replied, "Our enemies are capitalism and imperialism, not abstract painting." However, his acceptance has waned. To a 1967 exhibit of modern paintings, Fidel contributed a bull, seven cows, and an antiaircraft gun.

One of the major problems with the arts under communism is that there are no jobs outside the government and that same government controls all the avenues of exhibition, publishing, and distribution. If an artist produces work displeasing to the state, he faces the dual threats not only of having his work buried, but also of having antagonized the government, a possible jail sentence as an enemy of the state. The famous 1968 case of Heberto Padilla, a Cuban poet, brought this problem home vividly to the island's artists. Padilla won the Writers' Union annual award in poetry but was attacked by the armed forces official publication, *Verde Olivo* (Olive Green), on grounds of "counterrevolutionism" and "insufficient commitment" of one of his poems. His award was denied as the charges continued into 1969.

For the painter, living and working without government subsidies, there is more freedom to experiment and paint in nonrevolutionary styles. The artist will still have his government job and salary, but it will not necessarily be involved with painting. Also, unlike writing, publication is not necessary for the canvas for it to be successful. A new government decision may change much of the former dependency on salaries and regular jobs to support artistic work. It is now possible for artists to sell their creations privately and keep the revenue, after a suitable tax has been paid. This small return to capitalism may offer some freedom of subject matter and style and could bring about significant changes in the roles of Cuban artists.

For some of Cuba's young artists, life is almost as good as it is for sports stars. In a western Havana suburb, on the grounds of the old Havana Country Club, a beautiful collection of buildings was constructed by the Revolution to house the National School of Art. Graceful brick domes form classrooms, while long, curved, covered walkways delight the eye and protect the students and their works from the weather. Each year over 2,000 students across Cuba take a series of examinations for a hundred openings in five specialties: dance (national and folklore), drama, ballet, plastic arts (painting, engraving, sculpture, etc.), and music. Although it is a university-level school, students can start very young. There are some seven- and eight-year-old music students, and some ten-year-old ballet dancers. Since 1976, the school has gradually begun to require its students to have completed pre-university years.

Inside the painting classroom dome, canvases are stacked so closely together that only a winding walk gets one around the room. A dozen college-age students are busy with large realistic canvases during this morning session. Periodically each studies the nude model in the middle of the room. She is also a student, beautiful, and patiently holding her pose for the painters. Soon, when their class is over, she and they will be off for other sessions in drawing, sculpture, or engraving. It is all considerably more liberal and enlightened than might be expected from a Communist country that stifles its writers and journalists.

The wonder is where all that talent goes after graduation. About the only art work publicly seen is that on billboards, motion picture

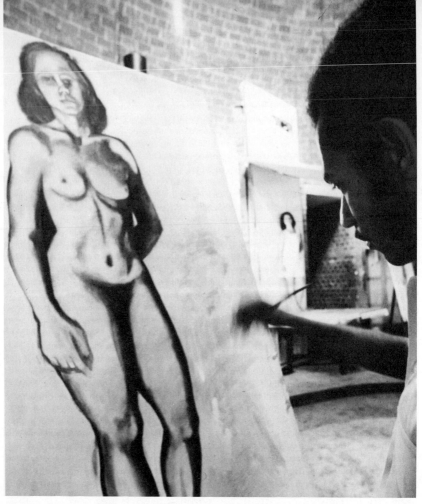

At the National School of Art, high school students are taught all the basic disciplines, apparently in a relatively free atmosphere. Nude painting is a regular feature, with live student models—although the administration insisted they be clothed for photographs.

posters, and government literature. Usually revolutionary in motif, such displays use bright bold colors and imaginative designs to transmit propaganda messages. Good enough to make Cuba famous for posters, they are still not the fine arts that might be expected from the years of training the young painters have received.

There is at least one public outlet that is receiving increased attention with the influx of tourists and the ruling on personal selling. Located on Cathedral Square in Old Havana, the graphic arts workshop brings together a group of artists each afternoon to work cooperatively producing handsome designs inked on large flat stones.

A clear policy about buying apparently is still being formulated, since tourists can purchase prints for about $30 one day and be turned down the following. As more and more visitors arrive, this will be an obvious place to separate them from some of their hard currency. Many of the graphics feature revolutionary subjects, which so far have been very popular with the foreigners.

Television's role in contemporary Cuba is almost completely different from its role before the Revolution, when it was as close as producers could make it to 1959 American TV. There was an existing nationwide network providing black-and-white programs across the island. All U.S. equipment was used and the stations were as commercial as owners could make them. A solid case can be made that many of the immediate advances Fidel Castro was able to make with his young revolution were largely owing to the existing television link throughout the country. With over a quarter of the population illiterate and no other mass communications medium in place, television offered Fidel the opportunity to explain his ideas and programs in his unique style. In his best father-teacher role, he would go on television for hours at a time and patiently lay out the latest innovation of his struggling government. It would be somewhat unfair to credit television with making the Revolution work during its most critical moments, but the task of communicating to and rallying the Cuban people behind him would have been incredibly more difficult, if not impossible, without it.

As an entertainment medium, television in Cuba today is in a strange limbo that reveals its 1959 roots intertwined with a curious blend of current Soviet and American technology. It should be first understood that Cuban television producers and filmmakers do not consider entertainment their primary obligation. Nor do they have to be commercial, show a profit, or attract the maximum audience. Since they have a monopoly, the audience will be there—there is nowhere else to turn for entertainment. Media roles are to support the Revolution, to inform the people as the government chooses, and to offer some entertainment, if it falls within the confines of the first two goals. Training in television has taken peculiarly Cuban turns. As important as television is to the island, there is no formal method of entering the field, and no classes are offered to learn its intricacies. The apprenticeship system is used with on-the-job training, the only way writers, producers, directors, cameramen, etc., gain access to the medium.

There are two television channels throughout Cuba. Unlike the BBC, which offers a "Home" and a "World" Service, both Cuban channels present similar material. Until the First Party Congress in December, 1975, TV was still black and white. Now, color is being introduced a little at a time, mainly through the use of Japanese equipment, even though the receivers are not for sale to the public. Japanese color sets are being seen more and more in hotel lobbies and other public places. Color is still considered special and gathers a crowd whenever it is on. Only events of unusual interest such as sports games, military parades, and government functions such as the opening of the first National Assembly rate color coverage.

Neither channel broadcasts all day. Usually both begin operations in the late afternoon and continue until about midnight. During that time each presents a wide variety of programs. News shows are in the style used by very small U.S. stations with limited facilities. The newscaster sits at a desk and reads the news. Occasionally there may be a minimally edited short film clip or a still photograph flashed on the screen. The niceties of rear screen projection, "chroma key" that allows an inserted action film or still photo to become part of the newscaster's scene, live mini-camera actuality reports, or professional news film have not come to Cuba. The result is a visually dull production that all too often matches the quality of the news being presented. Balanced reporting and fairness are not standards to be applied to the government presentations. All the government news is read in laudatory terms, all achievements by Cuba are recounted as victories over insurmountable odds, the accomplishments or activities of the Soviet Union and Eastern European partners are duly noted, and a few items are included to show the decadence and oppressiveness of capitalism, imperialism, and the United States. It is very difficult to come away from the evening newscast with a feeling of understanding what really happened that day.

Often there are interview shows, which again revert to the "talking head" approach, devoid of visual material. Children's programs usually are the puppet or "Romper Room" variety with adults hopping around playing with kids. All too often, somewhere in the production, one child is singled out to sing or recite a revolutionary number. Classes are taught on several nights and look very much like the old ETV programs common in the early 1960s. A few comedies find their way on the air and seem very popular. There are even some

"Ed Sullivan"-type variety shows with amateurs attempting to break into show business. And then, best of all for visiting Americans, are the old U.S. movies. In this case *old* means really *old*. Most are 1930 and 1940 potboilers, caught in Cuba during the Revolution and continually reshown. They are phenomenal favorites with fans who may have seen them twenty or thirty times each. On one night's programming there were no fewer than three scheduled. It is an amazing testimonial to both the films and to the Cubans' attitudes, but there is a very strong feeling that anything American is naturally better, and that includes old films. (As an example, on the black market, the best thing a Cuban can say about a product he is selling is that it was made in the United States.)

If all the television fare sounds dreary, that is simply because it is. The general quality of programming, technical accomplishments, and content of the shows borders on awful. Sports events, great Cuban favorites, are done fairly competently with several cameras in good positions, but there are none of the luxuries of instant replays or controversial commentaries such as Howard Cossell provides to U.S. fans. Since all televised programs are provided free by the government, one is happy just to be on the air. Without competition, only the pride of producing the best possible product keeps quality even where it is.

Television performers come from a variety of occupations, depending on the nature of the show under consideration. Since so many programs are instructional in nature, or interviews, specialists from government or industry are used. Singers, dancers, and musicians appear on television after beginning in restaurants or clubs, or on records. Technician training is mainly by apprenticeship, with young workers learning on the job.

Radio is even more popular than television, with all the old stations now operated by the government. Since receivers are considerably less expensive, and are free-purchase items out of the rationing system, radios are common. Daily programming, in AM and FM, parallels U.S. stations. There are news programs, popular music shows, classical music hours, interviews, an all-news station, and a variety of features, including comedy. As with television, performers for live programs generally come from other fields, while technical training is by apprenticeship. In addition to the large number of radio stations throughout the island, Cubans can easily receive Florida stations all the time and stations throughout the United States at night. Many Soviet-made shortwave sets are seen being carried, and they can receive programming from numerous nations. Apparently no attempt is made at jamming, and listening to the U.S. stations is virtually universal. Almost all Cubans complain about excessive commercials, since their stations carry none. In their place are propaganda messages.

In one area of the arts, the expansion and advancement has been nothing short of sensational. Dance has blossomed under the Castro government. Prior to 1959, serious students had to leave the island to find adequate instruction and performance opportunities. Alicia Alonso went to New York to study and became one of ballet's

Alicia Alonso has raised Cuban ballet into a position of world prominence. She brings her National Ballet of Cuba to Washington and New York in May 1978, as the first step in cultural exchanges since U.S.–Cuban diplomatic relations ceased in 1961.

brightest and most popular dancers. After the Revolution, she returned to Havana as Director of the National Ballet of Cuba, a post she still holds, in addition to her duties as a choreographer and lead dancer. Although ballet is just one of the dance forms revitalized in the Revolution, it is the one to capture the most attention. A substantial amount of that success is due to the electric Alicia Alonso.

Tall and ribbon-thin, she whisks into the room with the full authority of a person who leads people. She is dark and dramatic and could easily be mistaken for a Spanish dancer with clicking heels and swirling skirts. But the muscles are different—longer and lighter, with the lithe, graceful movements of a ballet dancer. She struggles a bit looking at the smaller objects on her desk. Only this betrays her lifelong curse of near blindness. For years she thrilled audiences she could not see, and once, when bright lights went on at the rear of the stage, she took her bows with her back to the theatre. Such courage and raw determination are almost paradoxical in such a fragile-appearing figure.

She 'sits in her office at the ballet school, a large photograph of Fidel behind her. Nearby a wood carving of Lenin decorates the desk, and numerous photographs of her in New York fill one wall. She is the dancer, the executive, the director, and one of the sparkling jewels of the Revolution. She is considered a national treasure, just as the Japanese regard some of their venerable artists. When she speaks, she is obviously relating the story of a dream come true, and of vast challenges still unmet. "It is impossible to compare what we have here now and what was here before and what I did in New York. Today, the only thing a dancer has to worry about is dancing. If he or she graduates from our school, he never has to worry about a job in dance. There are no money problems and no career problems. I, and all the other dancers, spent most of our lives worrying about paying for lessons and then finding a performing job. Now, everything is paid for and our only job is to do better artistically.

"Today, we have respect. It is impossible to imagine what that means to a dancer. Our boys have the admiration and respect of our people. You know how they were thought of before. This is a new thing in Cuba. One must have respect for his work. There is now a tremendous demand for dancers in Cuba. It's exciting and frightening sometimes, with all the responsibility.

"The Soviet influence has been beneficial for us and is a part of the

Soviet influence on the arts is evident in music and dance in Cuba. Emphasis and acceptance unknown before the Revolution are now common. In the spectacular National School of Art, constructed on the old Havana Country Club property, graceful domed brick buildings each house separate disciplines, such as modern dance.

growth in respect for dancers. It has brought an awareness of ballet and an enrichment. We have had Soviet dancers here to perform and to teach. Having ballet so popular and strong in the U.S.S.R. has meant an acceptance in Cuba. For us that has been an important bonus."

As she walked through the two large practice rooms, Alicia Alonso commented on the roles of her company and school. "Now we have two companies in Havana with ninety-five dancers. My goal is to have a dance company in each province. That has been started with classes in dance in the local schools. A dream of mine is to have a great number of dancers come to us here and learn and then return to the provinces and start new companies. We have annual exams and select only the best dancers for this school. In addition to teaching dance in the regular schools, it is also taught in the military, and we have two groups at the university. So, we have more interest and activity than ever before, but it is never enough for me."

Alicia Alonso and her National Ballet of Cuba have been chosen to be the first Cuban artistic group to visit the United States since relations froze between the two countries almost a generation ago. The eighty-five-member company performs in May and June, 1978, at the John F. Kennedy Center in Washington, D.C., and at the Metropolitan Opera in New York City.

Other kinds of dancing have received similar popular acceptance. There are a national folklore and a national modern dance company that perform throughout Cuba and travel internationally. Highly imaginative productions, fully costumed with specially designed sets, are gaining wide audiences whenever they dance. Recently both groups have been exploring the ethnic backgrounds of Cuba's black population and producing shows with African and slave influences. Numerous local dance groups are active throughout the island, performing both modern and folk numbers. There is a mediocre National Opera of Cuba, a National Symphony plus another symphony in Matanzas, a National Choir, four main drama groups located around Havana, and dozens of drama organizations spread over the island.

The dancing tourists are likely to see will trace few ties to either Africa or the Soviet Union. Las Vegas is a closer parent for the sparsely costumed, hip-swinging girls at Cuba's showplace nightclub, the Tropicana. There is simply nothing like the Tropicana anywhere

African and revolutionary themes predominate in new Cuban dances. The National Dance of Cuba, a modern company, presents "Iroko, the Myth of the Ceiba," based on black Cubans' belief that the ceiba tree houses demons. Modern, folk, and ballet are all dance forms that are flourishing since the Revolution.

Some of the numbers may have socialist themes, but the main thrust at the Tropicana is still lots of attractive girls, in small bright costumes, performing rousing dances.

else in the world. Before the Revolution it was a U.S. favorite, with a brash, beautiful show, lovely girls, and production numbers featuring dozens of performers on stage, above the stage, in the trees, almost surrounding the outdoor audience. It was just plain spectacular.

The happy news is that, except for the former casino, it is all still there. The girls have changed a little with two additions—more weight and bigger costumes—but the fun is contagious and there are still plenty of attractive dancers tossing their skirts around. It is Cuba for the nostalgic because this is the one place where, with eyes closed for a moment and then popped open for the full impact of the extravaganza, it could be 1959 again.

For the Cuban film industry, the old days will certainly not return. Throughout the island there is no more politicized and propaganda-oriented organization than ICAIC, the Cuban Institute of Cinematic Arts and Industries. Located in a downtown Havana office building with the mandatory security guard at the front door, ICAIC is responsible for motion picture production, distribution of Cuban films throughout the island, distribution of foreign films within Cuba, and distribution and sale of Cuban films overseas. Administering these multinational functions was recently deceased Saul Yelín, ICAIC's Director of International Relations, and the closest that Cuba came to having a "Hollywood type." In a bright, airy office with a marble-topped table, two Cuban-copy Barcelona chairs, and walls filled with cinema books from around the world, Yelín ran his operation sporting indoor sunglasses, a tailored tan guayabera, and a gold U.S. pen. Immediately, he corrected any misconception that Cuba might be producing entertainment films. "In the first place, Cuba cannot afford to make films just to entertain. That would be wasteful. In the second place, even if we had the money and resources, that is not our mission. Entertainment may be a by-product of our activity, and we certainly assume that our films do actually entertain people, but film is only efficient when it communicates, and then entertains, while transferring the message. It is getting the message across to the people that is important." Yelín's former boss at ICAIC, Alfredo Guevara, is now Vice-Minister of Culture. In his book-filled office and with his jacket characteristically draped over his shoulders, Guevara's position is that, "We cannot imagine films without Revolution. The Revolution affects all aspects of our lives. To have the Revolution in our films is perfectly normal."

From ICAIC's viewpoint, that message is widely varied. Cubans are almost fanatical motion picture freaks. They love movies and will stand in line for hours to see the latest release. It is quite common to see lines on Saturday nights winding around several blocks, meaning the people will have to wait for at least one additional showing and perhaps two before their turn to enter. On an island of under 9½ million people, the annual film audience is 35 million. Tickets are inexpensive, ranging from 80 centavos to one peso in Havana to 20 to 60 centavos in the country. ICAIC meets this demand with a steady diet of new pictures. It produces a weekly black-and-white newsreel of the type that television knocked out of competition in the United States some years back, between forty and fifty documentaries annually (seven to fifty-six minutes each, average length, twenty to thirty minutes), and about eight to ten short cartoons a year. Its feature-length films, over one and a half hours, can be on either fiction or documentary topics, and only a very few are produced each year. One recent offering was a feature-type documentary with actors, sets, etc., dealing with an alleged C.I.A. plot of some years back to assassinate Raúl Castro. The big hit before that was "Cantata de Chile" (Song of Chile), a full-length treatment expanding on a nineteenth-century workers' uprising at Chilean copper mines. Complete with horses, trains, numerous extras, battle scenes, and some elaborate sets, it is a considerable achievement for a small country's film industry. ICAIC even introduced the film in Hollywood premier fashion with floodlights on the theatre front, hundreds of invited guests, speeches, and floral presentations to the stars and to all the Chilean women in the audience. (The show was preceded with the then latest ICAIC documentary, "You Cannot Block the Sun With One Finger," a recounting of Fidel's recent trip to the twenty-fifth U.S.S.R. Communist Party Congress. When Fidel first appeared on the screen, the audience burst into applause. There were appropriate jeers at the images of Mao and Henry Kissinger and roars of applause when Fidel finished his filmed speech in Moscow.)

Using entertainers from throughout Cuba (actors, actresses, singers, dancers, musicians, etc.), ICAIC does a commendable job of producing films on relatively small budgets. Of course, with no union rules, overtime, high salaries, or profits, budgets are not really comparable to those of Western countries. ICAIC has placed a great deal more emphasis on training than has either radio or television in Cuba. The

Institute, one of the first established early in 1959 just after the Revolution, started from nothing. Alfredo Guevara remembers, "We had no equipment, no expertise, and no experience. We borrowed cameras from people around the island and used amateur cine groups as our nucleus. Now we are very well organized, with university graduates assigned to assist ICAIC directors in study-work systems while they are in their final years of class work. As they learn, they begin to specialize on the job. We have an intensive and unique program in Cuba of bringing in professors and specialists from around the world to talk to our students. We have had several film people from the United States do this."

Obviously, the Cuban productions alone would not be sufficient to keep films in the theatres. The bulk of the features shown are imported. On any given day Havana will likely be showing movies from the U.S.S.R., Czechoslovakia, England, Spain, Mexico, and especially from the United States. Typically, the lines will be longest for the American films. ICAIC never says how it gets the U.S. motion pictures, because the embargo forbids such trade and no revenues are paid to the Hollywood producers, but the route is well known. The films are pirated, usually from Mexico, but occasionally from another country. During a legitimate run at a theatre, the film is taken to a lab and duplicated. This dupe is sent to Cuba, where it is duped again several times for different theatres. The quality suffers enormously, but Cuba gets relatively new films virtually free. Alfredo Guevara realizes that the days of free films may be near. "We are going to have a real problem when U.S. relations come because we will then have to pay for your films. They are expensive, so we will have to be inventive in the future to solve this."

All too often ICAIC tries to get films that will show the United States in the worst possible light, such as those with gangster or race features. If the film is too favorable to American life, it might have a brief, printed announcement to precede it on the screen saying what the audience is about to see is not really true but only a bit of fiction.

One area where ICAIC justifiably receives considerable credit is in bringing films and some of the outside world to campesinos who had virtually no communication with the world until the Revolution. Naturally, the goal again was not to entertain or inform so much as it was to propagandize the people about the Revolution and its accomplishments and integrate all Cubans into it. In the early days it came to ICAIC's attention that there were people who had never seen a motion picture. The Institute organized teams to take the films and their messages to everyone.

Two men would leave in a truck that held all the needed gear. They would drive as far as they could and then transfer the equipment onto horses or donkeys. When the remote communities were finally reached, the projector, screen, portable electric generator, and films were put in place, setting the stage for a most incredible experience. ICAIC recorded the entire sequence in one of its most emotional documentaries, "Por Primera Vez" (For the First Time). Filmed in 1967 in the mountains behind the Oriente city of Baracoa, it shows the campesinos gathering for the totally mysterious event. Word quickly spread through the hills. Kids, many naked, and all without shoes, jumped and ran, practically overcome with excitement. As the equipment was being set up, an interviewer asked the people what they thought a film was. "Oh, I don't know," said one old woman, "but it must be very important to cause all this activity." A giggling child offered, "Films must be fun because everyone's laughing." The anticipation was almost unbearable as the community waited until dark. Through the dusk they came from their bohios, marching single file along the path, carrying their torches. As they were getting seated, many compared a film to a party, since it certainly seemed like a party to have everyone together. And then it started.

Oh, the ecstasy and wonder! Never had faces been so transfixed. They stared and smiled, and stared and laughed, unable to believe their eyes. With an absolutely brilliant stroke of planning, ICAIC had brought a Charlie Chaplin movie as the very first film the people had ever seen. They fell down laughing, pointed, fidgeted, and were suddenly transformed. No longer were they isolated from the world and never would they be again. It didn't matter that Chaplin was followed by revolutionary documentaries. Any government capable of bringing them such an invention must possess almost magical powers. And so it was that the Revolution, through ICAIC, brought the mountain people from out of the last century and made them a part of their own.

Tourism

9

We have always been ready for the United States.
We see all tourists as one, whether they come from Canada,
the United States, or Mexico. We do not expect any
problems. The Americans will come out of curiosity, for the
sun and surf, and will be well behaved. I am not
worried about their coming. Who knows, they may be our
biggest market in a year or two.

—Jesús Jiménez, Director
Cubatur

It was after midnight and still quiet inside the cave. Shadowy figures lingered by the overhanging rock entrance, whispering and nudging before the solitary guard motioned them in. Like Noah's creatures, they entered by pairs to join a waiting group already assembled in the darkened interlocking chambers. Candles flickered and then died back, briefly illuminating the huddled couples sharing their secrets. A few colored lights played across the rough stone ceiling, its reverberant dome gradually filling with more and louder nervous chatter. Word came from the five silhouettes in the room's center that the time had come.

An explosion of sound from the electric guitars signaled the beginning of the midnight show in Pirate's Cave, a natural oceanside cavern and popular weekend nightclub in Varadero Beach, Cuba's best-known tourist site. Spotlights illuminated the musicians, whose sounds soon had the mixed Cuban and Canadian audience on its feet, filling the small dance floor. Interchanging dancing partners and language in a style to make the United Nations envious, the revelers

A packed dance floor with bumping, undulating bodies is a Saturday night routine at Pirates Cave in Varadero. This most popular entertainment spot features live bands and many dark corners for couples.

continued their fun until almost time to have a good-morning swim in the crystal clear waters before breakfast. It was a night to relive in memories when the snow is two feet deep back in Toronto, and the kind of evening that Americans are once again planning.

President Carter's decision in March, 1977, made it possible and legal for Americans to vacation in Cuba for the first time since relations were broken between the two countries in January, 1961. (Between those years, only a few journalists, scholars, medical and technical experts, and government officials were allowed to visit with State Department approval. Leftist U.S. student groups organized as the Vencerémos Brigade made the trip illegally through Mexico without proper authority.) Although the economic embargo, called a "blockade" in Cuba, is still in effect to prohibit trade, Carter's order lifted any restriction for U.S. citizens to travel to the island and allows them to bring back the same customs-free purchases permitted from other countries—$100 total value of goods including 100 cigars and a quart of an alcoholic beverage. Formerly, any U.S. citizen desiring to travel to Cuba had to join a Canadian or Mexican tour. Now, with a summer 1977 Treasury Department ruling related to the embargo, which is still in effect, U.S. travel agencies can organize tours within the United States, and the 1977–78 winter season will likely be the first that substantial numbers of Americans will enjoy in Havana and Varadero.

Because Cuba has been off limits to Americans, there is a prevalent impression that it has been closed to everyone all these years. This is a source of great amusement to the Cubans, who have enjoyed an absolute tourist boom by the Canadians during the Americans' absence. In 1976, 60 percent of the total number of tourists in Cuba, almost 40,000, flew in from Canada. Russia and the other socialist countries provided 7,500, Latin America sent about the same number, and 6,000 came from Europe, for a total of 60,000 guests. On a typical day at Havana hotels, tour groups can be seen from Canada, Italy, France, and perhaps Holland, while businessmen check in from Tokyo, London, Mexico City, and now New York and Minneapolis.

Two kinds of package tours are currently available to foreigners, both organized by Cubatur, the country's government-operated tourist agency. Most popular are the flights directly to Varadero Beach, about sixty-five miles east of Havana. Long recognized as one of the world's most beautiful beaches, Varadero is a winter dream

To capitalize on its underwater appeal, Cuba is beginning special tours for divers. Its hundreds of miles of relatively unexplored coral reefs will be especially enticing to U.S. and Canadian swimmers. Alfredo Martinez of the new Institute of Oceanography collects a coral sample.

The world-famous beach at Varadero, renowned among international travelers before the Revolution, is currently filled with Cubans and Canadians. Its twelve miles of clear white sand and sparkling water make it the most popular vacation site on the island.

with over a dozen miles of pure white sand, and incredibly clear, blue water. A vacation favorite for decades, Varadero is now the center for Canadian tourists on holiday and is expected to be equally popular with Americans soon. International flights arrive at the airport only a few minutes away by bus and most guests are in the water within an hour after landing. A variety of accommodations are offered by Cubatur and are reflected in the package price now paid in Canada or Mexico. Charter air fares are added onto the Cuba fee by the travel agent, depending on distance flown. At the Internacional Hotel on the beach, a recently renovated prerevolutionary facility, one week costs about $320 per person including three meals daily, bus transfers to and from the airport, a "Cuba Night" party with entertainment, a seafood party, and some sightseeing. The air charter fare is additional. The Hotel Kawama is available for a similar rate. Much more common are the many motel-type accommodations along the beach for about $250 per week plus air fare, with the above features included.

More expensive and private are beach-front villas for larger groups. Meals can be catered for a family or several couples, providing a home rather than a hotel atmosphere. Of course, the main attraction is the beach, the center of Varadero's appeal. Boats and fishing equipment may be rented, but most people find lying in the sand activity enough. Generally, the surf contains an international mélange, with several tourists from Europe, the Soviet Union, and Latin America sharing the same wave. The Soviets will be the most difficult for gregarious Americans to decipher, since they seldom show any interest in conversation and almost universally hide their faces or turn away when a camera is present, a legacy of a lifetime of fear and distrust.

Entertainment ranges from the packed Pirate's Cave, where weekend reservations are a must, to the large variety show at the Internacional, usually good, but not as good as in Havana's nightclubs. Each hotel has one or more bars and there are numerous other well-marked clubs and bars along Varadero's streets. All payment must be in pesos when a registered guest is outside his own hotel. Bills are straightforward, with seldom a cover charge, and domestic drinks are reasonably priced. Beer is usually eighty centavos to a peso, and rum drinks anywhere from one to two pesos, depending on the drink's complexity. Daiquiris, old Cuban favorites, are always served frozen, whipped with ice in a blender. Cubans prefer *mojitos,*

Cubans join with Americans in finding the Russians puzzling and aloof. This Soviet vacationer at Varadero "takes her sun" in solitude.

Long a favorite hangout in Old Havana is La Bodeguita del Medio, whose success Hemingway ensured when he called their *mojitos* the best in Cuba. Angel Martinez was its owner before the Revolution and now works as its manager.

which include rum, lime, sugar, soda, ice, and the refreshing aroma and taste of mint sprigs. Imported drinks like Scotch and bourbon are ridiculously expensive. Occasionally on menus a listing will include a bottle of Scotch for $150 and cordials for $75. Be forewarned so there are no surprises.

Not to be missed is the old DuPont estate toward the eastern end of Varadero's peninsula. Now used as the Las Américas Restaurant, it shows some of Cuba's former luxury that the present government propagandizes as one of the reasons for the Revolution. The breezy, open-air dining rooms and quiet elegance provide a marvelous atmosphere for a memorable meal. Prices are above average, with lunch and wine running over $10 and dinner $15 to $20.

Since more Americans will likely be visiting Varadero than any other location, a word about Cuban attitudes toward tourists might be useful. In general, the Cuban people harbor a great admiration for Americans and a genuine curiosity built on years of isolation following the decades in which hundreds of thousands of U.S. citizens visited and worked in Cuba. The government has taken a stance of continuing to isolate tourists. Part of it is due to the currency problems and part of it is political. Since there is so much trafficking in black market goods, tourists are a prime source for new products. Cubans will ask to buy visitors' shoes for $50 or more, blue jeans for $30 to $60, etc. To limit this, officials try to keep tourists and Cubans apart. They realize the hopelessness of it, but they continue to try. The government does not want individuals wandering around Cuba, because of a long ingrained fear that subversion comes from the outside, that terrorists may come in as tourists, that Cubans will get overly curious about wages, availability of goods, and general working and living conditions, and because a guest might simply get into trouble. It is easier for the government to maintain control if such contacts are kept to a minimum.

Finally, the question of safety can be put aside. Tourists can walk around at will and have no fears about personal welfare. Street crime as we know it is virtually nonexistent. There is only one area of concern. Petty thefts are increasing and Varadero is one of the centers, almost entirely as a result of international tourism. Bathing suits, towels, sunglasses, cameras, and personal items left unattended are disappearing with alarming frequency. Stealing is due to the lack of these products in the tightly rationed economy. So far, thefts are confined to small things and are nowhere as serious or pervasive as in other vacation centers, but one would do well to be cautious.

In addition to the more popular Varadero vacation, there is a second package tour offered by Cuba, which begins in Havana. In the better Canadian tours, and the ones most likely to be offered to Americans, four nights of the week will be spent in one of the capital's three renovated hotels, the Riviera, Capri, or Havana Libre (formerly the Hilton), or at the nearby beach resort, the Marazul. The additional three nights of the one-week package can be either at the Colony Hotel on the Isle of Pines or at three separate locations during a bus tour of areas outside Havana. Currently, the Riviera choice and either alternative for the additional three nights costs about $350 plus air charter, while the nearby Marazul, located about fifteen miles east of Havana on the beach at Santa Maria del Mar, is $270 plus air fare. The average Canadian package cost is approximately $415 for a week at the Marazul, including three meals daily, bus transfers, two party nights, and air charter.

Obviously, winter is going to be the popular season for Americans, as it is elsewhere in the Caribbean and is now in Cuba for Canadians. The climate is ideal, warm and dry, in the months when the northern United States is most unpleasant. Since the Cubans are interested only in group tours, there is little chance of organizing an itinerary outside the approved schedule. Taxis are available and some roaming is being permitted, but changing hotels or cities is not done. Within the confines of the tour, travel is safe. Some Canadians have been surprised on the beach at night by machine-gun-carrying guards out patrolling for invaders, but no real problems have developed. Walking is safe day or night. Some Spanish is very useful in asking for assistance, since English is dependable only around the hotels. Even though every high school graduate has studied English, few speak it. Few logistical details will bother Americans, since airport formalities, porters, and buses will all be prearranged.

Choosing a hotel should be no problem for tourists since the travel agencies are aware of the status of existing accommodations. Havana has had no new hotels since the Revolution, but renovations have been made on the three previously mentioned hotels to conform to accepted international standards. Sadly, the formerly elegant Nacional, an old pink palace on the Malecón, is scheduled for renovation in 1978 and for the present should be avoided. Rooms there are usually not air-conditioned, salty water runs in the faucets, and the general appearance is rather shabby. The Riviera, Cuba's best, is remembered as a Mafia haven before Castro. The casino is gone, but the other features are just as good as many Americans will remember them. A gigantic saltwater pool, cabanas, two restaurants, spa, and the Copa nightclub help make the days enjoyable. Without the package tours, rooms cost almost $40 a night. More central is the Capri, also with former Mafia ties, a smaller but very agreeable hotel. A rooftop swimming pool offers fine views of the city and ocean. Slightly less expensive than the Riviera, the Capri is often first choice among business travelers because of its location. Only three blocks away is the Havana Libre, a favorite for delegations in Cuba on official business. Its Hilton heritage is evident in the lobby and room decor, and its mezzanine-level swimming pool is a popular meeting place for drinks. The beach-front Marazul at Santa Maria del Mar, completed in 1976, provides a tropical atmosphere close enough to Havana to visit several times during a week's stay. Palms and ferns decorate the large, open lobby area, while a saltwater pool on the

Americans will remember the kind of luxury that placed a gigantic saltwater pool beside the Malecón overlooking the deep blue waters of the Gulf Stream. The Hotel Riviera still exists, but most of the guests are Cuban now.

lower level, surrounded by the hotel but open to the sky, provides secluded swimming. The atmosphere is casual and the beach deserted throughout the week. For additional sightseeing or entertainment, taxis to downtown Havana run about six pesos and are readily available. As with the old Nacional, salty water runs in the faucets and should be avoided except for baths. One small problem is that the hotel leaks in heavy rains, fortunately usually only in the summer rainy season. When the problem was recently pointed out to Fidel, he mused, "I think perhaps our architects are becoming more concerned with beauty than function."

Generally, living in first-class Cuban hotels is convenient and pleasant. Tourists are spared almost all the everyday problems plaguing citizens. The hotels mentioned have their own water supplies and seldom experience the electrical blackouts that routinely darken homes and domestic hotels throughout the country. Although salty showers are manageable, the provided bottle water should be used for tooth brushing and drinking. Hot water may be unavailable or cooler than at home, but the climate is usually warm enough to make this only a mild inconvenience. Toilet paper and paper towels are common in the better hotels but in short supply elsewhere. Even though tipping is officially prohibited everywhere as a holdover from capitalistic days, it is the rare bellboy, chambermaid, or taxi driver who will refuse a gratuity of either cash or token gift. Laundry can be a real inconvenience except in the three discussed downtown hotels. Outside Havana, including the Hotel Marazul, it is extremely rare to find any laundries, and in-town operations can take several days when they are working. For short trips, it is best to plan for no washing. Even when laundries are available, they are expensive.

For the nostalgic tourist who is returning to Havana looking for some of the "good ole days," suffice it to report that they are mainly gone. No longer do pretty young prostitutes surround the hotels and parade on the main streets. The sexual exhibitions are only a faded memory to some of the elder residents, the "stars" having long departed for Mexico and south Florida. Gambling, one of the first casualties of the new Revolution, is unavailable to tourists, although playing the numbers is still a popular pastime for local residents, who use the Venezuelan winners for payoffs. Begging, practically a downtown staple in most Latin American cities, was prohibited years ago, its practitioners put to work.

There are two amateur exceptions to the above generalities. Recently, particularly in Havana, a few girls have been appearing once again in the evenings, looking for dates, and willing to trade their favors for goods rather than money. It is almost more a comment on rationing than on morals. The police occasionally pick up a few, but the problem is so small no one is overly concerned yet. Also, young boys, on their way to or from school, are developing the habit of lingering near tourist hotels asking for pens, cigarettes, or souvenirs. Hardly begging in the traditional sense, it still comes as a surprise to government officials who thought the children more socialistically indoctrinated than that. Still, when a youngster gets only one pen a year, it is extremely tempting to simply ask for another.

Of all the pleasures that visiting Cuba can bring, eating out can be one of the most enjoyable. This seems paradoxical since it is so widely known that food is rationed in the country. Obviously, both statements are true. Restaurant meals are one of the principal relief valves in the oppressive rationing system. A quick glance around any restaurant dispels any notion that the food is only for foreigners. Often over half the patrons will be Cubans.

Lunch at one of the new buffet tables can be a culinary treat, such as at the one provided by the Riviera Hotel. It is the most elaborate "Swedish Table" in Cuba; some of its overwhelming choices include three juices, milk, yogurt, three fresh fruits (such as bananas, pineapples, papaya, oranges, grapefruit, watermelon), two or three salads, two kinds of fish appetizers, tomatoes, cucumbers, potatoes, fried bananas, soup, bread, three main dishes (pork, fish, chicken, or beef), cheeses, French tarts, cakes, pies, custards, guava paste, and coffee. The spread costs eight pesos for either lunch or dinner, with beer an additional eighty centavos. For menu ordering, the Riviera also has the L'Aiglon Restaurant and a downstairs coffee shop.

Most of the other hotels have similar tables, although not as well stocked. And all the hotels have restaurants where meals on the package tours are served. For the first-time visitor, it is fascinating to observe how communism handles the problem of service. In a society ideologically striving for equality, the concept of one person waiting on another does not fit the ideal. Since the people who knew English and were used to working with tourists before the Revolution typically fled to Florida, creating a new industry of hotel and restaurant help has been a problem. The tourism ministry, INIT, has several schools struggling with training, but the results are spotty. Certainly the establishments have plenty of personnel. Two black-suited maîtres d'hôtel meet arriving guests at many restaurants, and separate people bring water, bread, take the order, and deliver the food. One morning in the Riviera's coffee shop, twenty-one people milled around in dowdy black uniforms, and it still took twenty minutes to get eggs. One could only wish the help would read INIT's carefully printed slogan on every placemat: "Your right is to enjoy; our duty is to serve."

Havana provides many eating possibilities outside the hotels. Easily the most spectacular view in town is at La Torre, a first-class restaurant atop the thirty-five-story Focsa, a prerevolutionary apartment building now used to house East European and Soviet technicians. Have drinks in the bar, located on the west side of the penthouse and overlooking the Malecón, the ocean, and much of the better residential areas of Havana. A move to the main dining room provides a panorama of the central city, El Morro fort, and bustling Havana Harbor. Dinner is almost secondary to the scenery, but the food is generally very good. Steaks, when they are available, are tender and tasty, and fresh seafood is usually listed. Since the restaurant is always crowded, reservations are required. Dinners with wine from either Spain, Portugal, or the Soviet Union will run from $15 to $25.

Tiffany lamps, fern-covered walls, a grand piano, and massive dark wooden Spanish colonial furnishings accent the most beautiful restaurant in Cuba, Las Ruinas. Recently constructed in Lenin Park, about fifteen miles south of Havana, Las Ruinas is a testament to good taste. Built around the ruins of a master's home on an old sugar plantation, it encompasses the crumbling stone walls as decorative details and utilizes space in multilevel expanses of eating, drinking, and viewing centers. Great floor-to-ceiling louvered doors admit sunlight and cooling breezes for the families who stop in after spending the day in huge Lenin Park. As in most restaurants, pianists entertain the dinner crowd with pre-1959 U.S. tunes, still the favorite quiet music throughout Cuba. If lobster and shrimp (which are never sold in stores) are available in Cuba, they will likely be served at Las Ruinas. However, in line with other good restaurants, the prices are high. Dinner for four, with lobster or steak, drinks, dessert, and wine, will cost between $80 and $100.

Many other good restaurants are scattered throughout Havana.

Cuba's most elegant restaurant now is Las Ruinas in Lenin Park. Maître d'hôtel Ovideo Chávez serves a frosted *guyana,* a tropical rum drink, to a Cuban guest spending Sunday afternoon in the park.

The "1830" is located just west of the Riviera, directly on the ocean. Housed in an old mansion, it is quiet, usually empty, and offers dependable meals. The Conejito, just down the street from either the Capri or Havana Libre, specializes in rabbit main courses. Directly on Cathedral Square in Old Havana, El Patio offers a Spanish flavor with a central fountain, garden area, and open-air-sidewalk dining out front. Inside, air-conditioned rooms have full meals with delicious seafood. Around the corner is an old Hemingway favorite, the Bodeguita del Medio, an intimate place whose owner for thirty-six years, Angel Martinez, stayed on after the Revolution to be manager. He proudly conducts tours around the walls crammed with pictures and signatures of the many people who have enjoyed good food here.

Nearby, another prerevolutionary vision emerges on a quiet corner. None of the people waiting on buses give the building a second look. It has no special meaning. A window is cracked, the paint is peeling from a faded sign across the glass, and the wooden doors are badly in need of attention. Inside, plaster drops from a decaying ceiling, a few bare bulbs cast their shadows onto empty, fragmented display cases, while four lonely customers sprawl against the once elegant polished bar, its wood a stranger to care for over a decade. Linda Darnell, Tyrone Power, Victor Mature, and Alice Faye all stare from behind glass under a sign that says in English, "You should have your picture taken at Sloppy Joe's, the best souvenir of Havana." The famous old watering hole, which hosted America's rich and celebrated, is only a shell now, just a corner bar that didn't even have a bottle of beer to sell.

Better cared for is the Floridita, a bar made famous by Hemingway when he said it made the best daiquiris in the world. The reputation still holds—the drinks are good. More importantly, the Floridita provides the proper atmosphere for getting the tourist in the right frame of mind to see more of Ernest Hemingway's life in Cuba. More remembrances of "Papa" exist around Havana than anywhere else in the world. Curiously, the government, while berating the United States generally, has always reserved a special place for Hemingway, accepting him as one of its own.

From the 1930s on, Hemingway divided his year among the United States, Spain, and Cuba. For $18,000 he bought the "Finca Vigia," a small villa on a hill with a pool, about forty minutes outside Havana. From there, he would drive to Cojimar, on the ocean, where

A historical backwater, Sloppy Joe's bar in downtown Havana recalls its livelier days as the most famous drinking establishment in Cuba. It is now run down and dirty, and only the movie star photographs on its walls authenticate its former appeal.

he kept his boat, and would fish in the Gulf Stream. Customarily, Hemingway spent six months each year living and working in Cuba. When he left in 1960 and went to Spain briefly, it was to be his last stay. At home in Idaho, whatever demons tormented him finally won, and he killed himself with one of his shotguns in 1961.

The home is now maintained as the Hemingway Museum, open to the public. Everything is just as he left it on that last visit. Old *Times* and *Newsweek*s lie across the bed in his corner bedroom, while across the room his glass-topped desk remains covered with souvenirs, snapshots, military patches, shotgun shells, and wood carvings. A bullfight painting dominates the living room along with a table of partially filled bottles: Bacardi, Gordon's, Schweppes. Two walls of books fill the library, overpowering a small Picasso plate with a bull's face. Mounted African animal heads attest to his lifelong passion for hunting. Beside his toilet, a complete bookshelf holds contemporary reading matter, and on the opposite wall, penciled diary entries record his morning weight, one of the fights he was always losing.

For Hemingway fans, a worthwhile side trip is to the little fishing village of Cojimar, only four miles east of Havana's harbor entrance. There the men of the fishing cooperative paid for and erected a memorial to their friend, who made them and their town world famous as the home port and site for *The Old Man and the Sea.*

For most visitors, the principal attraction of Havana will be the opportunity of seeing communism and the Revolution close up. However, there are numerous other possibilities for sightseeing around town. A walk through old Havana is a must to see the remnants of the protective Spanish wall, the aging stone Cathedral, Museum of the History of the City, Fine Arts Museum, and the old capitol, now the Academy of Sciences. Overlooking the water, across from El Morro, the former Presidential Palace, an elegant building in the Spanish style, has a new life as the Revolution Museum. Under President Batista, whom Castro overthrew, the palace became a symbol to the rebels of the opulence, oppression, and thievery they swore to replace. To reinforce the symbolism, Fidel chooses to live in an apartment and suburban home, and work in the government's new central office building. The relics of the struggle against Batista, and much of the visual history of the Revolution, are now housed in the former palace. Photographs depict practically every step of the

Ernest Hemingway remains a great favorite in Cuba, not only for his writing skills, but because Cubans think of him as partly one of their own. "Papa" spent part of each year in his comfortable home outside Havana. He fished, drank, ate, wrote, and seemed to greatly enjoy his months on the island. His home, kept now as a museum exactly the way it was on his last day there, features his souvenir-laden desk with photographs of wife Mary, letters, rifle shells, and war mementos.

The Revolution Museum occupies the old Presidential Palace on the waterfront in Havana, last occupied in 1958 by Fulgencio Batista. Relics, mementos, and photographs of Cuban history are displayed, with a strong emphasis on Fidel's revolutionary movement.

fight, a large model illustrates the precise movements of all participants in the Moncada Barracks attack in 1953, and guns, uniforms, hats, souvenirs, books, patches, stamps, and keepsakes are arranged under plastic domes, to be viewed in reverence by the populace as if they were splinters from the "True Cross." Out back, tanks, airplanes, and a miscellaneous collection of war machines chronicle the Revolution's progress from ragtag guerrilla bands to Third-World leaders. And, incredible though it may seem, the world's largest pheasant under glass, the original *Granma,* that creaking yacht that transported Fidel, Ché, and their eighty followers from Mexico to the Sierra in 1956, rests in its new transparent home, viewed in silence by constant lines of people reminiscent of the Lenin tomb crowds. For a museum utilizing photographs for over half of its displays, the height of inconsistency is prohibiting cameras in the presence of *Granma.*

Cameras and all types of fun are allowed and encouraged at Havana's weekend recreation center, Lenin Park, located about fifteen miles south of town. A recently completed amusement park, purchased for over a million dollars from Japan, is the big draw for children with its colorful ferris wheel, carrousel, flume ride, and tiny cars. Picnic areas, rowboats, a rodeo, aquarium, rental horses, narrow-gauge railroad, and amphitheatre are just some of the numerous features at this unique Cuban park. For tourists, it is the ideal place to see residents at play. After a leisurely Sunday afternoon

This small steam train pulls passenger cars around the perimeter of Lenin Park, Havana's favorite family recreation center.

of activities, dinner at the nearby Las Ruinas completes a full and interesting day.

Entertainment is more than daylight walking and looking. Cubans like to have a good time and will gladly spend their few pesos for live entertainment and drinks. Fortunately, tourists are welcome to join in. By far the most elaborate club is the flamboyant Tropicana, briefly described in the last chapter. Two bands, dancing girls in the trees, flashing lights, aerialists, singers, and a fast-moving show all blend to create a magic night under the stars. Although reservations are always requested, the huge club is seldom fully booked. Dinner is about 9 P.M. with the show at 11 P.M. For visitors, the meal with a couple of drinks and the show costs approximately sixteen pesos. Usually half the audience is composed of workers paying a fixed eight-peso price, rewarded by their unions for outstanding achievements. Each of the large city hotels has a nightclub with late night entertainment and variety shows. The best is at the Riviera's Copa Room. There contemporary Cuban television and recording personalities perform in a Miami Beach or Las Vegas style revue that is loud, bouncy, and fun. Show times are at 11 P.M. with dancing afterwards until very late.

Shoppers accustomed to bringing home presents will find few places to spend their Cuban allowance. By far, the most desirable products for Americans will be rum and cigars. One of the problems

Cubatur is trying to solve is how to separate tourists from more of their money when rationing restricts purchases outside the approved hotel shops and the island society is so short of hard and soft goods even for its own people. Various souvenirs are being tried, but so far the results are dismal. Tee shirts emblazoned with a sun and a "Cuba Sí" are the current rage, while posters are consistent sellers. Attempts at cheap Mexican-style pottery, wooden desk sets with Lenin's portrait, and three-dimensional postcards with rum bottles have not caught on with the foreigners. There is no indigenous craft industry, and all efforts in the economy have been addressed to struggling with domestic consumer demands. There are a few sales of guayaberas, the open Cuban shirts, but the $25 price tags discourage many travelers. Cuba should be seen and enjoyed for what it is, with shopping best left for other islands.

For any tourist, a chance to see Fidel in action would be the best souvenir of all. It is easier and more predictable to see the Maximum Leader than in most countries. So many mass public rallies are held in the Plaza de la Revolución that visitors can often join in with the half million Cubans for a look at civics in action. All such events are free and accessible without tickets. On January first, the Revolution celebrates its takeover in 1959 with a military parade and foreign policy speech. May Day is the international day for Communists and brings a grand parade. July twenty-sixth is the anniversary of the Moncada attack and an important event. September twenty-eighth commemorates the founding of the Committees for the Defense of the Revolution and usually produces another foreign policy address, while December second marks the landing of *Granma* and the founding of the National Assembly. While Fidel may not talk at every event, he is always present when in the country, and usually speaks publicly on several other occasions during the year.

Although the emphasis now is on international tourism and its inherent "hard currency" bonus, most of INIT's time and facilities are utilized by domestic Cuban travel. Only 60,000 foreigners visit the island while over 3 million Cubans use hotels and other accommodations throughout the average year, a new business resulting from paid month-long vacations for workers, more excess money, and a substantial construction program to diversify resorts throughout the country. Until the package tours are expanded or individual travel is allowed, most tourists will see only the Varadero or Havana hotels. From one viewpoint, that will be fortunate, because service and quality vary widely outside the two areas. Accommodations in the old "commercial" hotels are inferior in every way. The new hotels, planned for each province, are still meant for business rather than resort use, but are clean and attractive. For instance, the Hotel Camaguey has a pool, serves good fresh fish meals, and is several grades above the aging Grand Hotel in the middle of town.

No matter where one travels in Cuba, the general level of accommodation will be more closely related to what we accept as motels. Services are limited, there are no laundry facilities, hot water is rare, the restaurants have fixed meal hours, and interruptions of electricity and water should be expected. Still, there are some visually exciting and interesting places that give a fuller flavor of Cuba than that found in Havana.

Among the most popular short excursions from the capital is the three-hour drive to the Bay of Pigs, where Cubans refer to the fight as Giron, after the town where it began. Cubans sign up for regular bus tours of the area, located on the island's southern, or Caribbean, coast in Matanzas Province. Beginning about twenty-five miles north of the principal landing site, stone markers record the names of Cuban defenders who gave their lives on the spot. At Giron, a museum displays some of the captured U.S. equipment, airplane parts, a tank, photographs and memorabilia from the reported 160 "martyrs" who perished in the April, 1961, fight. Over 200 of the exiles, called mercenaries here, died in their struggle to "liberate" Cuba from Castro and communism, while 1,100 were captured. Later President Kennedy agreed to pay a ransom of over $25 million for their release.

One of Cuba's most interesting motels, Guamo, also commands one of its more unusual natural sites. Access to this honeymooner's dream is about thirty miles north of Giron, from a parking lot that serves the motel as well as the country's only working crocodile farm. (The idea is to see if the reptiles can be grown economically for their meat and hides. About 37,000 of them wallow around in huge pens beside the road.) There a boat takes guests on the twenty-minute ride first through a manmade canal and then across Treasure Lake. On its eastern shore, looking just like the Indian village they were designed to duplicate, individual units rise on stilts above the interlocked series of islands. Each guest has his own thatched-roof home and a boat, in

Construction for tourism is booming throughout Cuba. The idea is to fill units with Cubans on vacation in the summer and foreign travelers in the other months. This motel at Guamo is set on a series of small islands, with each pair of rooms in a separate building.

case he would rather paddle to dinner instead of walking over the arched wooden bridges. To complete the decor, a real Indian village with life-size statues shows how the original inhabitants of the region conducted their daily activities.

Another two hours to the east, backed up against the Escambray Mountains, is Cuba's real live outdoor Spanish colonial museum, the city of Trinidad. Long forgotten and isolated, the town failed to change. From its founding in 1514 by Diego Velázquez, Trinidad

To preserve its historical Spanish heritage, Trinidad's museum presents an early home to show the style and internationalism that were common in Cuba's earliest days. High ceilings, louvered windows, and an interior courtyard all contributed to the coolness of the rooms.

Tile roofs, barred windows, and cobblestone streets are relics of Spanish influence in Trinidad, the forgotten community that is now preserving its past by restricting renovations that will alter its appearance.

developed as Cuba's third city, until Havana was settled and became Spain's treasure port. Most of the remaining center of town was built between 1715 and 1780. Now declared a national treasure, the city must maintain its exterior appearance, with cobblestone streets built of ballast brought by Boston traders, grand stucco façades fronting directly onto narrow walkways, and captivating children playing in the barred and glassless "bay windows." The city museum, housed in a stylish home built in 1705, features a typically Andalusian entry, great open patio, and articles indicative of the wealth of the period, cosmopolitan furnishings from Spain, the United States, France, and Germany. A walk through the streets at dawn is a step back through time.

Another full day's drive to the east brings the hardy Cuban visitor to Santiago, the island's second city in size and importance. This hot Oriente port town is perfect as a jumping-off point for the rugged Sierra Maestra Mountains, within view of the harbor, and smaller ranges to the north and east. Around the industrial city, rum is still made at the old Bacardi plant (now called Caney); the Moncada Barracks are now a school and museum displaying the early

Revolutionary Struggle; El Morro, the sixteenth-century Spanish fort, is open for touring; and tiny Siboney Farm shows where Fidel and his 1953 rebels trained and gathered for their first fight. The Las Americas Hotel, constructed in the new concrete style, offers in-town accommodations, while the more stylish Versailles Motel has a fine swimming pool, attractive rooms, and a wide dinner menu choice.

Thus far, all the sightseeing locations have been east of Havana. Two attractions should get the mobile tourist out to the west, to Pinar del Río Province. It is here that Cuba's best tobacco is grown and dried. For the cigar enthusiast, Pinar del Río is like coming home to the mother lode. Thousands of farmers tend their small plots more as gardens than commercial crops. Heavy thatched drying barns, windowless and closed, are almost overpowering with their constant tobacco aroma. The other sight is one of Cuba's grand natural wonders, the area around Viñales. Great mountainous clusters appear to have been tossed about by some giant hand, with sheer rock walls appearing to leap straight up from the valley floor. In this peculiarly

Unusual mountain formations make the area around Viñales in Pinar del Río a favorite vacation site for Cubans. Most small farms in the region are still privately owned and produce some of the finest tobacco in the country.

Many caves are found in the honeycombed mountains around Viñales. In the José Miguel Cave, INIT has constructed a bar and refreshment area. Paths lead off into the mountain's interior.

limestone region, said to be duplicated in Puerto Rico and China, centuries of erosion have left only hard caps on the soft mountains, eliminating the slopes. As a result, cracks and caves texture the towering cliffs, with palms and other trees growing directly from the sharp walls, hundreds of feet up. Remarkable views of the valley are available from north-facing rooms at the Motel Jasmines, a delightful new facility done in neo-Spanish style. As with all the motels away from Havana, rooms average $15 nightly, and only occasionally will top $20.

From this brief description, it should be obvious that there is more to see and do on the 759-mile-long island than can possibly be accomplished on a brief vacation. Cuba should be experienced piecemeal to fully appreciate its potential. For Americans, the first accomplishment will be just to get there. Afterwards, as relations stabilize, additional visits can bring out the lesser-known details of Cuba's geography. Columbus may have been correct when he looked ashore in 1492 and called it "the most beautiful island ever seen."

Sugar

10

At the time of the Revolution, we thought it was
sugar that kept our people poor. We have tried many crops
and looked into even more. But we always have to
return to sugar, because of the money it can bring. We do
not like being so dependent on a single crop, but
that is just the way it is.

—*Fidel Castro*

Hector was up with the sun. After coffee, he packed an extra tin of water because he could see it would be hot today. As he walked toward the road where his workers' bus would pick him up soon, he thought, as he did each morning, what life might have been like if he had stayed in school. Just as he got to the part in his daydreams where he listed the things he would buy if he had more money, the bus arrived and he was lost in the laughing and talking that accompanied the long ride. Billowing black clouds told him when they had arrived. The burners must have started later than usual in the night for so much smoke to persist. One end of the field was actually in flames. Too bad, he thought, that will make it even hotter. With machete flashing, he was at work, one cut to separate the stalk from the ground, a few slashes to remove the few remaining leaves, and a trio of quick slices to make even pieces, about a yard long. Every hour or so, the growing stacks were picked up by the gatherers, as Hector and his fellow cane cutters moved slowly across the blackened field. Completely covered with soot himself, in late afternoon, he climbed back onto the bus, exhausted. With a few brushes he knocked some of the black from his orange tee shirt and cleared the faded letters, "Millionaire Brigade." His group was working as hard as possible to win the designation again this year. If they cut a million *arrobas* of cane during the season, 25 million pounds, they would get a substantial bonus and Hector could buy some of the things he had been dreaming about.

The Cuban government hopes that such long hard days for minimal pay may soon end. It would also like to terminate the country's almost total dependence on sugar as a supplier of desperately needed foreign currency. The reality is that neither situation is likely to occur. As Enrique Oltuski, who has held several ministerial posts, says, "We started the Revolution as sugar haters. We were sure if we put the island into other crops, we would solve our problems. Then we discovered the true value of sugar and could not switch to anything else." In 1959, sugar was mainly in the hands of a few American companies and large Cuban landowners. It was an efficient operation in general and profitable even at world prices of the day, which ranged from 2¢ to 5¢ a pound. For years, Cuba was the world's largest grower of sugarcane, with production at almost 6 million tons annually for 1958, 1959, and 1960. During that time, most of the crop went to the United States at a favorable price and was paid for in dollars. Before its association with the socialist countries, Cuba had no trouble spending the currencies it received.

In Fidel's 1953 courtroom speech, "History Will Absolve Me," he outlined his agricultural promises by saying tenants and sharecroppers on less than 166 acres would be given the land and the state would reimburse the landowner; 30 percent of the profits from industrial enterprises, including sugar mills, would go to the workers, and small tenant farmers would have the right to share 55 percent of sugar production rights with large farmers. As the country moved into communism, the large sugar plantations were nationalized and never distributed to tenants. They were and are operated by the state as a government enterprise.

Sugar provides Cuba with over 80 percent of its foreign exchange money. It is such a volatile commodity on the world market that no one ever wants to discuss the current production prices. A few advance details from such a large supplier could have tremendous impact on future sales. However, some conclusions are apparent. Cuba has been severely affected over the past year by a disastrous fall in world sugar prices. So much depends on that income that her first Five-Year Plan is already being altered and shipments of foreign-made equipment stopped.

In 1959, world prices were about three cents a pound. Almost all the 5.8 million-ton harvest, or *zafra,* was exported. As the Revolution consolidated the land, mills, and all other aspects of sugar production, vast claims were made that Cuba would finally be rich, with bigger plantings (no land left idle), more efficient use of manpower for cutting, full utilization of the mills since sugar could be diverted anywhere, and greater output because workers would know they were laboring for themselves and their government instead of some unseen landlord. It never turned out that way.

Sugar has been a terrible disappointment and embarrassment for the Revolution. After all the propaganda to the contrary, the reality is that, after eighteen years and with 10 to 15 percent more land in cane, production has been holding near the 1959 totals and only in 1977 crept up to 6.4 million tons. The sugar ministry places the blame on continuing drought in Oriente and the flight into exile of experienced sugar managers. Although both observations are partially relevant, even greater emphasis should be placed on mismanagement, inefficiency, and the undeniable human fact that production is higher under capitalism, where the profit motive spurs people to ever increased efficiency.

When the government was still in the organizational stage and attempting to cope with the flight of middle-management professionals, the 1963 sugar harvest dipped to 3.8 million tons, its lowest point since 1945. Massive efforts were implemented in all aspects of the enterprise and production slowly rose again. Then, at the highest levels of decision making, Fidel conceived and announced a plan that would have serious repercussions throughout Cuba for years. He said 1970 would be the year of the 10-million-ton zafra. More land was cleared and more cane planted. Fertilizers were purchased and people transferred from other work to assist. The goal became the national preoccupation with billboards asking, "What are you doing towards the 10 million?" The entire plan seemed all the more bizarre because of government efforts before the Revolution and between 1960 and 1962 to denigrate sugar's importance to Cuba's future. Fidel and Ché were widely quoted in 1959 and 1960 promising a sudden and considerable rise in living standards, a diminution of sugar depen-

dence, and rapid industrialization that would bring faster improvements in life-style than ever seen in any country. In every case, the
promises were unfulfilled.

Also unfulfilled was the 10-million-ton harvest. At the heart of the
plan was the need to divert hundreds of thousands of Cubans from
other jobs to help with cutting, transporting, and processing. Every
industry, and the military, was adversely affected for months.
Additionally, at the time when Cuba's future was being economically
determined, the estimated bill for the extra zafra effort was one
billion dollars to expand the industry's capacity to handle the
expected tonnage. The money had to come from other ministries'
programs and was never recouped by increased sugar sales.

As the zafra approached, it was surrounded by more and more
fantastic events. For historical significance, Fidel announced the 1970
harvest would begin July 26, 1969, the Moncada anniversary.
Because cutting would be under way in December, Cubans were told
Christmas Eve celebrating would be postponed until July, 1970, after
the zafra. Then the steady parade of dignitaries to the fields began.
Fidel would go out with slashing machete and cut for the TV and
newspaper cameras, and then stay on working for the rest of the day.
The Soviet Minister of Defense, Marshal Grechko, came and cut
cane, as did a group from North Vietnam, and the whole Cuban
cabinet. For the year it was de rigueur for all officials and visitors to
lend a helping hand.

In May, 1970, Fidel announced to the nation that the goal would
not be reached, and that 9 million tons would be all that could be
expected. As usual, he accepted blame for the failure and the
problems it had caused. These problems were astronomical, both in
psychological and material terms. The people had been promised
salvation, and it did not come. They were told their troubles were
soon to be over and that socialized sugar growing would show the
way. Instead, the experience brought new shortages, more rationing,
and the renewed realization that there were no easy answers and that
the government could be absolutely wrong. No one can measure the
long-term impact of such wide-scale failure. Even the 9-million-ton
estimate proved overly optimistic and the much heralded 1970 zafra
produced 8.5 million tons of sugar, a seemingly huge increase, but
inflated because it started so early and included some 1969 cane, and
went late enough to have some of the following year's crop too. All

the planners went back to work, trying to put sugar into its proper place again, and attempting to minimize the economic damage done by the grand experiment.

Sugar's lineage in the New World is inextricably intertwined with a fascinating trio of subjects: Spain, treasure, and slaves. Particularly in Cuba did these three combine to create one of the epic sagas of Caribbean history. From that October day in 1492 when Columbus and his crew became the first Europeans to lay eyes on the island until the Spanish defeat in 1898, Cuba was forced to serve her foreign master initially as a gathering point and supplier for the gold and silver fleets, and then later as an unsurpassed sugar producer. During the earlier role, sugar was only an infant industry. In the latter, sugar became king, and the black African slaves became the servants who made its production possible.

Even though Columbus is credited with the introduction of sugar to the Americas, many years passed before it achieved any significance. Unlike the other European powers colonizing the Caribbean, Spain was obsessed with treasure. As soon as it was certain that Cuba offered no quantities of gold and silver, Spain concentrated her efforts in Central and South America and plundered the riches of the Aztecs, Mayas, and Incas. Cuba might have been overlooked except for her strategic location. For security and supply purposes, Spain needed a port where the treasure fleet could gather and be made ready for the sail back to Europe. Havana was chosen for this task and Cuba developed to serve the rich convoy. It has been estimated that half the world's precious metals traveled this route through Havana.

Over the next three centuries African slaves began to be moved into the region in great numbers. England, in particular, was developing agricultural islands, and in the days before machinery, a large pliable work force was vital. Since the Indians had been eradicated throughout the Caribbean, slaves were the accepted answer. Once England defeated the Spanish Armada in 1588, effectively diminishing Spain's power and influence, Cuba's role gradually changed, setting a pattern that in time would see the island transformed into a gigantic sugar factory. Sugar and Cuba seemed made for each other, although the match was a long time being consummated.

As early as the 1520s there was some sugar mill construction, and by the seventeenth century, Cuba's eastern areas had thirty-seven mills operating with an output of over 300 tons annually. When the British captured Havana in 1762, they seized the entire year's sugar export on the docks, 500 tons, although the estimate is that actual production then was over 5,000 tons, most of which was smuggled to sell outside the Spanish system. At the time Cuba had about 100 plantations totaling 10,000 cultivated acres. In comparison, Jamaica, the nearest English island, had 600 working plantations and exported over a hundred times as much sugar. The pattern was set and nothing could stop the inexorable push toward sugar production.

In modern times, when sugar is so all-pervasive and cheap, it is extraordinarily difficult to grasp its significance to pre-Columbian Europeans. It seems that the original cane came from the South Pacific, and Polynesian legends deal at some length with the product. India was a prime producer for centuries, but research now indicates it imported sugar in the distant past. The sweet substance caught Europe by storm when it was first brought back by the adventurous traders who made their way overland to the Indies. In his stinging denouncement of sugar consumption, *Sugar Blues,* William Dufty says, "At the time of its introduction to Britain, sugar was prohibitively expensive, a courtly luxury in a price class with the most expensive drugs on the market today. At $25 a pound, it was the equivalent to a year's salary for a working man. Around 1300 . . . a few servings of sugar amounted to a third of the cost of a magnificent funeral feast. In the mid-sixteenth century, by the reign of Elizabeth I, the price had been cut in half. By 1662, Britain was importing 16 million pounds of sugar a year. The cost had been cut to a shilling a pound, which was equivalent to the cost of three dozen eggs. . . . By 1800 [Britain imported] 160 million pounds a year." There was never anything like sugar. Honey had certainly been collected and consumed for thousands of years, but the easily carried and stored sugar crystals were altogether different. The high price and appearance of luxury probably helped make it all the more enticing. As it happened, about the same time that sugar was being produced for a somewhat reasonable price, coffee and tea were also made available to the European market. Sugar blended with the pair perfectly, and the craze was on. The Caribbean islands, of all the countries, would be alternatingly locked for the next few centuries into the mixed curse and blessing of being sugar islands.

No way was imagined to develop the labor-intensive sugar business without the use of large numbers of slaves. It would take another century before people became sufficiently absorbed with the morality of the issue to seek action. So much money and national importance was involved that the principal preoccupation by governments and kings was how to get in on the action.

Cuba was always behind in development by comparison with England's islands. As the dominant naval, shipping, and trading force, Britain was naturally the dominant slave-trading nation. When Spain accepted the Papal Bull giving her rights to the New World, she also accepted the terms that gave Portugal claim to the new areas of Africa. Therefore, Portugal became the first supplier of slaves for Spain's colonies, to be followed by the slave traders from England. Then Spain decided to take the business back and formed the Havana Monopoly Company with exclusive license to bring slaves to Cuba. In the twenty years following 1739 that company brought in about 5,000 blacks for approximately $144 each—not a very high price by other standards of the day—who were principally purchased in Jamaica. Another estimated 5,000 were probably smuggled in.

Still, Cuba never seemed to have enough slaves to expand sugar production to suit the plantation owners. Capital was the problem and there was no organized way to finance the purchases. Spain was of little help, so Cuban planters depended on Cuban merchants to lend them the necessary money to buy slaves, land, and machinery. Probably 80 percent of the slaves brought in during the mid-1700s came in by merchant-advanced credit. Because of all the circumstances of sugar and slave evolution, and the economic difficulties in capitalizing it, one result would have tremendous impact on later Cuban society. Unlike all the other Caribbean islands, Cuba and Puerto Rico, the two Spanish colonies, had the lowest proportion of blacks to whites. Cuba, at this stage of development, had a population of less than half blacks. In contrast, on all the English and French islands, the average was 13.7 white and 86.3 percent slave. Additionally, Cuba had a sizable free Negro and mulatto population. In addition to about 32,000 slaves at the time, it is estimated that Cuba also had 20,000 freed slaves and mulattoes, living mainly in the cities.

The significance of this basically white Spanish heritage would later become apparent when Fidel Castro declared that there would be no racial discrimination in Cuba. In 1960, as now, the black population in Cuba amounted to about a fourth of the people. In comparison, numerous other Caribbean islands that developed with huge slave proportions are now almost completely black nations. The character of Cuba through the years and its character and attitudes today are easily seen as a product of the many peculiar slave traditions that the Spanish and Cubans fostered. First were the relatively small numbers of slaves. Then the Spanish, by losing their eminent position in the New World, were left with relatively small holdings compared with England and France, and thus never became the large sugar entrepreneurs that might have required bigger numbers and tighter organization. Cuba ultimately would become a huge sugar producer, always among the largest in the world, but without the strict rules that, for example, governed planter-slave relations on British islands. The Spanish-American islands, in a significant departure from the laws of other slave-holding areas, recognized the right of slaves to buy their freedom, and that of their parents or children. This was not possible in the colonies of North America or elsewhere throughout the Caribbean. If a slave raised or sold vegetables, worked part time in the cities, or used whatever skill and drive he had to earn and save some money, he could place a down payment on his freedom, and pay off the debt over a period of time. Obviously, this right also meant that the Spanish authorities recognized another right—that of owning property and accumulating capital. Such activities gave a different look and feel to Cuba, compared to the neighboring sugar islands. There was a relationship between blacks and whites that was not found, for instance, on nearby Haiti. Also in Cuba, unlike British colonies, where masters usually chose not to recognize illegitimate offspring, children from unions of master and slave were frequently set free. Slaves could request a new master if one could be found, and those slaves who lived in cities in merchants' households often enjoyed considerable privileges. They were even hired out to do day jobs, just as anyone else would work for a third party. As a result of these fundamental differences between Cuba, under Spanish laws and customs, and the other islands, it would later be easier to ease some of the racial issues that plagued the Caribbean.

During the final years of the 1700s, Cuba's sugar development soared. Numerous decisions and tax rulings eased the admission of slaves, more plantations were established, and both production and exports reflected the increase. Sugar exports averaged about 300 tons a year in the 1750s, rose to 2,000 tons in the 1760s, and exceeded 10,000 tons a year in the 1770s. The British colonies of Jamaica and

Antigua, large and efficient sugar producers in the past, were on the decline. The unfertilized land just could not go on with the heavy single-crop output. In contrast, Cuba kept opening up new land. Jamaica is basically a mountainous island, with relatively little land ideally suited for sugarcane. Antigua is flat enough, but it is small with no room to expand. The other British islands faced similar size and overuse limitations. The French islands of Guadeloupe and Martinique, on the other hand, might have been competition because of their large sizes, but their sugar exports went to France and did not compete with Cuba.

By the end of the 1820s, Cuba had become both the wealthiest

Using methods unchanged through the centuries, a cane cutter slashes his way through burned-over stalks, leaving short lengths suitable for the mill's grinder. The hot, hard, low-paying work remains the backbone of Cuba's sugar industry.

Modernization of the sugar production comes slowly to the countryside. Hand-cut cane stalks are loosely stacked in the fields to await ox-drawn carts that will carry them to nearby mills. Only the tractor hoist provides mechanical assistance.

colony of any nation in the world, and also the largest single producer of sugar anywhere. Her output in 1829 was 73,000 tons and rose to 160,000 tons by 1836. Cuba was now queen of the sugar islands, creating a dependency on the single product that continues today.

In many ways the physical conditions of sugarcane cutting remain much as they were in the 1700s. It is a hot, backbreaking job, slashing a machete through the undergrowth and leaves, cutting the cane into segments, and stacking them for removal to the mills. After a full day of such exertion, men are exhausted. Before the Revolution, the Cuban routine was much the same as that on the other tropical islands, a few months of cane work followed by several of unemployment. After the government socialized sugar, its first task was to alter the conditions of employment. Cutters, although generally lower paid, would be treated as all other workers, and would become yearly employees of the Ministry, complete with a month's paid vacation. It was practically an unheard-of advance and a promise fulfilled. But the obvious problem was what to do with the men for twelve months. Traditionally, sugar work was at best a five- to six-month job. An entirely new schedule was organized. Plantings were staggered to permit a longer harvesting season. Now, as before, the zafra is over in June. About a month is spent getting the mill and fields in condition for the following season. Then month vacations find employees traveling around Cuba, perhaps even spending a week or two at Varadero. After that, work begins on planting and getting the mill repaired and ready to open. Since cane, depending on the variety, field, fertilizer, and care, can last up to fifteen years before replanting, there is always a recycling of land for better yields. Currently, the Sugar Ministry is replanting seedlings every four years in an attempt to produce more sugar on the same acreage.

There is great hope that mechanization of the harvest will be the advance that will make sugar profitable. In 1959, almost 500,000 Cubans were involved in sugar, 400,000 of whom were in the fields cutting and hauling cane. Already, a 40 percent reduction in sugar workers, to about 300,000 people, has freed workers for other industries. Some of this results from centralized control, and some from the introduction of machines to do the cutting.

A sugarcane cutting machine is, like a wheat combine or a hay baler, one of man's more interesting inventions. Remarkable in appearance, it sweeps through a field of towering cane, with great

Cuba is basing much of its sugar future on machine cutters that eliminate slow hand-work. Still, less than a third of the harvest is machine-cut even though the 1980 goal is over 70 percent.

rolling clouds of dust and deafening noise, spinning its twin rotor blades as near the ground as the operator can bring them, sucking in the full stalk, where inside its dark innards knives, belts, and fans skin off the leaves, whack the stalk into proper lengths, blow the unwanted debris out one side, and disgorge the valuable three-foot sugary remains into an accompanying trailer. Used throughout the world to reduce considerably the overburdening costs of hand labor, the machines are both a trial and a boon to Cuba. The problems seem to be both the terrain and soil, and the machines themselves. All mechanical cultivation works best in flat areas. Cuba is partially flat, but much of her sugar land is on hills. The machines have a terrible tendency to dig into the soil on hills, particularly when driven by inexperienced operators. If the blades dig into the soil, a four-year or more planting is ruined and has to be redone. Then the machines themselves have not worked as hoped. In recognition of the importance of this experiment, the Ministry decided to have on-site tests of three different cutters, one made in Australia, another from East Germany, and one codesigned by Cuban and Soviet engineers and constructed in the Soviet Union. A thousand of the trio are on duty and cut 25.8 percent of the 1974–1975 zafra. As its part of the first Five-Year Plan, the Sugar Ministry planned to double the 1959 output by 1980 (to almost 12 million tons), and harvest 70 percent of the crop with machines. To utilize the machines at all, rows must be planted perfectly, and the small hills around each stalk eliminated so the machines can cut flush along the surface. All this takes years. It appears that, once again, disappointment will result from the effort, since guarded reports continue to note the difficulties encountered in keeping the Soviet cutters operational. At the end of the 1977 zafra a brief announcement said that about 30 percent of the sugar was machine-cut, not much improvement in two years.

To keep track of daily movements and activities, the Ministry of Sugar has a modern control facility in downtown Havana, complete with computers and wall charts that look much more like a military planning operation than an agricultural venture. Each province has computer points that transmit information on plantings, weather, mills, harvesting, transport, and any other relevant sugar information. The center evaluates daily, each ten days, monthly, by various stages in the year, and at the end of the total harvest. Computers store harvest facts, export data, shipping details, and all the information that sugar officials feel they want to make the right decisions about their precious crop. Their goal is simply stated: Cuba plans to have the highest sugar productivity per acre of any country in the world. It is a tall order, but they want to surpass Hawaii—that is their target. Sugar officials still say, disregarding the disastrous 1970 experience, that they plan to double the harvest with half the workers by 1980.

It is an interesting emphasis at this time, since the world suffers no shortage of sugar from other sources. In fact, part of the reason for Cuba's economic difficulties is that there is so much sugar production worldwide that the price is terribly depressed. No one knows what future effect continued research findings showing sugar's detrimental impact on human health will have on the total market. However, it is generally accepted that before the Revolution, Cuba produced about 35,000 arrobas per caballería. (In sugar, all figures are given in the old Spanish measurements where an arroba equals 25 pounds, and a caballería is 33⅓ acres.) What gives the Ministry hope is that there are areas in Matanzas Province where, with careful cultivation, use of fertilizers and irrigation, and replanting every four years, the yield is double, or 70,000 arrobas per caballería. That is 52,505 pounds of raw sugar on each acre, which is an outstanding production figure. That has not been duplicated around the island and is, at this point, only a goal. One other limiting factor is that Cuba's eastern sector, Oriente, a large sugar producer, has had several years of drought and is receiving only about half its usual rainfall. No new goals are likely to be reached as long as this condition remains.

Like a refugee from a Charlie Chaplin movie, the creaking old Camilo Cienfuegos Sugar Mill (built by Hershey Chocolate in 1919) still crushes cane stalks in Matanzas. Part of Cuba's sugar problem is that no new mills have been built since the 1920s and no replacement parts have been available since the 1961 U.S. embargo.

Of all the intriguing aspects of the sugar business, none is more bizarre than the archaic vestiges of another era, the venerable sugar mills. Appearing as some diabolical crosses between Charlie Chaplin's predictions of the machine age and an Environmental Protection Agency nightmare, some 150 of the hot, sticky plants spew out their jet black smoke throughout much of the year. In stark contrast with the new apartment and school construction, the latest sugar mill was built in 1927. Inside, gigantic wheels, rollers, and pistons creak and groan under decades of use and would appear more at home as silent movie backdrops. Since the machinery was made in the United States, the 1961 economic embargo brought an end to the spare parts supply. Cuba had to create a new facility, Planta Mechanica in Santa Clara, just to fabricate sugar mill parts replacements. About half of all the existing parts have been made there.

The sugarcane stalks are poured from railroad cars, trailers, and carts into one end of the mills to be passed through a series of crushers that squeeze the sweet juice into collectors. The remaining dry fibers, called *bagasse*, are retrieved to be used to fire the boilers that will reduce the juice to crystalline sugar. (The United Nations is funding a $5 million project in Cuba to see if bagasse can be converted into paper. The pilot plant is near completion and hopes are that it will ease Cuba's dependence on Canadian newsprint.) The process is

Mountains of bagged refined sugar wait in enormous twin warehouses at the Matanzas sugar port. The Soviet Union receives its Cuban sugar unrefined and in bulk, so these fifty-kilogram bags will go to other socialist countries as well as free world markets.

A West German mobile loader spirals sugar bags from conveyor belts directly into the holds of waiting ships. Eliminating handwork is one way Cuba hopes to save money.

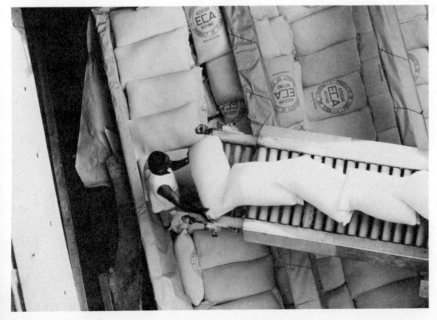

simple and relatively unchanged since colonial days. Then the boiling was in open caldrons and now it is inside pressurized boilers, but the output is the same. The first result of this crystallization is raw, or slightly brown, sugar. For some limited local consumption and for shipment to the U.S.S.R. that is a final step. (The Soviet Union takes raw sugar from Cuba so it can use its facilities for the extra step, refining it into the more familiar white product.) For most of its export sugar, Cuba does the refining.

From the mills, sugar moves, mainly by rails, to the various ports for shipment overseas. In the city of Matanzas, Cuba's most modern facility features a West German loading installation that transports fifty-kilogram bags of refined sugar (110 pounds) in a seemingly endless stream from the dockside warehouse up and over waiting ships, to let them drop by gravity down a spiral chute directly into the hands of workers inside the holds. The bags are then stacked where they will ride to Japan, Eastern Europe, or other markets. In an adjacent warehouse, it too the length of two football fields, a mountain of raw sugar rises almost a hundred feet toward the domed roof. Men and machines are dwarfed by the huge volume. When a ship is ready for bulk loading, sugar is conveyed by belt and blown into the hold, a brown fountain of crystals, bound for Russia.

Although Cuba has great hopes for a sugar future, the crop is so volatile in pricing and production that planning becomes practically impossible. After her output increased from 5.9 million metric tons before the Revolution to 8.5 million tons in 1970, the totals dropped again below 6 million tons. Estimates right up to the 1977 harvest were that it would not reach 6 million tons, but it is reported to have achieved 6.4 million. That will affect the 1978 estimates, which would normally have been below 6.5 million tons, and will now likely be revised upward. The summer 1977 world price centered around 8¢ a pound, very near the disastrous 7¢-a-pound figure it reached in September 1976, when Fidel announced to the CDR rally in the Plaza that it costs Cuba more than that to produce the crop. Still, their ally and benefactor, the U.S.S.R., has an agreement to buy sugar at above the world price and, although she can reduce the purchase price to Cuba to meet world conditions, has chosen to keep the support payment at thirty cents a pound. (The payment is in either goods or credits, and, since it is in a "soft" currency, cannot be used by Cuba to buy items she needs from Western countries.)

To appreciate the enormity of sugar's value to Cuba, and what
Soviet aid does, a calculation based on a presumed 6-million-metric-
ton harvest would mean 5.4 million tons available for export. (Ten
percent of the crop is domestically consumed.) If the Soviets paid 30¢
a pound for half of the export, the credit to Cuba would be
$1,785,240,000. And if the world price holds at 10¢ a pound, half the
harvest sold at that price would bring in $595,080,000 in hard
currency. The two sales total $2,380,320,000 for a year's sugar output.
Assuming the world price might again reach 20¢ and the Soviets
continued to buy at 30¢, Cuba would then gross $2,975,400,000.

Sugar is said to produce 85 percent of Cuba's foreign currency. If
we can believe a recent estimate that the country's gross national
product is about $7 billion, that means that sugar will produce nearly
a third of the G.N.P. this year. With the same proportion of a single
product to G.N.P. for the United States, that would mean the value
of that product would be $470 billion, a truly staggering figure.

Numbers aside, the fact remains that Cuba is at least as dependent,
and perhaps even more so, on sugar than it was in 1959. From
revolutionaries with a self-professed hatred for the sweet, it is an
ironic development. In a private interview with the author, Fidel
Castro observed, "We have looked very carefully at what we grow
and what we can sell to get the needed exchange to buy the goods we
require. Many crops will grow in Cuba's soil and climate. We
thought about corn and found that a hectare (2.5 acres) would
produce about $400 worth. We looked at rice, coffee, beans, and other
things and always came to the same conclusion. Sugar can produce
$7,000 a hectare, and so it is the most profitable thing we can grow.
So, with those figures, we decided to grow small amounts of various
items, but to mainly produce sugar and use the money from it to buy
the other food we need."

It is a tragic dependency. Cuba is trapped in a web it did not
originally create, but which it has not been able to break. Sugar
remains a capricious mistress, slavishly wed to fluctuating world
prices and oversupply. Also, like cigarettes, it is a product that, the
more deeply it is studied, looks increasingly dangerous. A growing
body of evidence indicates that, beyond containing empty calories, it
is actually harmful to health. As such, sugar represents the thinnest of
threads to grasp for a country's future.

Agriculture, Cattle, Tobacco, and Fishing

11

> We have made enormous strides in agriculture and
> intend to put much of our resources in continuing
> development there. In cattle and dairy production and
> fishing, the Revolution has taken infant industries
> and built them into important segments of our economy.
>
> —*Fidel Castro*

Maria reached beside her and pulled up a handful of filler. She had made the moves often enough to be unimpressed by the dark brown colors and heady aroma. A quick glance told her that the amount and quality were right. Then, two or three quick turns formed a cylinder, ready to be held in place by a leafy "cover." Forced into a six-slotted hand-carved wooden form, the familiar shapes emerged to await their final addition. Maria took a rich, pliable leaf, already hand-selected for its color and surface perfection, and carefully wrapped it over her creation. Deftly covering one end and clipping the other, she placed the cigar atop a growing pile. It had taken her less than three minutes to make, and it would sell for over a dollar to a waiting world market. Her cigars carry the label "Montecristo," one of the old names fondly remembered by U.S. smokers from before the Revolution. They are the finest that Cuba makes.

Maria is representative of but one of the many changes in agriculture since 1959. At the dilapidated old H. Upmann factory where she works, 215 other women handroll cigars. Before the Revolution, the craft was considered a man's preserve violated by only one woman. Other changes are on a grander scale, the most far-reaching innovation being nationalization of lands and the incor-

To keep production high, a minor compromise with capitalistic principles gives hand-rollers a basic salary plus bonuses for exceeding a given quota.

poration of almost all farming activities under INRA, the National Institute of Agrarian Reform.

At INRA's new hilltop headquarters about twenty miles south of Havana, Ilidio Sabatier, an economic section official, explained the acquisition of farms. "In 1959 we found our general land structure was much like other Latin American countries. Only 8 percent of the landowners had 70 percent of the land. Forty percent of that land was in sharecropping and 25 percent of the very best sugar acreage was in foreign hands. We spent the first five years of the Revolution trying to change all that.

"The First Agrarian Reform law came in May, 1959, only four months after the victory over Batista. That limited holdings to 1,000 acres. Then, 100,000 sharecroppers on that land were given two caballerías (66⅔ acres) and the right to buy up to five. The law authorized bonds for reimbursing the former landowners, but, in reality, almost all of them fled the country and were never paid anything.

"The Second Agrarian Reform law became effective in October, 1963. Its main purpose was to deal with the rural bourgeois, who were largely untouched by the first law. They were accused of being uncommitted to the Revolution, aiding counterrevolutionaries, and leaving land idle. This law limited holdings to five caballerías (166⅔ acres)."

It all sounds so cold and matter-of-fact on paper. The reality is that the government restructured ownership of the island. By issuing two laws, the INRA brought 70 percent of the entire land mass of Cuba under its control. A few people have been paid for their lands, but the vast majority simply could not tolerate the thought of living under a Communist government and left for Florida.

If a family supported the Revolution, it was allowed to hold up to 166⅔ acres under the condition that the owners remained on the land and worked it. (A few exceptions were made for larger holdings, i.e., where adjoining farms were operated by brothers.) Immediately, businesses like sugar and cattle raising that depended on great land tracts were obliterated. The smaller, special expertise enterprises, like tobacco and coffee, remained largely intact. In fact, even today over 60 percent of Cuba's tobacco is grown by private farmers.

Soil, climate, and expertise are credited with making tobacco from Pinar del Río what Cubans call the best in the world. Leaves are tied on rods before being hung in curing barns.

Pinar del Río, the country's westernmost province, maintains its reputation as one of the world's best tobacco areas. A combination of soil, climate, and personal experience in handling the delicate leaves gives cigars from the region their characteristic taste and aroma. Fields of broad-leafed plants are watched over so closely they could be compared more favorably to gardens than to large commercial enterprises. No harvesting machine threatens to intrude on this operation because only the human eye can determine when the leaf has reached peak condition. Each plot is picked at least five times a season by experienced workers who select only a few leaves each time. The very best, without imperfections, are then used as "wrappers" for export cigars. Lesser quality leaves are used for "filler," and the rest shredded for cigarettes.

Thatched curing barns, unchanged in basic design since the earliest Spanish tobacco operations, dot the landscape. To form a windowless building with relatively constant temperature and humidity, palm fronds are woven atop a sapling superstructure. In the dark, heavily scented barns, hundreds of thousands of newly picked leaves drape over long poles and hang just below the ceilings for thirty-five to forty days of slow curing.

The heady aroma of thousands of newly picked tobacco leaves fills the windowless curing barns of Pinar del Río, as the cigar wrappers slowly age in even humidity and temperature.

With 112,000 acres in tobacco, Pinar del Río produces 70 percent of Cuba's crop, or about 35,000 tons. Even though the majority of that production is done by private farm owners, it is still heavily influenced by INRA. The Institute prepares the campesinos' lands with equipment, sells the fertilizers and insecticides that are needed, and even provides manpower for planting, tending, and picking. The farmer pays for any supplies but receives technical assistance free. When the crop is in, INRA is the sole buyer. For the best grade of wrapper tobacco, the government pays up to 120 pesos per hundred pounds, up to 30 pesos for filler, and to 43 pesos for cigarette quality. Twenty-three pesos is the bottom price for low-grade leaves.

One of history's "accidents" was responsible for the first European observation of Cuban cigars. On his initial voyage in 1492, Columbus was so sure he had found China as he explored Cuba's northeast coast that he sent a party inland to deliver a personal note he carried from the King and Queen of Spain to the Chinese Emperor. After asking coastal natives, whom he insisted on calling Indians because of his belief that he had reached the Indies, he learned of a community in the interior. Mistaking it for Peking, Columbus sent his men marching toward a village where the city of Holguin now stands. Instead of the fabled capital of the Orient and untold riches, all the hapless Spaniards found were a few thatched-roof dwellings and a small number of peaceful natives. The note went undelivered as the visitors stared in disbelief at Indians who relaxed while smoking rolled tobacco leaves by holding a wooden tube, like a straw, to the nostril. Cuban cigars made their first converts.

Today's products are, of course, considerably different from the originals. At H. Upmann's, manufacturer of Cuba's premium brands, great care has gone into the protection of quality and reputation. Located in a dark, dingy factory near Havana's old Capitol building, Upmann turns out over 100,000 cigars daily, 67 percent of them by hand. Since all tobacco factories are operated by the government, the best tobacco grown on the island can be channeled here to produce the finest and highest priced export cigars. "Montecristo," "H. Upmann," "Romeo and Julieta," and "Churchill" are just some of its famous names. Besides Upmann's, three other factories produce export cigars and about one hundred make products for domestic consumption.

Upmann's creaking elevator takes the visitor up to two floors filled with workers sitting at long wooden benches. Open windows and fans barely relieve the oppressive heat, and many of the male employees strip to their undershirts. The women suffer in moist silence. Fast-moving hands constantly race the clock, because production above the stated norm results in bonuses, material incentives smacking of capitalism. Almost every worker is engaged in a different project, since Upmann's makes over a hundred various sizes and types of cigars. There are five lengths of "Montecristos," fat cigars, thin ones, shorts, longs, green, brown, and practically every combination of the above. The English prefer certain sizes, shapes, colors, and blends, Germans others, and Canadians still others. Upmann's keeps records of preferences and provides each country with its favorites.

In one back room, men stand before large open tables filled with twenty or more small stacks of similarly shaded cigars. To make a box

In H. Upmann's sorting room, skilled workers look over all new cigars and separate them according to minute color differences. Each box of premium cigars will contain only products of exactly the same shade. Fidel and a chart of the PCC's Central Committee keep this sorter company.

Ruben Morales reads the morning *Granma* newspaper as workers at the H. Upmann Tobacco Factory hand-roll expensive cigars. Traditionally, readers were hired by the workers to entertain and inform them during their tedious days. With Marxism, Morales works for the state and reads selections of newspaper articles and revolutionary literature.

of Cuban cigars visually uniform, they examine every wrapper, noting minute differences. Their precise matching of each boxful is a remarkable display of the eye's ability to discern color variations.

At the junction of two large work rooms, a contemporary variation of a venerable cigar tradition occurs daily before a brilliant red curtain. Traditionally, to relieve the boredom of handrolling tobacco, the employees would chip in to hire a "reader" who would entertain and inform them. That function now is a government-paid position, filled at Upmann's by Rubén Morales, who reads his morning prose from *Granma* and selected revolutionary and Marxist-Leninist tomes.

Boredom is far from the thoughts of workers in Cuba's newest enterprise. The Fishing Port of Havana is a swirl of activity as rows of refrigerated freighters unload thousands of boxes of frozen fish as well as whole tuna. Front-end loaders dart between the ships and three warehouse storage facilities, capable of holding 21,000 tons of fish prior to processing and distribution. The entire Port, which employs over 1,800 people, was a 50-million-peso gift in 1964 from the Soviet Union.

A false notion, commonly held, is that tropical islands are surrounded by rich fishing waters. Probably Hemingway and other sportswriters fostered the idea with great tales of man-versus-fish sagas. Although some sports fishing does exist in warm waters and the small reef fish make skin diving so appealing there, the vast majority of all commercial operations occur in the cold ocean waters of the North Atlantic, in the chilly Humboldt Current off Peru, and in the Northern Pacific. One of the ironies of the Caribbean, which lures divers and fishermen from over the world, is that the waters cannot support even small island populations, since plankton, the basis of the ocean's food chain, is largely a cold-water phenomenon.

Before the Revolution, Cuba's fishing was confined to small boats fishing close to the island. There was a Gulf of Mexico shrimp fleet, but the entire yearly catch amounted to only 20,000 tons. Conversely, the Soviet Union is one of the world's largest blue-water fishing nations. As the two countries joined in alliance, the Soviet Union provided Cuba with the technology, ships, and credits to broaden its fishing horizons. This year her thirty-five huge trawlers will put Cuba in about fortieth position among the 200 countries and territories that report annual catches. Cuba's ships will bring in almost 240,000 tons of fish, an incredible leap in eighteen years.

Frozen tuna fish are unloaded at the fishing port of Havana. Caught in northern waters by Cuba's deep sea fleet, the tuna pass before a docked Soviet ship on their way to freezers, where they will be kept until they are packed.

To accomplish this has meant organization of an entirely new industry. In a tidy photograph-decorated reception room just off the dock area, Deputy Minister of the Fishing Ministry Enrique Oltuski served old rum and cheese snacks while explaining fishing's impact. "Basically, we have four fleets. The thirty-five-trawler 'International Fleet' fishes in the North Atlantic, Pacific, and off the west coast of central and southern Africa. We started with Soviet ships. Now twenty-seven of our thirty-five trawlers were built for us in Spain and another five in East Germany. They all fish for fin fish in colder waters. Our tuna fleet is composed of twenty ships built in Spain and Japan and fishes a great deal off Peru. About 200 vessels are in the shrimp fleet. They were constructed in Cuba, Spain, and France and usually fish in the Gulf of Mexico. Finally, the coastal fleet has about 2,000 ships, all built in Cuba mainly of cement over an iron framework. They fish in close waters for lobster, shrimp, crabs, and some fin fish.

"This new business already employs 40,000 people and has an annual yield worth 120 million pesos. Most of that is exported so we can obtain hard currencies needed to buy products from other countries. In 1977, we will import about 50,000 tons of fish for Cuban consumption and export 35,000 tons. For instance, all the lobster, tuna, shellfish, and some fin fish are exported. In an economy where only sugar and nickel were produced for export, this has been a very important new addition." (The decision to export the desirable products of the new industry causes ill feelings inside Cuba, where people grumble that the country caught tons of lobsters, shrimp, and snapper, but they are available only in expensive restaurants and never in supermarkets.)

In 1977, Cuba will export about 35,000 tons of seafood products—mainly lobster, shrimp, and the more desirable and salable fish—and import 50,000 tons for domestic consumption. This Soviet fish shipment is being unloaded in Havana.

Fishing has brought Cuba to direct negotiations with the United States for the first time since relations were broken in 1961. It was caused by an international "Law of the Sea" agreement granting every country fishing rights to waters 200 miles off its shores. The United States accepted the terms in March, 1977, and notified all nations operating within those limits either to enter into a new agreement on catch limits or fish elsewhere. Cuba has been fishing within the new U.S. limit in the Gulf of Mexico, off the Florida Keys (where the total distance from Key West to Varadero is only about 100 miles), and off New England. Representatives from both countries met first in New York and then in Havana before reaching a new agreement allowing Cuba limited fishing rights.

The new 200-mile limit has severely affected Cuba's new fishing industry. According to Oltuski, "Cuba is hurt because we fish in other countries' waters. Until March we were off the Canadian and U.S. coasts. Then we retired to other places. Our 1980 goal is 350,000 tons of fish. Cuban scientists say 80–90,000 tons of that can come from our own waters. The rest must come from the cold waters of other countries. The new 'Law of the Sea' says all nations have jurisdictional rights over waters from 12 to 200 miles and can fish to their capacities in those waters. Any surplus fish they cannot catch can be divided among other countries based on 'historical performance.' That means a country can get a percentage of the surplus if it has a history of fishing there. We ask, must Cuba be forever punished for being underdeveloped before the Revolution? We have no 'historical performance' because we never had an international fleet. In 1976 we took 21,000 tons off the U.S. North Atlantic coast. In our negotiations we would be happy to get permission to take 15,000 tons now and 40,000 tons by 1980. We feel a developing nation should get special consideration. If the tradition holds of basing future catches on past performances, Cuba will be condemned to be undeveloped. We withdrew early in 1977 from U.S. waters and started negotiating for rights. By September there was still no agreement between our two countries, and that fishing delay cost Cuba between $4 and $5 million. We would normally have caught 20,000 more tons than we did, which has cut our total 1977 catch by at least 7 percent. We cannot afford such losses, and it is all because the United States has held up signing the papers."

Strangely enough, with all the interest and activity with fishing,

Cubans do not really like seafood. Largely as a result of tradition and their Spanish heritage (with a liberal dose of American influence), Cubans will always choose other food when it is available. Favorites are pork, chicken, and the highly prized beef products. The government is trying to change this attitude as it puts more and more efforts into different fish. Younger people are being taught to eat it through school lunch programs. It is somewhat forced on the public when no other meat is for sale in markets. Now the largest fish processing plant in Latin America is under construction across from the Fishing Port. It will handle two million cans a year, mainly cold-water fish that Cubans have never seen before, while another plant is under way to make fish cakes and fish fingers.

For normally provincial Cubans, nothing could be a greater contrast than involvement with the "International Fleet." The great trawlers are actually factory ships, built overseas, put on station in cold ocean waters, never to return until repairs necessitate it. The ships are practically self-contained, designed to drag miles-long nets, pull in the catches, separate, clean, and process the fish, and then box and freeze them. Seamen must endure these icy conditions for six months at a time, a difficult undertaking for warmblooded Cubans, who complain at home when the temperature drops below seventy-five degrees Fahrenheit. Since older sailors simply could not adapt to the alien environment, the government established the Superior School of Fishing near Havana to train younger boys in a four-year technical program. There they study on Soviet navigation, electrical, radio, and engineering equipment, have taped language lessons in English and Russian, and master the skills of seamanship they will later need.

More traditional, and personal, is the platform fleet that operates south of the island on Cuba's continental shelf. There the prize is what we call the spiny, or Florida, lobster, the *langosta*. Physically similar to its Maine cousin, the langosta has no claws. The leathery men who try to coax the lobsters up from their watery homes are the more typical Cuban sailors, born to the sea, and accustomed to dealing with it as an old friend. In small boats they leave from Batabanó, heading south in the warm, clear Caribbean waters that nurture the valuable crustaceans. Much more organized now, government research has told the fisherman where the lobsters are and how many to take without upsetting nature's balance. The men work for

To become officers of Cuba's expanding deep-sea fishing fleet, students at the Superior School of Fishing west of Havana must learn English and Russian. They are taught on new Japanese equipment donated by Canada.

Spiny lobster, the clawless tropical variety, is an important Cuban export. Traps are set in the warm, shallow waters of the Caribbean continental shelf. Using a glass-bottomed bucket, this lobsterman has snared a specimen from the trap below.

the Combined Fishery of Batabanó, one of six combines that fish the shelf. Their azure domain is divided into five zones, each covering about 400 square miles. One hundred thirty-eight of the small ships work the region. Each of the five zones has a collecting station, comprised of a utility building set on piers. The whole idea is efficiency so that the fishing boats can stay out ten days at a time without making the unprofitable trip back home. Every two days they cruise to a collecting station to unload their catches. Those are accumulated until one of four larger boats makes a run from shore to station and returns with the newly captured lobsters to be processed, cooked, and frozen for shipment to Canada, Spain, France, and Japan.

The seemingly complicated system works and saves manpower and ships in the process. Fishery scientists have established that a 10,000-ton harvest of lobsters is possible every year without damaging the species, and Cuba takes that amount. Traps are set in the twenty- to thirty-foot-deep water and checked on a regular schedule. When the traps are pulled in, several flapping delicacies are picked out and tossed into the water-filled storage hold. The routine is repeated in a systematic passage over buoy-marked routes until the ship is full and has to go to a collecting station for emptying. The ten days out, usually within sight of small islands or land, is as long and as far as the older men want to go. They seem happy to leave the cold weather and months-long voyages to the younger generation.

On a different, more domestically oriented path, Cuba's new cattle and dairy enterprises present an expansion story similar to that of fishing. Before the Revolution, there were ranches and farms producing beef and milk, but because of U.S. proximity many food items were brought by barge from Key West. Most middle- and lower-class Cubans did not include beef in their diets because of cost and tradition. Per capita consumption was considerably less than today and much of what was consumed was imported from Florida. As the Revolution began to provide secure jobs and salaries for everyone, consumption was universalized. What the presence of money could not completely accomplish, rationing did. After the government had proclaimed everyone equal, suddenly there were the demands of equality in the market, and even the poorest farmer wanted to try steaks and ice cream. It was obvious that the Cuban economy could not supply such widespread demand, so that rationing was introduced to limit meat and dairy products. Simultaneously, grand new development projects were inaugurated to make the island self-sufficient.

Interestingly enough, Enrique Oltuski, previously mentioned as a Ministry of Fishing official, started in the revolutionary government as Minister of Communications and moved on to a cattle-raising operation in Pinar del Río when the expansion needs were recognized. Bright, impatient, and eager to see the Revolution succeed as rapidly as possible, he was somewhat upset by one of Fidel's early decisions to bring Cuba's best milk-producing cows to Havana Province where milk was most needed. In an all-night discussion at his home of the "good old days," Oltuski reminisced, "I wanted to raise milk production in my operation and to do so I needed good cows. But Fidel had said no. I was sure that our superior farms, feed, and care would produce more milk than Havana and wanted to prove it. This was in 1964. So, while Fidel was on a trip to Oriente, I rented some trucks and went over to Havana and brought 1,500 of the best cows back to Pinar del Río. My idea was to show quickly how much better they would do there.

"Well, as luck would have it, one Sunday after Fidel returned, he drove out to a Havana farm and began looking for some of the cows that he recognized and knew by name. He walked around for a while and realized something was wrong. Fidel called over the manager and asked where his cows were. The man, a bit scared now, said Oltuski came and got the 200 best cows. Now that made Fidel mad. He went back to his office and wrote me a letter that began, 'Oltuski, you think you have the biggest balls in the country. But you don't. There is someone in the country with even bigger balls.' And he only knew about 200 of the 1,500 cows then. Naturally, he found out about the other 1,300, and when he did, he sent around the Minister to fire me and let me know that he thought I should be a common worker for a while. So I went to the Isle of Pines and was a cowboy for six months."

Improvement of the herds is on a more scientific basis today. So convinced is the government that Cuba can be self-sufficient in beef and dairy products, even with increased demand, that enormous efforts are being expended to increase the number of cattle and potential grazing lands, as well as to improve the individual breed of cow. One fascinating aspect of this work occurs about 40 kilometers southeast of Havana, at the Rosafe Signet Provincial Insemination Center. There 110 of the finest Holsteins in Cuba are pampered with the good life. Much of the herd originated in Canada, where Cuban representatives paid up to $20,000 a head for the best bulls they could buy. If the food, water, minerals, and care are all first-rate, nothing can compete with the Holsteins for milk production. However, they suffer from the heat and are susceptible to tropical diseases. Cuban cattle experts have found that a better breed for the island is 75 percent Holstein and 25 percent Brahma. It produces less milk, but handles the other problems better. Artificial insemination is the only practical way of ensuring that the best bulls are mated with Holsteins to produce a higher quality dairy herd and crossbreed with the Brahma for adaptability to the climate and yield better beef than the Brahmas alone can. (There is also some experimenting with crossing Brahmas and *Charolaise,* a successful Florida type, to make a new breed called *Charbray,* that offers meat production improvements. And on Isle de Turiguano, in the new province of Ciego de Avila, about 7,000 head of *Santa Gertrudis* cattle, a large, hot weather breed developed in Texas, are being carefully studied.)

Prize Canadian Holstein bulls are pampered in special barns at the Rosafe Signet Provincial Insemination Center in San Jose. Semen is collected and frozen for use throughout Cuba in inseminating Brahmas to produce a new breed of dairy cow more suited to the climate.

For a country that prides itself on its macho reputation, it is sad to report that sex has largely been taken out of the art of cattle breeding. It is considered unscientific, slow, terribly inefficient, and even dangerous to let a very valuable bull, capable of impregnating hundreds of thousands of cows artificially, out alone with a single female. Instead, the bull's precious semen is collected, analyzed, and frozen into small pellets, to be stored up to fifteen years until needed, or shipped around Cuba for building up the herds.

Collection is a sexual ballet, without consummation. Each of the Center's 110 bulls has two of his very own artificial vaginas. Brilliantly conceived, the eighteen-inch-long fiberglass tubes have a rubber bag interior and a collection vial at the closed end. Warm water is pumped into the area between the tube and rubber to give body temperature. Then air is pumped in too, to simulate the pressure that nature provides automatically. A lubricant is added, and the device is ready for action.

Each morning, the bulls are brought down a dozen at a time from their comfortable stalls to an open station backed by a glassed-in wall where technicians watch. A bull whose semen is no longer desirable is tied to one wall as a "mannequin," an animal to get the bulls excited but who will not actually be penetrated. (Cows are not used because they are too weak to withstand mounting by fifteen bulls a day. After a few days, the bulls seem not to notice that the object of their activity is a bull too. As one technician pointed out, "The bulls are much like people. So much is psychological and seeing everyone else doing it that they just go along.")

When a bull's turn comes, he is walked around the "mannequin," whom he sniffs, nips, and nuzzles. Out of habit, since the bulls come out twice a week, only a few seconds of this produces an erection. A waiting technician is ready with the artificial vagina and at the instant the bull mounts the "mannequin," his penis is diverted into the tube, a couple of strokes is enough, and the vial is filled with the new semen. Within seconds the fluid is inside the lab being examined under a microscope. If found satisfactory, it is immediately stained green to show it is from a Holstein, and quick-frozen in liquid nitrogen. The single ejaculation produces sufficient pellets for impregnating 150 to 200 cows and the Center is getting an 80 percent success rate in conceptions.

Approximately twenty-five extractions are done daily at the

Center, and nine other centers around Cuba are performing similar tasks. In all, the country is inseminating about a million cows annually. Many of the results of the work can be seen at the nearby Agrupación Genetica de la Havana, a 122,000-acre complex headed by a former wealthy Cuban landowner, Hermenegildo Curbelo. The farm has 54,000 cattle, now producing forty-one times as much milk as when it started in 1970.

Campañero Curbelo drives his jeep through the vast operation, overseeing the 176 herds that are kept as separate units, each with its own fields, barns, and milkers. Bouncing over the fields, he proudly recites his success figures. "The idea here is to serve as a dairy farm and as a genetic farm to improve the country's cattle. We keep 60 percent of the land for grazing. We provide the milk for Havana. In 1970 we began with 1.1 million liters for the year. Now we are producing 130,000 kilograms [286,000 pounds] of milk each day, over 45 million liters this year."

The thrust of Cuban cattle raising is toward dairy products and not beef. Typical of the contemporary look in dairies are these fields east of Havana, with white concrete posts and new feeding and milking barns.

When asked about his background as a wealthy Cuban, he nodded, "Yes, I guess I was rich. I personally owned 6,500 acres, had 2,000 cattle, and harvested millions of pounds of sugarcane. I was not a socialist then, but I could not agree with much of what I saw. I went to the university but I could see that the children of many of the workers on my family's farms would never get an education. I saw many things that I wanted to help change. Now we are doing some. In spirit, I am richer than ever before."

Even with the vast increases in output, rising population numbers and food demands have meant continued rationing of milk products. There is the consistent hope that the 1980 end of the first Five-Year Plan will end the limitations, but the reality is that there will be even more people then who will be asking for yet more food. The island's unexpandable borders are a vicious trap to a growing population. Such a restriction seems even more critical with the realization that twenty pounds of plant protein are required to produce one pound of beef, making any beef growing a questionable activity. And, because cattle take a great deal of room to grow, beef cattle raising cannot possibly produce the potential income sugar can; but when sugar prices collapse, as now, there is neither food nor salable sugar. As the economic planners grapple with the complexities of such dilemmas, consumers have to deal with shortages and rationing. Cubans under seven years old are allowed a liter of fresh milk daily while others can buy three small tins of canned condensed milk a month. Yogurt is unrationed in stores and ice cream can be purchased in Coppelia (brand name) retail shops for about 60 centavos a dip. Milk is unlimited in restaurants. Thus far, the Revolution has decided to deal with dairy products first and later hopes to produce enough meat to meet demands, but it is a slow process, and neither need has yet been met.

Citrus growing, the other important thrust in Cuban agriculture, is making the kinds of strides that planners love to report. Although numerous areas are planting new trees, it is on the Isle of Pines that the most dramatic changes have come. Long considered a "poor sister," it was designated the "Island of Youth" in 1966 and began a mammoth school-building program to house thousands of secondary students from Havana and Oriente provinces. Already thirty schools are in operation, and the total should reach eighty by 1980. After careful research to determine the best agricultural use of the island, citrus won out as being most productive. What used to be an offshore backwater with no economic or social importance has been completely transformed into an island of grapefruit trees. Since the program began, over 3 million trees have been planted in neat rows that surround each school. Another million seedlings are being prepared for planting this year. Since it takes about seven years for citrus trees to reach maturity and begin to bear productively, there is a period of waiting until the full explosion of output occurs. Two years ago the Isle of Pines shipped 17,000 tons of fresh grapefruit, mainly to Canada. By 1980, when many of the trees will be yielding, the export is estimated to be 150,000 tons. In all of Cuba, 59,700 metric tons of citrus products were grown in 1975 and the number jumped to almost 100,000 tons in 1977. The total will skyrocket as the young trees mature. In a hard-currency-starved economy, fruit was responsible for $15 million in foreign exchange in 1974 and considerably more today. As described in chapter 6, it is principally the students of Cuba who tend the trees and harvest the crop.

Other areas of Cuban agriculture are not as successful. It cannot be overemphasized that much of the difficulty results from high-level decisions to continue as a "sugar island" and buy needed foodstuffs with the proceeds. (In order to lessen the devastating effects of gigantic price swings in sugar prices, throughout 1977 the United States participated with some eighty other sugar-producing and consuming nations in European-based conferences organized to establish a price "corridor." The idea is to agree on a range, probably from 10¢ or 11¢ to 20¢, where sugar prices can vary and let market conditions fluctuate only in that narrow corridor.) The plan works when sugar is selling well but causes severe shortages when prices are down. For instance, Cubans dearly love their coffee, perhaps more than food. It is inconceivable to consider passing through an entire day without having a few small cups of the thick, sugary potion. Even with its climate, soil, mountains, and expertise, Cuba is a coffee importer, finding it cheaper to buy the beans with sugar income. This year caught the country by surprise, causing considerable suffering (emotionally, not physically) over a situation that brought sugar prices down and saw coffee wholesale prices reach $4.50 a pound in the United States. Looking at the incredible demands for her diminishing foreign currency income, Fidel announced at the CDR rally of October 28, 1976, that the people would have to sacrifice

In an attempt to lessen Cuba's dependence on imported coffee, a new enterprise at the island's eastern tip, near Point Maisí, has over 100,000 seedlings ready to be planted. Irrigation will be necessary on the dry lower slopes.

some of their coffee. The new ration allows Cubans one-and-a-half ounces per person per week, and the black market price has tripled.

Other foods present perhaps even more difficult problems. Coffee can be easily shipped in bags and has a stable shelf life. Fresh fruits and vegetables used to come to Cuba from the United States. Now, unless they are grown on the island, they are unavailable for the people. Although Cubans have never been particularly fond of fresh vegetables, their physicians are beginning to realize the severity of this dietary lack. Tomatoes and cucumbers are seen more and more in salads, but demands exceed supply so much that it is rare ever to find a tomato that was allowed to ripen before being served. Rice, a staple in the local diet, is still imported. Grown in paddies in Oriente and in a gigantic new irrigated operation in Pinar del Río, rice is yet one more item that drains off foreign exchange. Tragically, instead of consuming nutritious brown rice, Cubans produce and import polished white rice which has been reduced only to starch. The government hopes to start bringing rice from the United States when the trade embargo is lifted. INRA is responsible for providing Cubans with daily food needs. Throughout Cuba, government farms grow the various agricultural items that are distributed in the markets. Often these are large operations with only one or a few crops. In addition to these centralized farms, individual farmers also grow vegetables that are sold to INRA, the only legal purchaser. This combination of private and government farming supplies what food is available. Since shortages are common, the system obviously does not work very well. A few years ago there was a grand plan announced to surround each city with a green belt of agriculture that would produce the food for that area and eliminate some of the shipping expenses. Because of the lack of expertise, training, management, and proper land, the system failed and reverted to a nationwide program. Since there can be no private selling or price variations to meet demand, there is little incentive to produce fully. Small farmers cannot bring their food to market, but must sell only to the government at a set price.

One way to bypass the system is home gardening. Popular in some areas, it is not as pervasive as one would think. The main problem is land. Most Cubans live in apartments and do not seem to have the background, expertise, or incentive to grow vegetables in pots on their balconies. Sadly, what could be a food-producing area is either not used at all, or is reserved only for flowers. Another problem is the lack of seeds. There is no business in selling seeds to individuals, so anyone who wants a garden has to save his own seeds. Fruit trees are common in yards, producing mangoes, oranges, limes, guavas, etc., but Cubans do not seem to care enough about vegetables to grow them.

Despite all the impetus to industrialize the country, Cuba remains an agricultural economy, and unfortunately, not even a self-sufficient one at that. She could be, but, for a variety of reasons, most of her land and efforts go into sugar production. As long as sugar retains a superior role, money from its sale will have to be used to buy some of the other foods the people need. That decision is causing hardships with the population, where discontent with the system is already manifested primarily in grumbling about rationing and shortages. The people have been asked to deprive themselves and their families for eighteen years. More and more, they are asking why. Not only do they look at all the effort and expenditures for sugar, and then ponder the empty supermarket shelves, but they also are asking why so much money is being put into the new fishing enterprises so the best fish and all the lobster and shrimp can be sold overseas. (Grumblers erroneously say all the good food is shipped out to Russia. In reality, the government cannot afford that mistake. Desirable food products are sold to Western countries to get their currencies and not to the Soviets for their "soft" rubles.) Similarly, every time there are no oranges or grapefruit in the stores or juice in the restaurants, the complaint rises that the fruit is all being sold abroad. Cubans resent it and want some of the benefits to stay at home.

Another striking feature of Cuba's communism is that over 30 percent of the land remains in private hands. In the past that reality has been used to prove that the system is not repressive and that small farmers, who were credited with early support of the Revolution, would voluntarily come into the system when they realized its advantages. Now that may change. In a private interview, Fidel told the author, "We are discussing the problem of the integration of the land, because one third of it is in the hands of small farmers, and, for technical development reasons, we must integrate it. It has been discussed with the farmers and they have a lot of confidence in the government and this helps." It will be fascinating to see if such a proposal actually is implemented. First, it would destroy some of the remaining faith in the government to keep its promises. Second, if the Soviet experience is a model, it would actually decrease production. Private incentive is so often what makes the difference between inferior and superior performance. Defying the claims of increased efficiency, central planning, and control benefits, the hard fact is that people produce more on their own land when there is gain in it for them. Cuba thinks that will change when the "socialist mentality" becomes prevalent. It does not appear to have worked in sixty years of Soviet attempts. For the foreseeable future, Cuba must make many painful decisions about agriculture while continuing to feed its growing population.

Oriente's Sierra Maestra Mountains, the birthplace of the Revolution, still isolate many Cubans from the mainstream of socialist life. The government is slowly bringing electricity, telephones, schools, and clinics to some parts of this remote and beautiful region.

> Over the next few years our biggest problem will
> continue to be production . . . in all areas. The country and
> its economy are expanding so fast in all directions
> that we will have to keep production increasing to stay apace
> of this development. Our resources are really
> working people. Nickel and iron are our only minerals; we
> have no coal or oil to produce steel. But it is possible
> for Cuba to industrialize sufficiently to have other products
> and to use Cuban labor skills for manufacturing.
> Look what Japan has done.
>
> —*Fidel Castro*

The early sun adds its warm intensity to the rusty landscape. No life stirs among the craggy rocks, each piled high with a thick layer of omnipresent red dust. The plants are all dead and only a barren, eerie desert remains. For a second the wind calms and there is no odor. But just as suddenly it returns, noxious and choking, and in its path life has been defeated. No far-flung Martian landscape this; it is Moa, it is booming, it is nickel, and it is horrible.

Along Oriente's northern coast lies a surface of nickel almost a hundred miles long. Always recognized as sizable, it is now calculated as massive enough to give Cuba the third or fourth largest nickel reserves in the world. What the government has done is to continue the mining that was begun by the United States.

Nickel is a vital ingredient in steel making and important to other industrial processes. Years ago, the predominantly red soil of the region due north of Santiago was tested and found to be rich in iron and nickel. Since iron ore was available closer to power and processing facilities, it was the nickel that other countries wanted. First the ore was shipped out unprocessed, but World War II threatened U.S. supplies and the two countries cooperated in letting the U.S. government build a processing plant in Nicaro to extract nickel from the iron ore dug from the hills just south of town. Heavy concentrations of pure nickel, up to 1.3 percent, assured a large-scale steady production.

Men are dwarfed by the enormity of Soviet trucks and dragline at the monstrous nickel mine near Moa on Oriente's north coast. Blessed with one of the world's richest nickel deposits, Cuba plans great expansion of its exploitation, as prospects of U.S. markets grow brighter.

In 1959 another plant, located a few miles to the east at Moa, was nearing completion when the Revolution took place. Built as a private enterprise by a U.S. firm, Freeport Sulphur, it was nationalized before it could open. The company has an outstanding claim against the Cuban government for $88 million, which is the fourth largest claim of a total of a $2 billion bill for expropriated property.

In an attempt to capitalize to the fullest on its limited resources,

Cuba runs the two mines and plants twenty-four hours a day. In 1958 the export from the Nicaro plant was $28 million. With two plants in operation, the exports reached $164 million in 1974, and it is estimated that this year 40,000 tons of nickel will be shipped at a minimum value of $192 million. The reason the total is so difficult to state accurately is that the nickel officials refuse to disclose plant outputs and the Soviets are said to pay Cuba considerably more than the world market price of $4,800 a ton.

Although the returns to the island are enormous, so too are the environmental costs. Developing countries are so vitally concerned with production that the long-term damage they do to their limited resources is beyond calculation. Eighteen years of mining and processing without concern for reclamation has taken a ghastly toll. Great sweeps of the coastal regions around the two towns look as if some supernatural blight had stricken the people and their environs. The pervasive red dust covers and penetrates everything. Three days later, after two baths a day, the color is still caught in hair and ears. The officials joke that it shows up on white shirts a week later in Havana. To the people who breathe it all day, it is no laughing matter. At Nicaro, so much of the dust is blown out by the prevailing winds from gigantic smokestacks that a red streak is visible across the land for miles. Several of the roads in Moa receive such quantities of gases from the plant that newcomers gag and choke on the spot. The director acknowledged the problem by saying that incoming workers were bothered by it for a few days, but got used to the gas.

It is a staggering situation that places thousands of people in dangerous conditions every day. And the nickel plants and mines are certainly not unique. True, they are probably among the worst examples, but the lack of concern and adequate protection for workers is visible throughout the country. At the drop of an English phrase, any Cuban is quick to jump at the opportunity to condemn exploitation, both past and present, by capitalism and the United States. A hundred examples can be cited to show how the working man has been used without regard for his welfare, solely to make a profit for the unfeeling corporation. But it might be well to examine the role of exploitation a bit further. Without a doubt, history is full of many authentic cases of companies and governments immorally exploiting people in less fortunate circumstances. In Latin America, in particular, the United States has a record that can be criticized.

However, an honest look at contemporary life under a regimented system will reveal a considerable number of equally bad abuses. The nickel employees, though their working conditions are unhealthy, unpleasant, and even dangerous, have little recourse. Strikes are prohibited, quitting is not permitted, job transfers are possible but time-consuming when they are allowed, salary increases are not negotiable, purchase choices are severely limited by rationing, larger consumer items are not available without a peer vote and cooperation with the system. Who, then, is being exploited and who is the exploiter? How much is it necessary to relinquish as a human being to have some of the other benefits of society? Communal ownership and state-paid education and medical care are certainly desirable for many people. But at what price to the worker? One has to look seriously at a system that allows such conditions to exist. And then, the obvious question arises—are working conditions better or worse and are the people happier or not because of the social experiment? Only time will provide the full answer.

Some answers about present conditions are available now. Cuba is having to curtail some of its Five-Year Plan industrial expansion because of the loss of sugar income. If sugar recovers soon, the delays may not be too serious. But, as the months of lower prices continue, postponements will have a domino effect through the economy, damaging many interrelated areas and adversely affecting the Plan's

Mountains of marble are being cut away on the Isle of Pines to supply Cuba's booming construction program. Hammers make the holes for small dynamite charges used to split the stone. Typically, no eye, ear, or breathing devices are used for the workers' protection.

goals. Priorities will have to be set to see which construction to continue and which to put off.

Questions that intrigue Western observers concern the long-range aims of Cuban industrialization. For years the stated plan was to build up the economy so it could be self-sufficient in numerous industries. Some diplomats who viewed the figures felt there was a great deal of overproduction capacity built in. That gave rise to the theory that Cuba hoped to become the "Japan of the Caribbean," a heavily industrialized island with few natural resources which would import raw materials and export finished products. Now a new theory is being suggested, fostered by none other than Castro himself. In May, 1977, he met with a group of Minnesota businessmen and suggested that perhaps Cuba could provide factories and workers to turn out goods for U.S. firms. It is an incredible departure from the typical government line about "Yankee imperialism" and the "oppression of the masses." It is just possible that this "service country" concept is Fidel's latest experiment to cure Cuba's economic woes.

Until quite recently, industry in Cuba meant maintaining and running those industries that were vitally needed. Most of the facilities were in place at the time of the Revolution and subsequently nationalized. Only a relatively recent departure is allowing the country, through massive aid from the Soviet Union and help from the Eastern European socialist nations, to build entirely new plants.

For a country cut off from its major supplier, great gaps had to be filled by creating new industries. Furniture is too expensive to import, so Cuba is making its own in factories like the one at Alamar, which fabricates basic wooden designs of beds, chairs, dressers, cabinets, and tables. Plain and completely unadorned, the furniture is functional and serves the needs of a commodity-starved population. In many other areas where goods were universally imported, the Cubans are looking for ways to make them domestically. Newsprint is brought now from Canada, and is expensive. Cuba is using U.N. money to pay for a project to determine whether the paper can be made from bagasse, the dry, stringy remains of pressed sugarcane, presently burned to power the sugar mills. Some pipes are being made locally, even though there is no basic steel industry. Plastic is imported, but newly purchased machines are transforming the raw plastic to Cuban needs, for instance in new beer cartons. Porcelain is still basically an imported item, but some stainless steel plumbing fixtures are being made in Santa Clara. Many items are reprocessed for later use, such as paper, cans, glass, aluminum, iron, and steel. Several Cuban cement factories provide the domestic supply, but asphalt is produced solely from oil and is made from the Soviet crude that meets all the islands' needs. Many other building supplies—paints, plaster, tiles, and accessories—are being manufactured locally as expansion permits, and the government plans call for independence from imports in practically all areas.

Among the industries in existence in 1959 and seized by the new government were the telephone company, transportation firms, a television network, two oil refineries, the electric power company, and numerous sugar mills. The Cuban Electric Company alone was valued at $267 million in 1959 dollars. Few countries have been fortunate enough to begin a revolutionary government with so many undamaged and well-developed facilities.

The oil refineries, owned by Shell in Havana and Texaco in Santiago, are still in full operation, refining all of the country's petroleum needs. The oil now comes from the Soviet Union, at a price estimated at half the current world value. The power stations are also still functioning, although not as well. Their aging generators are increasingly difficult for the Soviet and Cuban engineers to keep running. Much of the glassware, including bottles for beer, soft drinks, milk, and food, is made in a dilapidated Owens-Illinois plant in San José. The problem is that the Cubans did not and do not have funds for constructing all new plants. They have skimmed by with the prerevolutionary facilities, and time is beginning to run out. Many of the plants have been overloaded with night and day use and need replacement parts, repairs, and updating. The Cubans take great pride in having kept them operating all these years without U.S. expertise and equipment, but the equipment will not perform miracles. The closest to a miracle has been the continued functioning of the 150 sugar mills, the newest of which is fifty years old.

Although much of the industry is so old that its day of reckoning is near, there are many new enterprises. Between Havana and Matanzas, at Santa Cruz del Norte, a sparkling new plant turns out 30 million liters of Havana Club rum annually. Largely an export and restaurant brand, Havana Club costs Cubans, when they can buy it in shops, between $15 and $30 depending on age. (The old Bacardi factory in Santiago is still in operation, making a brand now

Handcraftsmanship remains in the small natural-sponge industry, centered at Batabanó on the Caribbean coast south of Havana. Workers trim off the rough edges and shape the soft sponges, which are still valued above the plastic imitations.

called Caney that is mainly for domestic consumption.)

In Santa Clara, the capital of the newly created province of Villa Clara, the National Industry for Domestic Services (INPUD) operates a 1,700-man plant to build home appliances. It is an industry that did not exist before the Revolution because all such products were easily imported from Florida. Ché Guevara dedicated the plant before taking leave for his fatal excursions, a fact proudly noted in a small park to one side of the building. Using domestic and imported components, such as locally made sheet metal sections and refrigerator motors from East Germany and the Netherlands, workers build stoves, sinks, pressure cookers, refrigerators, and grain and meat grinders. Obviously, this single plant cannot satisfy a country's demands. In 1976 it turned out 45,000 refrigerators, 52,000 propane stoves, and 150,000 pressure cookers. No doubt twenty times those amounts could have sold. The decision to limit production is one of those governmental compromises that must be weighed in terms of future benefits and current discontent. Any money diverted into consumer goods, either in building a factory to make them or adding personnel and raw materials to existing plants, means that another facet of the economy will be deprived of funds. Thus far, Cuba has opted to allocate funds to basic development and construction projects and skimp on consumer happiness.

Some industries have grown from rudimentary operations that functioned before the Revolution. Building small ships was a relatively unimportant enterprise until imports were cut off by the embargo. Starting in 1962, a shipyard in west Havana, named Chullima by Ché after a Korean winged horse, constructed wooden boats principally for Gulf of Mexico work. They were traditional, handmade, seventy-five-foot-long boats. In 1969 the technique changed and the yard constructed Cuba's first ferro-cement ship, a forty-nine-footer of steel and cement. These ships are still very much in use in the Gulf and by the south coast "platform fleet."

Welders fabricate one of a new fleet of steel shrimp boats at the Chullima shipbuilding works in Havana. Formerly limited to constructing small wooden boats, the industry now has experience with both metal and concrete vessels.

The big step came in 1971 when the shipyard made its first all steel boat, again seventy-five-feet long and designed for shrimping. It was such a success that all construction switched over to the metal ships in 1973. Last year eighteen of them were turned out, and the goal is to be able to make forty annually by 1980. After plates are spread out over the ground at the riverside boatyard, hard-hatted welders with cigars poking out past the smoked glasses fit pieces together like a giant jigsaw puzzle. Partially completed ships appear as stage sets, their rooms filled with performers but no front walls. Sparks fly past the electricians as the welders move from room to room and task to task, oblivious of the fascinated audience outside.

A concept being tried to gain more industrial efficiency is illustrated by Nuevitas, a new city on Camaguey's northern coast. Here, a whole area has been set aside for an industrial center, complete with apartments, shopping facilities, and factories. Nuevitas, an unimportant port before 1959, now has three major plants and thousands of new residents. A cement factory announces the entrance to the city with its belching white smokestack. Nearer the water are a Soviet-assisted fertilizer plant, one of three in Cuba, and a thermoelectric power station, built with Czech technology. The 1,800 workers who operate the fertilizer factory (average age twenty-one years) make 120,000 tons of ammonia and 235,000 tons of urea annually. Miles of pipes and tubes, a plumber's nightmare, connect

Four Soviet technicians work with Cuban operators in the control room of the new fertilizer plant in Nuevitas, a designated industrial city on Cuba's north coast. Built with Soviet technology, the plant provides much needed fertilizer for a growing agricultural production.

the various operations. Even though the plant was completed in 1975, there are still Soviet technicians on duty to aid the Cuban operators with certain details.

Just down the road on the bay, the 128-megawatt power station is about to have its power increased by 50 percent. A new generator, scheduled to be operational by 1980, will meet the growing electrical needs of the region. Inside the plant, where the heat is so unbearable that breathing is sometimes difficult, Cuban technicians monitor power demands and output on rows of Czech meters. An oil-burning plant, it receives its Soviet petroleum by ship after it has been unloaded in Havana. Electrical generation is a continuing problem for Cuba with all the existing old equipment. Currently, there are seven of these newer plants, and construction on the country's first nuclear plant is scheduled to begin within a year.

Industry is both a hope and a curse for Cuba. So much of its limited capital is being spent on industrialization that there is little left for consumer products. Naturally, the government has to continue saying that the shortages are only temporary and, once the new plants are producing, things will improve. There is unquestionably some truth to that, but the people are wondering about the benefits of a new steel plant, a nuclear reactor, and the other esoteric projects when what they want is simply some more food and appliances.

From this control room, electricity generation is monitored at the Nuevitas thermoelectric plant, built with Czech technology. One of seven such installations in Cuba, the plant now produces 128 megawatts of electricity powered by burning Soviet oil and is being expanded by sixty-four megawatts of additional output scheduled for completion in 1980.

The U.S. Naval Station at Guantánamo Bay

13

> We have taken no measure of hostility toward the
> United States. We have no base on American territory. All
> circumstances are the other way around. If the
> United States is not using the base against us, then we have
> to ask why it is still here.
>
> —*Fidel Castro*

The young marine crouched lower in the elevated wooden outpost. "Christ," he said to no one in particular, "I know I heard something."

"You've been out here too long," his companion replied, "I didn't hear a thing."

"No, I'm sure I did . . . there, listen, it sounds like someone walking."

As the two heads slowly emerged over the top of the open port, its front panel tauntingly painted with a huge American flag, a sudden flash of light and dull thud of an explosion electrified the air.

"I knew it," the teen-ager gasped. "This is it. Get on the horn and see what's happening."

The older marine called the command post by the Northeast Gate, listened for a moment, and tried to calm his friend. "It's nothing to worry about. Another deer just walked through the minefield."

"Yeh, then what about those sounds?"

Just then another rock landed near the outpost and a heavily Spanish-accented voice jeered from far beyond the barbed-wire fence, "Hey, Yankee, why don't you go home where someone wants you?"

And so the confrontation politics of life along Guantánamo's fence continues. Calmer now than a few years ago, the fence is still a tense area, much like the Berlin Wall, where communism and capitalism meet every day over a thin white line.

The U.S. Naval Station at Guantánamo Bay is an anomaly—the only American military base in a Communist country. Over the past eighteen years it has often faced the glare of publicity as it became the focal point of Cuban-U.S. conflicts, only to be forgotten as the crisis of the day passed. To the military personnel on base, the tension is never fully overlooked, for there is the ceaseless awareness that a superior force lies just beyond the protective fence.

The U.S. Naval Station is comprised of forty-five square miles of land on both sides of Guantánamo Bay, located on Cuba's southern coast, near the eastern end of Oriente. From the air it looks much like any other military facility, with an operational jet runway and one unused airport, berths for many of the Navy's largest ships, repair buildings, administration and recreational structures, water tanks, a golf course, personnel housing, fields of radar and radio antennas. But there is a difference. Not completely noticeable at first, the unique feature of Guantánamo requires a moment to appreciate. It is the fence, 17.4 miles of steel fencing on the perimeter, followed by a no man's land and then another fence on the Cuban side. Part of the area between the two barriers is mined by the Cubans to discourage

Guantánamo Bay claims the distinction of having the only U.S. military facility inside a Communist country. Looking inland from the sea, the forty-five-square-mile U.S. Naval Base is largely composed of water. The upper bay is controlled by Cuba and has a regularly used shipping port. The jet airport in the lower left is active as are the numerous docking facilities along the bay's eastern shore.

any more exiles. U.S. mines protect the single road into the base. In several strips there are also vestiges of the "Cactus Curtain," an earlier attempt to foil escapees by growing huge cactus plants right in front of the U.S. fence. In the desert climate of the region, the chain-link fences stand out like scars on the landscape, a constant reminder that there is still trouble between the countries.

Currently about 6,000 people call the base home. This is down considerably from the 14,000 who lived there in 1968. The Navy says it keeps only the people there who are needed to fulfill the training mission of the facility. That means approximately 2,000 Navy personnel and 1,800 dependents, almost 500 Marines to provide security, about 1,000 Jamaican laborers, and some Cuban exiles. The most commonly heard complaint is not about the Cubans on the other side, but that the Navy is pulling out so many people that swimming pools are closing because there are no people to take care of them. The Marines have a much more serious gripe. Unlike the sailors, the enlisted Marines are not allowed to bring dependents, so there is a serious shortage of women and nowhere to go for dates. There is one compensation. Gitmo, as the base is called, is considered a ship by the Navy when duty time is calculated. Many men gladly take the first year there and sign up for another because that typically means six years before any more ship duty is scheduled. Only a few isolated bases in the world share this status.

The Navy brass cringe a bit when Gitmo is called a country club base. However, it is true that additional considerations have been made to provide some home comforts for the personnel there. A special services bulletin lists fourteen sports and activities, including golf (on a nicely kept but dry course), bowling, fishing, boating, tennis, softball, baseball, soccer, cricket, football, and others. There are movies, theatres, numerous bars, restaurants, officers' and enlisted clubs, beaches, workshops, hobby centers, and an endless round of parties. It is not a bad life and it is all operated by the U.S. Navy, and has to be by law.

The treaty that gives the United States rights to the base was signed in 1903 by the two countries. At the time, Cuba had just gained its freedom from Spain. It is still a contentious matter whether the U.S. military presence with Teddy Roosevelt was a vital role in final independence battles. The U.S. position is that we freed Cuba. Current Cuban history instruction is that the United States came in

To keep its personnel and their families active, happy, and out of trouble, the Navy supports fourteen sports and recreational activities at Guantánamo. Marblehead Lanes is open nightly and is usually busy.

at the last minute when the rebels were ready to win anyway, took unnecessary credit for the victory, and forced an agreement on a weaker Cuba that gave the imperialistic United States illegal rights to meddle in Cuban affairs. No matter which side of that hopeless argument is taken, the fact is that the United States did ask for rights to establish four bases on Cuban territory. The Cuban government cut the request in half, granting rights to two bays, and in 1912 limited it to only one, at Guantánamo. The United States asked that the bays be ceded to it for an agreeable payment. Cuba denied that request and agreed instead to a rental.

The actual terms of the 1903 treaty (updated in 1934) concerning Guantánamo are interesting in view of the hard feelings that had developed at the time over U.S. intervention; over the terms of the Platt Amendment, which gave the United States certain rights over Cuban policy; and over the U.S. position concerning the Isle of Pines, which was kept from Cuban control for years. The most important features of the joint agreement are that sovereignty remains with Cuba; that the U.S. lease is indefinite as long as the terms are met; that a continued U.S. presence is required; that no private businesses can operate on the base; that it cannot be a fugitive haven and fugitives must be delivered on demand; that the lease price (as established in 1934) is $4,000 annually in gold coin; and that Guantánamo Bay must be open to sea traffic.

Captain John McConnell, Base Commander at Guantánamo, says, "We adhere to the treaty religiously. For instance, we have no businesses here that could be considered in competition with any Cuban business." That particular feature of the agreement was originally inserted to protect local Cuban businessmen who hoped to make considerable profits over the years providing all the needed services to the base. Sovereignty over the base is also unquestioned. The land is Cuba's and the U.S. position is that the Navy can legally remain just as long as it continues to live up to the treaty terms. Any child born of Cuban parents on the base is automatically Cuban, and offspring of U.S. citizens can choose between U.S. and Cuban citizenship. The $4,000 rental fee is paid yearly, although only the 1959 check was cashed. The remainder of them have been deposited in a Swiss bank. The reason is that Castro has never recognized the legality of the treaty. He says it was forced on Cuba and has no legal status. That view brings up an interesting point concerning the return of fugitives. Over the years since 1959, hundreds of Cubans have asked for exile in the base and 373 remain as residents. If Castro requested their return as fugitives, the Navy's position is that they would probably have to be returned. (Politically, it would be a scandal in the United States.) But, since he has never recognized the treaty, he has not enforced its terms.

Carlos Brú is called the senior exile in Guantánamo. For thirty-five years he had been a U.S. Navy employee and is one of the fortunate Cubans with Civil Service retirement benefits. In 1966 he and his family lived in Guantánamo City, on the Cuban side, and he commuted each day to his base job. For months they worked on their escape plan. His wife and children applied for a ninety-day tourist visa to Mexico, but one married son could not be included in the group. The family decided, after long discussions, to go without him. As soon as the group was safely in Mexico, with their one thirty-pound suitcase, Carlos Brú walked through the Northeast Gate and declared himself to be an exile. Soon he was able to bring his family to the Naval Station, where they now live. Says Brú, "Soon I will be able to retire and then we will all move to the United States. I'm lucky because I have worked without interruption since before 1950. Anyone who started after that, or who works in a 'non-appropriated' job, like in the base exchange, is not covered by government retirement."

In 1976 there were 75 families composed of 373 Cubans who were living as exiles in Guantánamo Bay. Brú explains, "There have been two kinds of exiles here. First, there are the single people, men and women, who came and stayed and who left their families behind in Cuba. Second, there are people like me who were able to get their families out with them. So many years have passed we are now getting another group . . . children of exiles who live here are growing up and getting married and also having children. So we have new families.

"The exile movement started a year after Castro took power. People left because they couldn't stand the system, because they feared being jailed for one reason or another, and because they needed dollars to exile other family members. The only way to accumulate dollars was to live outside Cuba. The common denominator in all this was the belief that the system would not last long. No one suspected Castro would hold on. We all thought Cuban communism was a temporary thing. There are a number of people here who would say if they had known it was going to be permanent, they would not have come. That's especially true of people who left without their families. They are very frustrated now."

Most of the people who are exiles in Guantánamo were in some way involved with base employees. Many of the workers, like Carlos Brú, came in to the base one morning and never returned. Others had tourist or business visas to go abroad, declared themselves exiles while away from Cuba, and then settled in Gitmo. Some made it the hard way—by jumping the fence. That is dangerous, and several who have tried have been caught or killed in the process. The last successful escape was in 1974. Understandably, neither side is anxious to discuss the attempts, the successes or the failures. The ones who do become exiles have a choice of remaining in Gitmo and working for the Navy, or relocating in the United States. Most stay on to be close to their families and friends. In past years the resident population has been higher, but deaths and relocations gradually diminish it.

Equally interesting is the other Cuban group in Guantánamo, the daily commuters. In 1961, 3,000 Cubans came to base jobs each morning. They were the skilled laborers who had spent years doing the machine shop and electrical work as well as the unskilled personnel who kept up the physical plant. Beneficial to both countries, they provided the basic work force for the Navy and brought in millions of dollars in U.S. currency to the struggling government. Even though the two countries broke relations in 1961 and some minor disturbances occurred around the naval station, the situation was relatively stable until February 6, 1964. For the stated reasons of protesting several U.S. fishing incidents, Castro cut off the water and electrical services to Guantánamo. Water barges from Puerto Rico and some portable generators provided temporary facilities while the Navy constructed a seaside plant to desalinate ocean water and produce all the power the base needed. Still, President Johnson went one more step. He ordered the firing of 2,000 of the Cuban commuters to decrease any U.S. dependency on the foreign work service. (To replace them, contracts were let in Jamaica and hundreds of Jamaicans now do most of the unskilled jobs on the base.) Castro said he would allow no new commuters but that anyone currently employed would be allowed to work. He also publicly noted that the United States was not providing retirement benefits for the Cuban workers and offered any Cuban who was working for the Navy and who did not receive benefits all the services he would have gotten had he been employed inside Cuba. By 1969 the number of commuters had declined to 343 and in 1976 only 150 Cubans made the daily round trip.

The life of the commuter is not easy. He must get up each weekday at about 4:30 A.M. and take a bus from Guantánamo City or a ferry across the bay from Caimanéra. Then he is transported for arrival about 5:15 at the outer gate on the Cuban side. Each man walks into the small guardhouse located just out of sight behind a hill across from the Marines at the Northeast Gate. There the men line up alphabetically and begin a one- to one-and-a-half-hour wait while each individually enters a room to undress before a guard. If found to be hiding nothing, he dresses in his "transit clothes," and walks the quarter mile through a three-sided fenced tunnel called the "cattle chute," where he emerges and crosses a single painted line on the concrete. He is now on the U.S. base, where he picks up his photo-ID card from the on-duty Marine, walks to the waiting bus, and is driven to his job, where he usually changes clothes again. The commuters are expected to enter by 7:15 A.M. in order to begin work at 7:30. The entire process is repeated in the afternoon at 4:15, when the workers return their passes to the Marine guard, walk through the cattle chute, wait and undress again at the guardhouse, get dressed, and return to their homes. Women used to commute also, but quit after

This single Northeast Gate is the only route between Communist Cuba and the U.S. Naval Base. Each day about 150 Cuban "commuters" enter and leave on their way to and from work at the base. The distant sign was the Cuban guardhouse, but a new one has now been built behind the hill out of sight of the U.S. Marines.

the twice-daily search was instituted.

Although there has been trouble between the commuters and the Cuban government in the past, most agree that any present difficulty can only be called minor harassment. The long waits are thought to be a device to unnerve the workers. Occasionally, during one of the searches, a guard will ask a commuter for some information or for a small thing—perhaps a copy of *Playboy* or a piece of clothing. The commuters think there is a hope that the guards can get them to break a rule. Once hooked, the next step is presumably to do some spying. It makes an interesting game because the Cubans think the commuters bring information to the U.S. Navy and the Navy thinks the commuters keep the Cubans informed of base activities. Either way, the commuters lose.

Since the United States is no longer coaling steamers in the Caribbean or defending the Panama Canal with ships, it is reasonable to ask why we place so much value on Gitmo. Captain Jason Law, Commander of the Fleet Training Group at the Naval Station, has given that considerable thought and has an impressive list of reasons. "This facility takes ships directly out of the shipyard, whether it is a new ship or a refitted one, and does the shakedown, getting the crews and ships ready for duty. We do 95 percent of our training at sea. Each year we move 20,000 sailors through here on training duty. For this mission, Gitmo is vital. It has advantages that the Navy would find very difficult to replace: 1) We have almost perfect weather—no rain, no fog, no snow, and no delays. 2) The waters off this station have very little sea traffic, which is an important consideration for large ship maneuvers and live ammunition firing. 3) There is little air traffic around here, so we can shoot pretty much at will. 4) This is a forgiving harbor, deep and wide, which is important when training "green" crews. 5) There is very deep water just off shore. The sea drops to 400 fathoms just outside the harbor. That means we can leave the dock at 5:00 or 6:00 A.M. and be on station in an hour or less, shoot all day, and be home at night. 6) There are no distractions on base—no leave, no women, only work. We can train intensively when everyone knows there is nowhere to go and nothing else to do."

As compelling as those are, the Navy is apprehensive that its base will be bargained away when a political solution is reached on Cuba. Captain Jack McConnell, the base commander, has said, "When we get back to normal diplomatic relations with Cuba, we'll probably have to give this base back." If that occurs, no one knows where the Atlantic Fleet will get its training. There is no other warm-water port where ships can be on station in so short a time, train all day in relative safety, and return at night. Any other facility would require considerably more time to accomplish the same goals.

Beyond those tangible advantages, Gitmo is really a symbol. Certainly it would be missed by the U.S. Navy, but it is not vital to American survival. The physical plant, built largely in the 1940s, is estimated to be worth $321 million, and there would have to be compensation if the base were abandoned. From the Cuban standpoint, the Naval Station is symbolic as a permanent reminder of Yankee imperialism. Government propaganda constantly reminds Cubans that the unwanted base is there because the United States was strong enough to force it on them in 1903 but that no treaty should remain in force forever when one party wants out.

There is another concern. The United States is fearful that such a fine facility as Gitmo would offer great advantages to the Soviet or Cuban navies and would ultimately be used to the detriment of this country. The U.S. Navy would not like to relinquish any base that might be used against it. As unsavory as such a thought is, it may become reality.

More than anything, Gitmo is a thorn in Castro's side. It used to be a larger irritant than it is today. For the past few years the Cubans have chosen to say little in public about it. It is now likely that they believe they will be able to negotiate it back under their control and the less said aloud, the better. Their plan seems to be working.

The Government of Cuba

14

> The highest political responsibilities are in the hands
> of the Central Committee of the Communist Party. The
> Constitution itself recognizes the leading role of the
> Party. The Party lays down the state political line, and it is
> supposed that the state, through the National
> Assembly, will carry out that program. If that did not
> happen, the Party would be discredited, and there
> would be a political crisis.
>
> —*Fidel Castro*

A hush bordering on reverence spread over the overflow crowd in Carlos Marx Theatre. Only seconds before, thunderous applause had resounded for minutes as the participants were overwhelmed by the historical significance of the event. Before them, the recently acknowledged leaders of the country, stood the object of their adoration and attention, their Maximum Leader and Commander in Chief, Fidel Castro. Resplendent in his new red-and-gold-braided military uniform, he stroked his beard, graying now, and looked out over the National Assembly delegates. The historical impact of the moment seemed to cause a slight hesitation. He could see his brother on the front row, and the few remaining comrades in arms from the Moncada Barracks attack. There were friends who had survived the Sierra Maestra, and others who had been with him since the earliest days of victory. And now, the theatre was filled with the Revolution's first national representatives, ready to assume office on this twentieth anniversary of the landing of *Granma,* December 2, 1976.

From his prepared text, Fidel read first his greeting and then issued

235

a characteristic, but ungracious, swipe at the United States at a moment when other business seemed more pressing. Then a review of the Revolution's history and Marxist-Leninist philosophy, a statement of current problems, and a report on the decision to revise military ranks brought the speech to its emotional conclusion:

"A formal act is all we have left: to state that, at this moment, the Revolutionary Government transfers to the National Assembly the power it has held up to now. Thus the Council of Ministers invests this Assembly with the constitutional and legislative functions it exercised for almost eighteen years, the period of the most radical and deepest political and social transformations in our country's life. Let history judge this epoch objectively!

"As for me, dear comrades, I am a tireless critic of our own work. We could have done everything better from the Moncada up to today. The light that indicates what could have been the best choice in each case is experience, but unfortunately the youth who start along the hard and difficult road of revolution do not have it. Nevertheless, this helps us learn that we are not wise men and that for

In a return to partial representative government, the National Assembly was formed December 2, 1976, in Havana's Karl Marx Theatre. Delegates to this assembly—scheduled to meet twice a year—and those to the provincial assemblies were all named by municipal assembly members, who are the only elected officials in Cuba.

each decision, there might perhaps have been a better one.

"With extraordinary affection, you attribute great merit to your leaders. I know that no man has exceptional merits and that we can learn great lessons every day form the most humble comrades.

"If I were to have the privilege of living my life over again, I would do many things differently from the way I have done them up to now; but at the same time I can assure you that I would fight all my life with the same passion for the same objectives I have fought for up to now. COUNTRY OR DEATH—WE SHALL OVERCOME!"

Between the first day of 1959 and that moving assembly in 1976, Cuba had been ruled under what could be described as emergency powers. Now, a new phase of the country's experiment in government has been entered, with a just-passed Constitution, a completely new political and administrative organization of the island, and recently formed assemblies at the municipal, provincial, and national levels. Elections were held on a nationwide scale for the first time since Batista, and the slogan now is that the Revolution is being "institutionalized."

The impetus for the changes was the actions taken at the First Party Congress in December, 1975. When the Congress, which had been promised for a decade, finally materialized, among other actions it promulgated the first Five-Year Plan with numerous economic and social goals and approved a new Constitution, the first Cuba has had since 1940. (This document was largely the work of Blas Roca, the old-line Communist who is now President of the National Assembly.) Placed before the people in early 1976, it was ratified by 97 percent of the voters. Of course, there was no opposing constitution to consider.

This 1976 Constitution forms the law of the land and establishes the format of a completely new governmental system for Cuba. Among its numerous features, it provides for elections, three levels of public assemblies, and new national officials, and clearly places the Communist Party as the dominant force in Cuban life. It is also an attempt to break up some of the heavy central bureaucracy and return partial control to local organizations.

Before the nationwide program was put into effect, an experiment was conducted in Matanzas Province. There Poder Popular (Popular Power), as the plan is called, was tried to see whether it was feasible to let people vote for municipal assemblies and run their own affairs. Using this single province as a model, the plan was organized on a national level.

The whole intricate scheme was designed in Havana as a total government package. Few in the countryside had any idea what was happening or how it would work. True, the new Constitution laid out some of the details, but the implementation was elaborate and difficult to understand. The first thing the people were told was that there would be elections again. Reading the Constitution showed that only one level of the assemblies would actually have popular votes. While municipal assemblies would be elected by the people, the national and provincial assembly delegates were to be chosen solely by municipal delegates. *Democracy,* a word that got bandied about a great deal in 1976, was obviously a system that could not be fully trusted.

Then the rules started filtering down from Havana concerning how the municipal delegates would be picked. Nominations were to be made in each CDR. The government used population as a base for defining delegate areas in each town, and required at least two candidates for each position. Nominations were open to anyone, but there could be no campaigning. After neighbors were picked to run, their pictures and brief biographies were posted on the streets for all to see.

October 10, 1976, was set as election day and thousands of delegates were chosen. If individual districts failed to reach a majority vote, runoffs were held on October 17 for the top two candidates. It is after this vote that democracy began to get submerged. On October 31, the municipal assemblies across Cuba met to elect their own

October 1976 marked the first nationwide election under Castro. Candidates were known solely by posted photographs and biographies in single locations.

officers and a Municipal Executive Committee of six or seven members, and to elect delegates to the provincial assemblies. One provincial delegate could be elected for each 10,000 people in the municipality.

As if things were not already moving too rapidly, just two days later, on November 2, the municipal assemblies met again in each town and elected deputies to the National Assembly. This time they elected one deputy for each 20,000 people in their cities. Obviously, if the original delegates to the municipal assemblies were thought to be the most qualified people in the country, who would be named to the other two assemblies? The answer is they kept naming themselves. And they automatically fell back on the most secure and convenient solution: they named Party leaders.

To further complicate matters, on November 7 all the provincial assemblies met. Their first function was to elect executive committees to administer and operate the assemblies. In Havana Province, an assembly of seventy-seven voted for a seventeen-member committee of which nine are men and women workers who are employed in various jobs and eight are paid professionals who will spend full time on assembly business. All eight professionals are Party members.

It is practically incomprehensible to imagine forming a complete government in so short a time. The first elections of the Revolution were held on October 10, and all municipal and provincial assembly organization was completed by November 7. Only the final meeting was necessary to complete the triad. On December 2, in an old Miramar movie theatre renamed after Karl Marx, the delegates took their seats to become Cuba's single legislative body. Nothing was left to chance, and ballots were passed out for the three assembly leadership posts with the names already thoughtfully printed in. Besides listening to opening speeches and getting organized, the principal business was ratifying new national officials, who were also automatically approved without comment.

Even though there had been speculation for a year that Fidel might use this opportunity to step away from the daily operations of running the government and, as his Soviet counterparts do, assume Party functions only, he stayed on. The Assembly unanimously accepted the Party's recommendation that Fidel Castro be named President of the Council of State, which carries with it the constitutional titles of Head of State and Head of Government, and that he

Leaving nothing to chance, the ballot for National Assembly officers was preprinted for the delegates.

also be President of the Council of Ministers. On both councils, brother Raúl Castro, who is also in charge of all Cuba's military forces, was chosen to serve as First Vice-President. Of the seven top officials of the Council of State, all male, there are two old-line Communists. Of the ten leading members of the Council of Ministers, there are no women and one old-line Communist.

Criticism immediately arose that nothing had really changed with the new government arrangement. As far as real power is concerned, nothing had. The significance is that it is a beginning. There is now a permanent apparatus that could, perhaps, someday become more democratic. Already there is speculation among Cubans that the national and provincial assemblies might someday have popularly elected delegates. But real power is so tightly held that even such a basic decision would have to come from the top Party leaders.

Although many of the details are still to be worked out, some aspects of the assemblies are known. For instance, the National Assembly is scheduled to meet twice a year, probably in July and December, for an indeterminate period, and is the only body in the land that can pass laws. It is expected that some requests for new legislation will come from within the body, some from the Council of State, and some from the Party. Great issues of national policy almost surely will originate only from the PCC. The Assembly's first meeting lasted only two days. No one knows whether future sessions will take longer, but if the point is just to come to Havana and rubber-stamp programs that are already prepared, such misuse of the deputies' time will certainly lead to discontent. It should be obvious that these are not professional lawmakers. Still, once they have been given the duties, there will be some pressure for them to actually perform.

The provincial assemblies are supposed to meet three times yearly, in February, July, and October. Each session is designed to establish a semblance of democracy with elections, assemblies, and delegates. In reality, no serious work can be done in one-day sessions, and the infrastructure will allow the delegates only superficial involvement in lawmaking and administration. That will be done for them by the executive committee professionals. And the PCC, at the national level, will continue to set the general policy in all-important areas. Although there is no particular reason for Communist governments to operate solely with the strict no-dissent, one-party control which is virtually universal, it is a model they have chosen. The rest of the world does not expect changes in their systems, but finds it always slightly surprising to see them establish elaborate schemes that do not relinquish any significant power and use the word "democracy" to describe the plans. Such verbal shenanigans only create confusion when "republic," "constitution," "freedom," "elections," and "democratic principles" describe such vastly conflicting functions. One can only wonder why they bother. Why did Cuba choose to go to the trouble and expense of establishing an elaborate new government when the result will be virtually the same as it was a year ago? The answer is locked in the minds of a very few island leaders, but there are some guesses.

In order to look legitimate and gain a position of leadership among the hemisphere's nations, Cuba needs to achieve the U.S. recognition it has sought for two years, diminish some of the fear surrounding its international activities, and show that it has a government with popular appeal. No matter how much support the Cuban people may give to their system, a revolutionary government in office for eighteen years without elections begins to look alarmingly similar to the hated military dictatorships that Castro uses as examples of beneficiaries of U.S. assistance. After a generation of "emergency" rule, it is simply time to institutionalize the regime. Naturally, it should be completely obvious that the PCC and Cuban government would create a system to keep power and control where it was. The only things really altered are that the Cuban people can now feel a bit more involved with governmental activities, and many of the smaller more local issues, like water hours, school construction, and commercial details, may be handled in the municipalities instead of from Havana. As far as daily life is concerned, the average Cuban will notice little to signify there is a new government.

When Fidel and his victorious band arrived in Havana in 1959, one of their first acts was to rid the country of the existing Batista government and form a revolutionary replacement. Between then and December, 1976, the principal administrative duties on the island fell to the various ministries that were created within a Communist framework. Over the years, the Cubans have divided governmental duties into a dizzying array of organizations, with a flare for acronyms that would put to shame the best FDR abbreviators of the 1930s. MINCOM (the Ministry of Communications) is followed by MINED (the Ministry of Education) and so on through the alphabet past MINJUS, MINAL, MINAZ, MININBAS, MINCEX, MININT, etc. After those come the institutes, such as ICAP (Cuban Institute for Friendship with the People), ICAIC (Cuban Institute of Cinemagraphic Arts and Industry), INDER (National Institute of Sports, Physical Education, and Recreation), INIT (National Institute of Tourist Industries), and many, many others, including INP, ICP, ICA, ICR, INDAF, INRA, etc.

Ministries will remain and will continue to be the basic governing units. Once policy is determined by the PCC and the highest levels of leadership, any necessary laws will be presented to the National Assembly for passing. Items which might affect only one area of the island will most likely be left to the municipal and provincial assemblies of the region for their consideration and actions. Rather than creating a system of checks and balances, of deliberation, debate, and compromise, the new Cuban governmental apparatus places a layer of representation between Havana and the people, but gives it no power to act or dissent. Realistically, how could it have been otherwise? Who would expect a Marxist regime to reestablish a democratic society any more than a monarch would voluntarily establish representative goverment?

In the case of Cuba, republican government would have made a fascinating experiment. In reality, Fidel Castro is still an enormously popular figure. The public would follow him virtually anywhere. It is by the sheer weight of his personality and leadership that Cubans have willingly endured the economic deprivations of the past generation. Of course, there is also the restraint of a massive military presence, but an honest evaluation would reveal there is no great pressure for revolt. Cubans have certainly accepted Castro and seemingly even accept the tenets of Marxist-Leninist thought. Why then must there be government-imposed restraints? Why do freedom of travel, of the press, of thought, of dissent, and of moving and acting openly in society have to be curtailed by Communist governments? No one brought the present system to Cuba by force, as was the case in the Communist countries of Eastern Europe. The Cubans who chose to remain with Castro in the early 1960s did so voluntarily. If they like the system and if the system is beneficial to their welfare, why restrain their basic freedoms? If the ports were open again for emigration, most observers believe that no more than a million of the current 9½ million Cubans would leave. (Although that would be a very high percentage of exiles, it would still demonstrate that the vast majority of Cubans had again chosen to stay.)

Cuban officials who deal with such questions produce answers with a spurious ring. They say that Cubans cannot freely travel overseas because they do not really want to and because the Western world has conspired to make their pesos worthless. Since the government cannot afford to transfer pesos to hard currency for vacation travel, the people are refused permits. The argument is refuted simply by the hundreds of thousands of Florida exiles who would gladly send dollars for relatives to travel if only the Cuban government would allow it. The real reason is more likely that Cuba wants to limit exposure to other peoples at this time and to avoid the risk that many of them would stay abroad when their visits were over.

The value of the free press in society has been proven consistently in its role as a watchdog over the government, and in its providing relatively unbiased information to the population. After Watergate, few in the United States would question the service performed by a diligent and free press. Since enterprises are operated by the government in Communist societies, and since dissent is seldom allowed, the function of the press is entirely reversed—it becomes an arm of the state. One would have to ask how any critical or dissent role or watchdog activity could ever be possible under such a structure. When sixty years of Communist history with the press is viewed, the answer is that none is allowed. In a private interview, Fidel Castro dealt with the issue by explaining, "In a capitalist country, the freedom is to own the property of the press. But it is the owner who is free to say what he thinks and not everyone in that society. We know from writings about Cuba that people who agree with us are often suppressed and our critics are published. I know of many cases of such restrictions in the Western world. Here, we are restricted by paper, which we have to buy. We only have two newspapers and still we use too much paper. Our concept of criticism is within the Party and the organization of Poder Popular. We want freedom at those levels and have not achieved it. Our press is not very critical. On the other hand, we have a different philosophy from the liberal philosophy. We consider the construction of socialism as a transition period in which one class is prevalent over the others—the dictatorship of the military. In this transitional stage, until classes are eliminated and a new society established, we do not permit dissension against the system."

To institutionalize all the practices and beliefs of the Marxist years into a new document, Cuba created its new Constitution. Although loosely patterned on the U.S. model, its effects are remarkably different. In the preamble, normally reserved for the grandest statement of nationalist principles, Yankee imperialism is denounced, Fidel's leadership lauded, the *Granma* honored, the Soviet Union credited, and the values of Marxist-Leninist doctrine mentioned twice. The role of the Communist Party is specified in Article 5, which states that the Party is "the highest leading force of the society and of the State." Articles 49 and 50 guarantee free health care and education. And Article 51, in a strange addition to a national constitution, guarantees the right of the people to physical education and sports. The Constitution is made even more popular, since Article 8 in a long list of guarantees says, "No one [shall] be left without access to studies, culture, and sports," and Article 38 includes a section stating, "The State promotes, foments, and develops all forms of physical education and sports." With three distinct inclusions, it is apparent that the writers of the Constitution wanted to make sure everyone understood that sports would be available to all.

Other interesting features are found in Article 10, where a direct attack on the Guantánamo Bay treaty says Cuba "considers illegal and null all treaties, pacts, and concessions which were signed in conditions of inequality . . ." and in Article 12, which states Cuba "considers wars of aggression and of conquest international crimes; recognizes the legitimacy of the wars of national liberation . . . and considers that its help to those under attack and to the peoples that struggle for their liberation constitutes its internationalist right and duty." That particular statement was in response to Angola and a declaration that there might be more such adventures. That, and a line in Article 10 recognizing Cuba's right to use violence, are some of the items of concern to the United States as normalization of relations seems possible.

Two articles concern work: Article 19 says, "In the Republic of Cuba rules the socialist principle of 'from each according to his ability; to each according to his work.' " and Article 44 notes, "Work in a socialist society is a right and duty and a source of pride for every citizen." Then there are some restrictions. Article 38 includes, "Artistic creativity is free as long as its content is not contrary to the Revolution," and the concept of freedom of religion is guaranteed in Article 54 with the stipulation that "The law regulates the activities of religious institutions. It is illegal and punishable by law to oppose one's faith or religious belief to the Revolution; to education; or to the fulfillment of one's duty to work, defend the homeland with arms, show reverence for its symbols, and fulfill other duties established by the Constitution." Press freedom is dealt with in Article 52, which says, "Citizens have freedom of speech and of the press in keeping with the objectives of socialist society. . . . The press, radio, television, and other organs of the mass media are state or social property and can never be private property. . . . The Law regulates the exercise of these freedoms."

Various articles deal with the National Assembly and its functions. Article 69 states that its deputies are to be elected by the municipal assemblies, and Article 70 sets its terms for five years but allows it to extend itself as a body if there were "exceptional circumstances." From its own deputies, according to Article 72, the Assembly will elect the Council of State, consisting of a President, a First Vice-President, five Vice-Presidents, a Secretary, and twenty-three other members. (It is the President of the Council of State—Fidel Castro at the present—who also receives the twin titles of Head of State and Head of Government.) The important Article 73 spells out twenty-six duties of the Assembly, giving it the power to elect the Supreme

Court and the Attorney General, to pass and nullify laws, and to appoint the Council of Ministers "at the initiation of the President of the Council of State." So that no one misunderstands where power lies, Article 122 subordinates the court system to the National Assembly and to the Council of State.

Of course, the whole complex organization that Marxism brought to Cuba with the Castro Revolution was entirely new. There is an upsetting trend, largely fostered by the Cuban exile community in south Florida, to think that the island was the picture of prosperity and democracy before then. It is hoped that some of the previous chapters have helped dispel the belief that the overall welfare, education, health care, and economic stability of pre-Revolution Cuba were all that bright. The country was developing but was not fully developed. It was moderately prosperous, with a distinctly wealthy class, but with vast sections of the country locked in poverty. There were sufficient communication, transportation, and industrial facilities to make the governmental takeover relatively easy and keep Cuba somewhat self-sufficient at a higher standard of living than enjoyed by many other Caribbean and Latin American nations. However, with all these advantages, Cuba has practically no history of democratic self-government. One of the premises of Hugh Thomas's monumental work *Cuba: The Pursuit of Freedom* is that

Pleading his own defense in a traffic death case, the witness makes his point before a five-judge panel. Cuban justice is largely concerned with thefts, crimes of passion, and crimes against the state, a catchall category that includes cheating on the rationing system and activities against the government.

despite attempts to capture it, the elusive right to be free continues to evade the unfortunate country.

Perhaps the ultimate cause for that failure could best be studied by a psychologist, who could deal with mass phenomena, rather than by a political scientist. (Naturally, any country that uses the phrase, "From Havana, Cuba, first free territory in America," to open its radio programs is likely to disagree with the suggestion that freedom is yet to be achieved.) Other nations in and out of Latin America escaped the colonial yoke and went on to democratic systems, although some have experienced a cyclical return of military dictatorships. But there is something vital missing in the Spanish-heritage countries that has kept them from developing fully. There seems to be none of the preparation for freedom that Britain, for instance, was able to impart to its colonies. And, worst of all, there appears to be a passive acceptance of the systems that makes great popular uprisings exceedingly rare.

To fully comprehend what the struggle has meant to Cuba requires reviewing, long before Batista, the era of Spanish rule. The personality of the island and its development are to this day, along with Puerto Rico, the results of being the last Spanish colony in America. Wars of liberation, led mainly by Simón Bolívar, had long freed Central and South America from foreign domination, but, for a variety of reasons, the leaders of those fights decided to spend their time and energy developing their mainland areas and left Cuba on its own. The island did not lack for patriots willing to die for the cause of freedom. Protests and uprisings have a long history. Carlos Manuel de Céspedes started the Oriente revolt that led to almost half a century of conflict. Toward the end of the nineeenth century, the torch was carried by Cuba's leading writer, spokesman, and activist for freedom, José Martí, the Apostle. Killed in battle, Martí is revered by exile and Communist alike as the driving force behind the ultimately successful movement. (Non-Communist Cubans despise the Revolution's taking Martí's name and memory and incorporating them into Marxist ideology. The government says Martí began the long march toward freedom that is still continuing.)

The year 1898 marks a fascinating period of involvement in Cuba by the United States, one that continued unabated until the diplomatic break in 1961. As the fighting between Spain and the rebels became heated and serious, the United States sent a battleship,

Occupying an important position along Havana's Malecón, the monument to the U.S.S. *Maine,* which honors the American sailors killed in the controversial harbor explosion resulting in U.S. involvement in the 1898 Cuban fight with Spain, was the site of anti-American demonstrations in the 1960s. Students toppled the metal eagle that adorned its pedestal.

the *Maine,* to Havana in case it might be needed for the protection of U.S. lives or property. Unquestionably, there was strong public and government opinion in the United States at the time that Spain should leave Cuba. There was even a movement, never very large, that suggested the United States should annex the island and perhaps even make it a state. The idea had been around Washington for decades and Thomas Jefferson had even considered doing it. In any event, no matter how corrupt one might believe U.S. governments have been or how devious their activities, there appears to be no historical evidence that they even planned acquisition. Had there been such a plan, Cuba would almost surely not be a Communist country now but the fifty-first state.

The event which brought matters to a head occurred when the *Maine,* at anchor in the mouth of Havana harbor, blew up, killing 260 sailors. Yellow-journalism newspapers in the United States had a field day, calling for, and even demanding, war. (William Randolph

Hearst would later brag that it was *his* war.) The people who were seeking war, including Assistant Secretary of the Navy Teddy Roosevelt, immediately claimed the Spanish had blown up the battleship, and they wanted retribution. Later suggestions would be made that the United States blew up the ship deliberately to provide an excuse for declaring war. Recent research into the disaster indicates the explosion came from within and was most likely an accident. In any event, the Spanish were almost surely not to blame.

President McKinley was not one of the officials calling for war. In fact, he decided to make one more effort to seek a peaceful solution to the increasingly dangerous situation by approaching Spain with a purchase offer. The United States would buy Cuba's freedom for $300 million. It was the fourth time that the United States had actually made overtures to Spain for such a purchase. Spain refused, and there seemed to be no other prospect for averting the conflict.

The sorry little war came and centered around Santiago, where Teddy Roosevelt led his band of Rough Riders up San Juan Hill and into military history. After brief land and sea skirmishes, Spain asked for peace, and the United States gained the undying enmity of the Cubans by refusing to permit the presence of their rebel representatives or flag at the ceremonies. In the process, the United States also took control of Puerto Rico and the Philippines. McKinley held meetings to decide what to do with the new possessions. It was determined that Cuba and the Philippines would ultimately be autonomous, while Puerto Rico would remain a part of the United States. Fighting lasted only two weeks with a loss in American forces of 698 officers and men. However, in the following year of occupation, disease claimed an additional 5,509 U.S. lives.

The Cubans felt cheated. Their decades-long struggle to rid their island of colonialism had ended, in their view, with victory snatched from their hands at the final moment by a stronger United States. After fighting and dying for their cause, all they had to show was a U.S. military government, which stayed until 1902. Although there was a constant fear among the Cuban leadership that the Yankees might stay or annex their country, the messages from Washington continued to direct the proconsul to prepare the island for a stable government. In addition to providing stability, the military also performed a service of immeasurable value. Yellow fever had struck Havana annually since the mid-eighteenth century. Dr. Walter Reed headed a commission to find the cause and cure. Operating on a Cuban suggestion, Reed determined the disease was caused by the stegomyia mosquito, and the U.S. forces eradicated it in 1902.

One continually aggravating feature of U.S.-Cuban relations began in this early military period. Congress prohibited U.S. businessmen from operating on the island in the hopes of limiting exploitation. However, a market opening up just off Florida's shores was too much of a temptation for the Yankee traders. They came alone and as companies, with a "hot deal" or a sizable offer. Speculators, penny merchants, and giant corporations all looked in on America's newest possibility. The United Fruit Company, already a force in Central America, bought 200,000 coastal acres for $400,000. From that beginning, there was no end in sight.

By this time, the U.S. message was clear to Cuban governments: the Monroe Doctrine will protect you from outside domination and we expect you to set up democratic institutions and govern yourself. Teddy Roosevelt, now President of the United States, feeling he had a special hand in the freeing of Cuba, declared, "Not a European nation would have given up Cuba as we gave it up." Roosevelt had a longer view of history, he felt, and he desired that the United States consolidate the territory it had and wisely use its strengths. He sought no annexations. In his 1906 annual message, Roosevelt said U.S. desires for Cuba included only the wish that she "prosper morally and materially."

With U.S. promises to protect and defend it, there were great hopes that Cuba would use its resources and flourish, but since the country had no history or experience in democracy, the institution failed almost immediately. In 1909, Jose Miguel Gómez entered the new office of President as a poor man and left a millionaire. Graft and corruption were established companions to power. Mario García Menocal arrived in 1913 worth perhaps $1 million. By 1921, when he left office, he had an estimated $40 million. Sugar and corruption, corruption and sugar. Those were the twins of the period. Cuba was expanding its sugarcane production steadily, often one-third of total world production, but the fruits of that prosperity were being stolen and the condition of the peasant remained poor.

One interesting development of the time was the eruption of student unrest. Beginning in 1923 and continuing until 1960, when the Castro government effectively stopped it, much of the political thought and radicalism originated on the campus of the University of Havana. For years, the students were responsible for the effective criticism of the sitting governments, for street violence, and for a rising acceptance of communism as an alternative. They would be the proponents of change, often risking their lives to achieve it, from the 1920s, through the Batista era, and into the early Castro days.

Sensing the times, Gerardo Machado campaigned in 1925 with promises of peace and prosperity. A complex man, he had a criminal record (which he had burned) for cattle rustling, only three fingers on his left hand (a legacy of his days as a butcher), and a reputation as a good, but perhaps quasi-legal, businessman, who operated a Havana pornographic theatre in the days when most Americans had never heard the word. All his lofty promises were quickly ignored as his regime plunged into a corrupt dictatorship. Murders became common and unrest among the students, as well as their parents, began to rise. The 1927 Pan American Conference, held in Havana, invited President Coolidge. In a surprising hands-off policy of letting Cuba do with its government what it wanted, Coolidge called Cubans "independent, free, prosperous, peaceful," and returned to Washington. With his guests barely out of Havana, Machado took his government on a grisly course by having four students accused of being Communists thrown from El Morro, with weights attached, to be eaten by sharks. Opposition and additional killings once again increased, and the U.S. felt trapped, damned whether it took action or not.

Machado used the occasion of the 1928 expiration date of his term in office to grant himself a six-year unelected extension and to bestow upon himself the title "Illustrious and Exemplary Citizen." The situation deteriorated consistently until it was intolerable on any level. Cubans were appealing to the United States for help, the American community was frightened, and U.S. investments were threatened. President Franklin Roosevelt sent Ambassador Sumner Welles to Havana to work out a solution and to see what might be done with Machado. The people were ready for a revolt, largely spurred on by Communist groups and the knowledge that the United States wanted Machado out. Protesters brought the country virtually to a halt. When Machado fled to Nassau with seven bags of gold, there was great expectation that Cuba might once again try for good government.

The U.S. intervention proved disastrous. Despite Welles's best intentions, events conspired to make his moves for the United States turn the course of Cuban history forever away from its dream. Welles had forced out of office a despot with no popular backing. Then he was responsible for putting into the presidency yet another man with no appeal, Carlos Miguel Céspedes. Had the president been stronger, or the government better supported, the next event, the "Sergeants Revolt," might not have occurred.

Only a month after Machado's hasty departure, a group of army sergeants became fearful that their pay would be cut and started talking about being upgraded to officers without being tested. Such insubordination would normally have been dealt with quickly, but in the unsettled times of September, 1933, it rapidly developed into a heated argument in which one of the most talkative sergeants, Fulgencio Batista, told an officer that he was no longer in command and appointed a sergeant as a replacement. More audacious actions followed, and the sergeants found themselves in command of an army base and with a large and growing following. The ease of the takeover was appalling, and the U.S. community once again became fearful and asked this time for U.S. military intervention. Sumner Welles evaluated the situation and advised Washington that the United States should intervene with some show of force, but Roosevelt overruled him. Batista asked Céspedes to name him chief of staff for his support, but the president refused. In a highly confusing period, Céspedes was removed as president and Dr. Ramon Grau named to the post, but the military revolt captured all the attention. Army officers, objecting to Batista's takeover, holed up in the Hotel Nacional and threatened to fight if attacked. It was the opportunity that Batista needed to become a strong man, as his men shelled the hotel from land and sea until the officers were forced to surrender. Batista, the sergeant who had now appointed himself colonel, had filled a vacuum and become Cuba's newest leader. He would thoroughly dominate Cuban politics from 1934 until 1959.

Between 1934 and 1940 Batista filled the presidency with puppets under his control. He himself was elected for a term in 1940 and ousted elected President Prío in a coup in 1952. He remained in the post until Fidel Castro fought his way to victory after the Moncada attack in 1953 and in the Sierra Maestra from 1956 until 1959. Batista's rule was only the epitaph on half a century of almost universally pitiful and criminal rule that left Cuba bereft of stable political institutions.

One can only ponder what went wrong. How could the country of so much promise both fail and be failed at every turn? Part of the answer lies in the Spanish legacy of corruption and struggle for personal gain. And a great part is attributable to the unavoidable proximity to its gigantic neighbor, the United States. As long as Spain owned Cuba, U.S. influence was minor. When the colonial period ended at U.S. hands, the vacuum created was impossible to fill as long as the United States voluntarily refused to consume the island. And a great deal of the problem resulted when the United States failed to define a permanent, long-range political plan for Cuba. Normally, one would not be necessary for a sovereign country, but the economic impact of U.S. investments made Cuba special. One estimate has U.S. firms and individuals owning over 10 percent of the island's land mass after World War II. In every way, U.S. involvement in Cuban life was pervasive, yet the United States refused to enter Cuban government except to stand as a possible threat when things ran out of control. Both Cuba and the United States were mainly concerned with maintaining a safe, calm climate for business investments. That simply did not turn out to be a sufficient goal, and the Cubans were never able to adequately develop the strengths and skills needed to establish the kind of government the United States wanted for them.

With that background and the desperate need for reform, Cuba in 1959 was ripe for one of the most remarkable revolutions in history, constructed with almost no power base, with little financing, and without an overall plan except a call to action for the overthrow of Fulgencio Batista. But the Revolution had one overriding attribute— the captivating personality of Fidel Castro.

Fidel Castro

15

> I would like to study. I would like to write. I would
> like to meditate . . . to think. And above all, I would like to
> be the owner of myself.
>
> —*Fidel Castro*

The bearded leader pushed his chair back a bit, stretched, and lit his fourth Cohiba of the evening. Outside, a tropical downpour obscured the nearby trees just past the open doors. Even though he had been talking for hours about his dreams, aspirations, and plans, he showed no loss of enthusiasm. The cadence of rain beating on the metal roof caused him to pull his chair closer now, so his quiet voice could be more easily heard. After a few puffs on the eight-inch *cigaro*, Fidel Castro continued his explanation. "You asked about my work. In our new government, the amount of work that will belong to me will be increased. In some ways that will make me more of a slave to the state conscience than I already am. So, personally for me, that is not a very satisfying prospect. I like real work. I do not like formal work. But the amount of formal activities I will have will grow and the real work will grow, too. Of course, no revolutionary has the right to say 'This I like' and 'This I do not like.' I would say that a revolutionary is a slave to beauty and a slave to work. He does not have the right to say, 'I am going to work on the thing I like best.' For me, working posts are something I accept as a duty and not as a pleasure."

The Maximum Leader sat in a small wooden house, nestled in the middle of an experimental farm about twenty miles south of Havana. In addition to being one of his favorite places to give interviews, the farm is also a preferred hideaway for relaxing. Before dusk he made a quick tour to check on the dairy herd, a new patch of grass from the United States that may become Cuban cattle feed, and a wide variety of tropical fruit trees whose yields are checked for commercial possibilities. This continuing concern with agriculture is based on both duty and interest, manifested by his ability to recall hundreds of crop statistics on Cuba's current and future farm outposts.

When darkness came, a piece of fruit and glass of milk were all the fuel needed to power him through a discussion lasting until after midnight. The talk had begun in the late afternoon at the Hotel Riviera. As is typical of Fidel, a certain amount of secrecy accompanied the meeting. No advance warning, no appointment, and no firm time were ever given. When the call came, it said simply that Fidel would be at the hotel entrance in seven minutes.

The initial meeting with Castro was somewhat surprising because he is larger and taller than I expected, and he was more formal than reports had indicated. That wore away after a few hours, but the stiffness and proper governmental stance contrast with the popular opinion of the man. He arrived on the scene in his usual working outfit—starched and pressed green fatigues, a pistol strapped to his side, and pants stuffed into polished black boots. No official limousine awaited this entourage; instead he sped up in a green Soviet jeep complete with an AK-47 automatic rifle hooked onto the dashboard and a pair of communication radios bolted in place. Two backup jeeps filled with armed troops provided security.

Some of the formality ended after only a dozen blocks when Fidel ordered the driver to the back seat so that he himself could take the wheel. From that point on, he was the amiable Fidel, waving to pedestrians who recognized him and yelled his name, and conducting his own interview on conditions in the United States. His inquisitiveness about the United States was insatiable as he began asking such questions as, What is President Carter really like? How about Ford, Reagan, and Rockefeller? Do many politicians keep secretaries on the staffs for sex? Is Carter popular in Georgia? Is he as popular as Ted Kennedy? Will Chappaquiddick continue to affect Teddy? Is the United States becoming more conservative? Is Watergate finally over? Each response was recorded, almost visibly logged in for future recall.

As the jeeps rolled along through the agricultural countryside en route to the farm, Fidel changed the subject to Cuba and looked a bit into the future. "Over the next few years, our biggest problems will continue to be in production. Our population and economy are expanding so fast in all directions that we must keep production increasing to stay apace of this development. The island's only real resource is working people. Of course, we have sugar, nickel, and iron, but we have no coal or oil to produce steel or power our electrical plants or cars. Our only truly valuable economic products are agricultural, and they depend on the weather and world prices, both of which are beyond our control. We lament our dependency on sugar but can do little about it since our soil and climate are so ideally suited for the crop and it is normally better to grow sugar and use the profits to buy other things we need. However, we do feel it is possible for Cuba to industrialize sufficiently to have other products and then to use Cuban labor skill in manufacturing."

Upon arrival at the small farm, Fidel went to the fields to see some of the crossbred Holstein and Brahma cows and found the entry gate locked. As he worked with the wire in an attempt to open one end, one of the soldiers rushed up with his pistol, ready to shoot off the lock. Fidel declined the offer, and worked the gate free as he continued to look into Cuba's future. "Naturally, we cannot predict what will happen to us because so much depends on others. Certainly we intend to continue in our movement toward communism. We also plan to expand our economy, better the lives of all Cubans, and seek the goals of the Revolution. Concerning the United States, we do not feel the future is up to us. After all, we have no blockade nor have we expressed any aggression against the United States. We trade with Europe now, thousands of kilometers away. Obviously, it would be better and cheaper to trade with the United States. You have the things we need and we have products you could use. We would like to see those things happen and also a lessening of tensions."

After eighteen years of hostility, such statements have come so swiftly that they make Cuba-watchers incredulous and enrage the Florida exile community. In the first few months of the Carter administration, faced with deteriorating conditions caused by Angola and the cancellation of the anti-hijacking treaty, Cuba-U.S. relations made dramatic recoveries resulting in a mini-tourist boom as American travelers were granted access to the island for the first time since 1961. What had seemed so impossible only a few months before

1977 suddenly became viable, with diplomatic "interest" sections opened in both capitals, and more developments promised.

After inspecting the cattle herd, Fidel settled into the small house and waited for the approaching storm. When asked about his role in the new government structure, he responded, "The thing I cannot do personally is to take my liberty and renounce my obligations. On the other hand, I like many things, such as our new programs and the state work. I think the unhappiest man is the one who is burdened by too many responsibilities. Some people enjoy power, but when you look at it as a pressure, as a responsibility you have been assigned, it is not pleasurable at all. It is hard, hard work. Later, I hope I will have enough life, enough energy to do the other things that I like better. I would not like to dedicate myself to advising others, because there are already too many advisers. I would like to study. I would like to write. I would like to meditate . . . to think. And above all, I would like to be the owner of myself.

"I think the system forces the revolutionary to have responsibility for life. I personally think that there should be a limit in time in which men have to exercise that responsibility. Historical experience up to this point has shown that they stay until they die, or until there is a political crisis. The main reason for that, in my opinion, is that in exercising high responsibilities, men have many opportunities to become vain, to become like gods. That is a risk, especially in the revolutionary experiences in which men who have important roles in the starting of the revolution acquire great prestige and charisma, which become power. Sometimes such power is a risk, because men are still men. It is important that the men who have these responsibilities are the most conscious of the danger. How have we avoided the danger? By sharing the responsibilities, the facilities, and by developing collective direction. Never will there be anything superior to collective direction. The most intelligent of men can make many mistakes. Unfortunately, the historical experience of revolutions has shown that collective leadership and distribution of powers and responsibilities have not developed. There have been concentrations of power and that concentration has brought about negative consequences for the revolutionary movement. In Cuba, that collective direction is provided by the Central Committee of the Party."

It all sounds considerably neater and more organized than it really is. Fidel speaks of collective leadership, but in reality policies and

Fidel's three trademarks—cigar, beard, and fatigues—are all visible in this late afternoon portrait at the experimental farm he uses for relaxing and entertaining. His curiosity is insatiable, and he asks interviewers as many questions as he is asked.

programs are virtually impossible to implement without his approval. This one-man rule has strengths, as long as the decisions are wise, and many weaknesses. There is no written record of the Revolution or governmental plans because everything is constantly in a state of change. History becomes, in a Communist society, what its leaders say happened rather than what actually occurred. Fidel has changed directions and altered his statements on so many occasions that truth now becomes, in *Brave New World* fashion, the truth of the day. For years he told everyone he and his associates were solely revolutionaries, before declaring his Communist intentions in 1961. Former friends of his now in exile have verified his original statements. Now, Fidel is telling TV correspondents that he has always been a Marxist. He probably means he had socialist thoughts before becoming a Communist, but history is being distorted in the process.

Who is this man who has captured the world's attention for a generation and has been the object of systematic assassination attempts? Fidel Castro Ruz was born in Oriente Province August 13, 1926. He was the second child in the second family that Angel Castro fathered. Angel was an interesting character, who obviously had considerable impact on young Fidel. He had come to Cuba with the Spanish army near the end of the 1890s revolt that resulted in the Spanish-American War and Cuba's eventual freedom. He always felt that the United States stole a sure Spanish victory.

With this background, and employment at the United Fruit Company, Angel developed a sizable hatred for the United States and must have passed some of it along to his children. Proud of his Spanish heritage, he did not feel particularly Cuban. For his work he chose the northern coast of Oriente, the most primitive area of the island, which in the early 1900s was practically isolated from regular Cuban thought and culture. This isolation and the independence of the province's small farmers gave Oriente the distinction of birthing all of Cuba's revolutionary movements.

Angel's land and monetary transactions are shrouded in mystery and appear to have an air of illegality about them. Fidel confided once in an interview that his father never paid any taxes on his land or income. The place he built was southwest of the Bay of Nipe and the town of Mayarí, along the Nipe River. As an example of the underdevelopment of the region, as late as 1953 fewer than one percent of the people had ever taken a college course and only half the people over six years old had ever completed the first grade. But Angel Castro was different, and his cleverness was put to use in consolidating "Manacas," a 10,000-acre sugarcane plantation that employed 500 and had a quota of 18,000 tons annually. Even at a low 2¢ a pound, the gross would have been $720,000.

Angel had married a teacher, and the couple had a son and daughter. Fidelity, however, did not seem to be one of his virtues. In the mid-1920s he employed a cook from Pinar del Río, Lina Ruz González, and they too began having children. The offspring of this second family were named Ramón, Fidel, Juana, Emma, and Raúl. Since Angel was rich, he began searching for the proper education for his family. Settling on a Catholic school in Santiago, he was told by the registrar that baptism and confirmation would be required of the children and that Angel would have to marry his common-law wife, Lina. Since his first wife had by this time died, Angel complied and off the children went to Santiago.

Fidel adapted to the Jesuit schooling amazingly well and almost immediately began excelling in debate and athletics. So well did the tall, muscular young man do that in 1944 he was named Cuba's best school athlete. This talent and training would serve him well later in the Sierra Maestra. His interest in sports clearly shows today, since he stops to play in almost every game he passes.

Considered rebellious by his family, young Fidel developed his argumentative skills for use both at school and at home. When he was only thirteen he tried to organize a sugar strike on the farm against his father. By the time he was eighteen, although he was basically getting along with his father, he accused the older man of abusing his power in his dealings with people. Looking back, one can make a case that his basic character traits were formed early and that a resentment of authority was evident both in family and at school.

The real turning point in Fidel's development came when he entered the University of Havana. It is absolutely impossible for Americans to comprehend fully the politically charged atmosphere, radical thinking, and actions of that institution when the most serious campus events of the 1950s in the United States were "panty raids" and Bermuda shorts as female attire in the classroom. At the University of Havana, students felt they were the political activists of the nation, and had a substantial influence in national affairs. They were quite used to violence as a means to achieve their goals. Since the uprisings of the 1920s, university students had employed shootings, fights, kidnappings, and other techniques. In this boiling pot, Fidel Castro became a catalyst.

No sooner had he arrived on campus than he got involved in a celebrated fight with the Student Federation president. Then, to prove he would do something no one else would, he rode a bicycle full speed into a stone wall. One of his distant cousins, now an exile in the United States, told the author that her grandmother had several times informed her as a child that the young Castro boy was "crazy." Fidel's brand of craziness and the turmoil both in the country and at the university were meant for each other. Fidel fell into politics, the campus hobby, with the same zeal that he had earlier displayed for athletics. He entered law school for no other reason than his speaking and debating ability which made the law logical to him at the time. Later he regretted the choice and wished he had learned something more practical for his purposes.

From the very beginning he was active in opposition politics but was not the leader of any group. On more than one occasion he was implicated in shootings, but there was never enough proof to send him to jail. Then, in 1948, a most peculiar event occurred that seems to have been a turning point in his career. The Pan American Conference was scheduled to meet in Bogotá to be re-formed as the Organization of American States. Because General Marshall would represent the United States, students from Argentina and Cuba planned a protest. The Argentinian dictator, Juan Perón, paid for the trips. Fidel was one of the Cuban students who showered anti-U.S. leaflets from the balcony of the meeting hall. He was taken to a police station, warned, and released. Then, during a demonstration, a loved and respected antigovernment leader was killed and Bogotá was wracked by rioting and lawlessness that left over 3,000 dead. Although many charges have been raised over the years about Castro's role as a Soviet agent and an instigator of the fighting, it appears that he was just what he said he was, a student protestor who was caught in a terrible event that he probably approved but did not control. In the melee he received sanctuary at the Argentinian embassy and was flown back to Havana on a cargo plane. In any event, the experience seems to have had a strong impact on Fidel, who was impressed by the protest, the fighting, the speeches, and the near success brought on by violence.

Back in Cuba, Fidel settled down somewhat and married Mirta Días Balart in October, 1948, over her family's objection. Continuing his studies, he received his law degree in 1950 and joined a firm. However, he did little practicing, and that often for poor clients. There were constant complaints during that period of never enough money for his family, now growing with the birth of Fidelito in 1949.

Continuing his political activity in the Ortodoxo Party, Fidel's inconsistency was such that no faction could fully call him its own. He was still not a political leader, although power clearly fascinated him. One friend, Alfredo Guevara, worked on converting him to communism, to which Castro laughingly replied, "I'd be a Communist if I were Stalin." The Communist movement in Cuba had a checkered career. Sometimes it would work with the government, but often it opposed it. Most of the politically active students were antigovernment. Still, the Communists held some appeal, and brother Raúl flirted with the Party's youth organization for a while. But, in Fidel's own words, at that time he was simply anti-Batista and wanted to unite all the country's forces against him. He did not see his role as organizing a movement or even being the leader of the Ortodoxo Party. He thought he would be a good soldier and help bring all parties together to overthrow the dictator. He was out of college, without a platform, without an organization of his own, and without professional clients. Now Fidel Castro conceived his grand plan of action that almost brought about his death and was the first stop on his road to total domination of Cuban life.

The idea was audacious to the extreme. Fidel's scheme was to launch an attack on Cuba's number two army installation, the Moncada Barracks in Santiago, which normally housed 1,000 fairly well-equipped and trained soldiers. He saw this attack as both a means to gain badly needed arms for a continuing struggle against Batista and as a spectacular single act that would incite the spark for a revolution. He planned to train about 150 participants who would then simultaneously attack Moncada and a smaller installation at nearby Bayamo. It would be a young group, mainly in their twenties, with only a few married.

After Cuba became a Communist country, and the middle class, who had supported Castro, felt betrayed, there were wild charges that he had been a Marxist all along, even at the Moncada. Actually, in 1953, when the Moncada attack came, Fidel was probably further from communism than he was at any time since he became a university student. The Communists did not plan the attack, did not participate in it, and even condemned it as a futile gesture after it occurred. As an example of Castro's thinking at the time, he prepared a radio proclamation that was to be delivered if he was successful at

Moncada. In part it said, "The Revolution declares its respect for the workers ... and ... the establishment of total and definitive social justice, based on economic and industrial progress under a well organized and timed national plan. ... The Revolution recognizes and bases itself on the ideals of Martí. ... The Revolution declares its absolute and reverent respect for the Constitution which was given to the people in 1940. ..."

Had he been successful at Moncada, Castro planned five laws. First, he intended to restore the 1940 Constitution, and until elections, to run the country through the Revolutionary Movement. Second, he planned to give tenants on farms of less than 166⅔ acres title to that property and to let the state pay the old owners for it. This would have involved about 80 percent of Cuba's 160,000 farms. Third, workers would share a third of the profits of sugar mills and other large, nonagricultural businesses. Fourth, sugar plantation owners would produce only 55 percent of the crop, with the remainder shared by small farmers. And fifth, land, property, and cash obtained illegally or by fraud would be confiscated. Obviously, this was not a Communist plan in any traditional sense. Since the attack was unsuccessful, the laws never went into effect.

If ever there was an almost perfect disaster, the Moncada attack has to be it. After recruitment and some training around Havana, the group went to Oriente, where a small farm at Siboney was rented for additional training. Only six of the group knew the ultimate aim. Unfortunately, very few of the participants knew Santiago, and that would turn out to be a costly mistake. In the early morning of July 26, 1953, Fidel was ready. His final pep talk explained the mission to the group—how it would be a strike for freedom. Since it was carnival night, the soldiers would likely be drunk and hungover at the 5:30 A.M. attack.

Fidel had bought whatever he could from a total budget of $20,000. Shotguns and .22 rifles were the principal weapons for the poorly trained group, and some sergeant's uniforms were purchased to fool the gate guards. Fidel sent one contingent of 28 to Bayamo and used 134 for his Moncada attack. The idea was to have a large body of fighters force their way through the main gate, while a smaller group, led by Raúl, would control the roof of the Justice building next door and a doctor with a few men would capture the hospital across the street to be ready to tend any wounded.

Things went badly from the very beginning. Cars carrying about half the force got lost coming into Santiago and failed to show up at the gate. Men in the first car jumped out and yelled to the guards, "Make way for the General!" and grabbed the stunned soldiers' rifles. The signal was that the other rebels would leave their cars when Fidel, in the second automobile, stopped. Obviously, the plan was for them to be well inside the gate when that happened. Instead, Fidel either drove into a curb accidentally or deliberately ran into two soldiers (depending on whose account is believed) and his followers left their cars too early. Incredible confusion followed and the surprise element, so vital when fewer than 100 poorly armed men are attempting to overpower 1,000 soldiers, was lost. Small arms firing was brief and fierce as undressed soldiers in bed were frightened into action by the frantic attackers. Fidel called for a retreat, and he and his men as well as Raúl and his men began to retire, leaving some wounded and others to be captured. The contingent in the hospital never got the word to leave and later tried to hide as patients when the troops searched them out. In the brief battle two rebels were killed outright and one died from his wounds. Several others were wounded and left behind. The rebels killed 33 soldiers and wounded several. Although the relatively small number of rebel deaths would seem to make it a somewhat successful military venture, there is more to the story. Forty-eight of the participants escaped altogether and 32 were kept alive and brought to trial. All the rest of the 162 original activists were tortured and murdered by the soldiers during the following few days. Fidel and Raúl both briefly escaped only to be captured within the week. In that time, the unspeakable violence had occurred behind the Moncada walls and its publicity outraged most Cubans. What could easily have been condemnation for the Castro brothers and their attack became extreme criticism of the army and Batista as President for allowing the captured youths to be tortured to death. The officer who saved the barracks, and would normally have been a hero, was arrested and brought to Havana.

The government was not interested in providing Fidel with a forum for justifying his attack and tried various means to prevent him from testifying. However, the trial did proceed in October, without press coverage. In his own defense, Castro gave a brilliant, ringing denouncement of the Batista government in speeches that were ultimately published as his famous *History Will Absolve Me.* There he outlined his plans for revolution, his proposed laws, his motives, actions, and the crimes of the dictatorship. Although he justified his attack as a legitimate expression of rights against a tyrant, he was sentenced to fifteen years, Raúl to thirteen, and the remainder to lesser terms. The entire group would serve their time at the notorious Isle of Pines prison.

Unlike many others, who were never seen again after entering the circular prison buildings, Castro and his band received proper treatment and were even housed together in a special section away from the regular inmates, who were cramped in two-man cells. There the rebels could read, study, and talk, and it seems that much of Castro's revolutionary development came during the jail experience. After serving twenty months, the group was released under the conditions of a general amnesty that Batista issued as an election present to Cuba. Once freed, Fidel began writing antigovernment articles. Soon he became suspicious that Batista was preparing a bullet-riddled car for his body to be found in after a trumped-up police fight charge. So he left for Mexico to prepare for the next phase of his revolution.

In 1955, Fidel came to the United States to raise money and support for his cause. He visited New York and talked with many U.S. and Cuban citizens about his program, but the only real source of income was from former President Prío, who had been deposed by

Five circular units formed the "Model Prison" on the Isle of Pines that housed Fidel and his 1953 rebels for twenty months. Many other prisoners never emerged alive from the notorious facility, patterned after the U.S. prison in Joliett, Illinois. The bars are gone now, and the installation is used as a museum to commemorate past abuses.

Batista and whose only common bond with the young revolutionary was a fervent desire to rid Cuba of the dictator. Prío's money was used to buy what has become one of the strangest symbols of any revolution, the aging fifty-eight-foot fishing yacht, *Granma*, owned by an American couple. In late November, 1956, Fidel crowded eighty-two men onto it in Mexico and set out for Oriente, a long and miserable journey with overcrowded conditions, seasickness, and the embarrassment of having the ship's first officer fall overboard. But much worse lay in store for the adventurers. There was to have been a coordinated effort, led by the able Frank País and timed to coincide with the landing, to cause serious disruptions in Santiago and thereby divert attention from the boat and its passengers. Also, landing at Niquero would provide a solid beach to disembark on, and waiting friends with help and supplies. Since the *Granma* was late, it missed coordinating with País's activities, which were largely successful, and by landing at *Playa de los Colorados*, a swamp, it missed the planned rendezvous. It took the men three hours just to reach hard ground without all their weapons and supplies. A government plane flew overhead and soon a naval vessel was firing from the sea. Everything had gone wrong. It was December 2, and they had been scheduled to arrive November 30. The plan was for them to disrupt towns in the isolated southwest corner of Oriente, to be followed by País's armed attacks in Santiago, both designed to give the illusion of large-scale fighting, then calling for a general strike to show disapproval of the government. País's activities were over; Castro, poorly armed, was in the wrong place and about to come under attack, and there was no plan for this contingency.

Part of the group became lost as the party slowly worked its way inland toward the Sierra Maestra, where there might be some sanctuary. In the late afternoon of December 5, while hiding in a sugarcane field, the rebels were betrayed by a guide and attacked by an army force that seriously depleted their ranks. Most of the captured guerrillas were shot. The survivors separated. Fidel and a few followers escaped and continued to make their way upland. On December 17 they were joined by Raúl and the four men with him. By December 19, all the survivors were together, a total of fifteen men of the original eighty-two. In addition to the Castro brothers, there were the remarkable Ché Guevara, the Argentinian physician who served both as medical officer and revolutionary ideologist, and

Camillo Cienfuegos, a lovable character who became a principal architect of the guerrilla conflict. Of course, there was some support around the island, but at that moment, the success of the Revolution hinged on that tiny, ragtag band of hungry rebels.

It was at this low period, when the army would periodically bomb the mountains around them and there was the constant fear that troops would come up through the trees, that Fidel made a public relations masterstroke. Havana was reporting that he had been killed, that his effort was doomed, that there were only a few fighters, who would soon be exterminated. Fidel felt that his cause would benefit greatly if only he could get his story out to a foreign publication. That would give him international recognition as well as show Havana that he was well enough entrenched to get a reporter across and back through the army lines.

Enter Herbert Matthews of the *New York Times*. The contact was made and Matthews was driven to Oriente. There he walked up the last few miles to the mountain command post and interviewed a confident Fidel Castro, who explained the tremendous support he had from the people and his plans for Cuba after victory. All the time Raúl was casually parading back and forth below them with the same group of men, giving the impression of a large force. Fidel said his *Granma* contingent was the hard core that had been supplemented by other followers. In reality, on that day only eighteen men made up the entire 26 of July Movement in the Sierra Maestra. Matthews's articles created a sensation in Cuba and made Fidel Castro an international figure. In a world constantly seeking heroes, Castro was painted as the romantic freedom fighter against the wicked tyrant. Batista called the reports lies and said Matthews could never have gotten through his lines. The *Times* then printed a photograph of Matthews and Castro together in the mountains, making them both celebrities.

The fight was far from over, but the military morale and general government support began to diminish. The movement gathered more money and volunteers across Cuba and slowly the tide turned in Castro's favor. He sent out columns of men to the Sierra Cristal and to Las Villas Province. By the end of 1958, when it was apparent that final victory was coming, Fidel called his guerrilla leaders to the Sierra Maestra to plan their future actions and discuss taking over the government. Some fighters met him for the first time during that session, although they had been risking their lives daily on behalf of his beliefs. During the night of December 31, Batista took as much money as he could and flew to Miami, leaving the country in the hands of the 26 of July Movement. Celebrations erupted everywhere with wild shooting and yelling, while the rebels went to police and army installations, collected weapons, and told the men to go home and wait for further word. The island and its economy came to a standstill as Fidel slowly made his way from Oriente by car to arrive in Havana a few days later for a gigantic rally in the Plaza. It was happy, chaotic, exuberant, and a bit wild as people drank and screamed and made love for days, reeling under the promises that all their troubles would now be over.

As with all honeymoons, this one had to end. It came first with the universally negative press reaction to the Cuban show trials of a few hundred "murderers," "torturers," and "criminals" of the old regime. Although Americans no doubt expected some killings, they were unprepared for the huge public trials with people screeching for blood, and the convicted being hauled off and shot. They saw it all in *Life* and on their new evening news toy, the television set. Off on such a bad foot, Fidel compounded his image problem with the United States by announcing the first Agrarian Reform law that took land from big owners. Immediately the charges of "Communist" were hurled at him and he resented them. Every social reform he discussed was called a Communist plot by his detractors. The message was becoming clear to him and his new government: you can be anything you like and do anything you like in Cuba, but you cannot create a Communist country.

This unfortunate beginning was followed by the tragic meeting in Washington with Richard Nixon, the continued expropriation of property (largely U.S.-owned), the second Agrarian Reform law, taking over the refineries, and the break in diplomatic relations in 1961. Almost tumbling on top of each other came the Bay of Pigs invasion, with all its ramifications and ransoming of prisoners, and the Cuban Missile Crisis, which brought the United States and the Soviet Union nose to nose with nuclear arms. Throughout all this, Castro continued to maintain his magnetic grasp on the affections of the average Cuban, who would follow him anywhere.

Fidel's mistakes in government have been both costly and considerable. The misery of a one-strong-man system is the lack of a counterbalance for errors. Without opposing forces that make compromises and reconsideration integral, monumental miscalculations such as the 1970 sugar harvest disaster, Ché's Bolivian fiasco, and serious economic priority decisions are as much the rule as the exception. It is still too early to determine whether his new African experiments will be beneficial or detrimental to Cuba. Although he has publicly assumed the blame for many of the crises, a different form of government might have avoided some of them.

At the root of the problem is a kind of intellectual hypocrisy on the part of both Fidel and the government that bothers one. In dual cases, there is an assumption that he and his government know what is better for the Cuban people than they do themselves. As an intellectual man, Castro has an inquiring mind and demands intellectual freedom for himself. He reads widely, travels, and has access to the world's information, yet he has denied that same access to the Cuban people. The assumption is that information is safe with Castro and the leaders, but unsafe in the hands of the people. This is the elitism that communism causes but publicly denies—a separation of the governed and the governors. Fidel Castro would be stifled under the same rules he applies to the mass of Cubans.

Later in the evening, when the discussion again turned more personal, the concepts of luck, death, fate, and risks for a revolutionary became topics of interest for Fidel. "When the number of times I could have been killed are considered, it does seem that luck has played an important role. My death at some point might have meant the failure of the effort we were making. There were such points in the Revolution. Fortunately, we solved this a long time ago. At certain points individuals play such an important role that the death of a single individual may change the course of events. What satisfies me most now is the reality that the Revolution does not depend on me. The work of the Revolution will not end with the death of one man, or two, or three, because it was once the idea of a few and now it is the idea of a whole people. One, two, three, or even ten leaders may die—that would be an inconvenience similar to that encountered with the loss of a man of experience—but the course of history cannot be changed. It is one of the things that most tranquilizes me. No one could die well if he knew that whatever he had been fighting for all his life could end with his death. But everything has risks—driving, indigestion, diving, flying. It doesn't bother me. I have been lucky

May Day paraders pass before the reviewing stand, carrying a larger than life portrait of Fidel in the Sierra Maestra. Although "cults of personalities" are prohibited and official pictures of living leaders are banned, there are hundreds of thousands of Fidel images throughout Cuba.

and am lucky. But consider when a man is born, it is by a very great chance—one out of a million possibilities."

Even when it was pointed out that he was the founder and symbol of the Revolution, Fidel insisted that it would continue without him. "There is no personality cult here. There are no official photographs. No street and no farm bear the name of any leader."

While technically true, the fact is that Fidel's presence is everywhere on the island. There are rules prohibiting the likeness or name of any living Cuban being on stamps or money, but engravings of Fidel coming ashore from *Granma,* arriving in Havana aboard a tank, and speaking to a Plaza mass rally have all appeared on the backs of paper money issued by the government. Most of the posters and huge murals are reserved for dead heroes, both Cuban and Russian, but there is plenty of adulation remaining for the Maximum Leader. His face and words are the principal decoration of every home, office, and building in Cuba. Although the government does not print such pictures for the walls, there seems to be no shortage of them available for the population. Billboards carry Fidel's messages and admonitions, the newspapers are filled with his activities, and the movie theatres offer documentaries and newsreels of his movements. Whenever he appears on the screen, a spontaneous cheer erupts from the audience. If he honestly believes there is no personality cult now, it is staggering to think what Cuba would look like if the decision were made to create one.

In fact, Fidel Castro is so much the personification of today's Cuba that the country and the man are now conceived of as one. Only his first name is needed for instant identification, either on the island or abroad. Even the official Communist newspaper, *Granma*, where some extra respect might be expected, refers to him constantly in headlines as "Fidel." Stories such as "Fidel and Brezhnev Conclude the First Joint Bilateral Conversations" and "Reception Honors Fidel" are two recent examples. Only inside the article is the need felt to completely identify the Maximum Leader. There, in one breath, he is referred to as "First Secretary of the Communist Party of Cuba and President of the Council of State and Council of Ministers." Sometimes the newspaper uses the simpler "Commander in Chief." Around the country no one ever uses anything but "Fidel." Last May Day, when thousands of workers marched in front of the platform holding the Party's Central Committee and guests, there were no yells or cheers, but as each section approached, there was a simultaneous crescendo of a chant, "Fi-del, Fi-del, Fi-del, Fi-del!"

After midnight, the conversation turned to the published reports that the United States, through the C.I.A., had made numerous attempts on Castro's life. Fidel dealt with the situation seriously, although with a good-natured air. "Whenever I see a security escort, I mentally count the costs. Of course, it is really not too expensive, but it is an account that I would like to pass along to the U.S. government, which forces us to take so many measures. For example, when I go fishing, I have to take along two military boats. So the costs of fishing are increased. Our two navy ships see if there are any submarines or frogmen about trying to attach explosives to my boat. Then things I eat or drink have to be checked to see if they're poisoned. I can't even receive gifts. I used to think these measures were exaggerated and I would protest against the security measures. But some of the things the C.I.A. has done did not even occur to our security personnel—incredible, incredible. Once I went into a cafeteria to have a chocolate milkshake. The man there had a poison pill the C.I.A. had sent him. He kept it in the refrigerator. He went to get it and I guess it had frozen because it didn't dissolve, so I came very close to having a milkshake with C.I.A. poison in it. Oh, I could write a book about it. Exploding cigars, poisoned cigars, powder to make my beard fall out, bazookas, grenades—there have been some close calls. But I think that has stopped now. In any case, I still have to take measures."

Castro's imposing figure has once again become familiar in American magazines and television programs. The beard, somewhat grayer now, still remains, a holdover from the Sierra and now a symbol of the Revolution. Fidel says he plans to keep it until it turns completely white, and then he will make a decision on shaving. Green fatigues are his uniform, also a symbol from the mountain days. Now they are starched and neat, with a commander in chief's shoulder insignia, but they are still army fatigues and he wears them almost everywhere. The only other clothes anyone ever sees him in are tailored military uniforms that are used on official occasions.

For security reasons, not much is known about Fidel's private life. Such mystery has built a mystique that he somewhat savors and encourages. He likes the role of the elusive character who keeps no schedule, who appears from nowhere and disappears again. Officials say his itinerary and dwelling are kept secret to protect his life, but there seems to be some enjoyment of the image that makes mysterious even the commonplace.

He has at least four homes around Havana. There is the principal residence, an apartment in the Vedado section, which is shielded from the top to prevent any unnecessary spying from the telephoto eyes of the C.I.A.'s snooping photographic satellites. He uses two houses in the city's suburbs and the experimental farm already mentioned. Where he is at any time is never announced. Even the important speeches in the Plaza go unheralded so that he is never committed to an appearance. He merely shows up, whether to address half a million Cubans, or to play basketball with secondary school students during their physical education class. *Granma* publishes photographs and articles *after* he has appeared and does not print advance schedules or appointments. Whether his trips are by jeep, helicopter, private jet, or boat, they are revealed later and then only if he chooses to do so.

Rumor has given him a reputation over the years as a lady's man. Divorced years ago from his only wife, Fidel is never seen in public with a woman. Gossip constantly links him with Celia Sanchez, a companion from the Sierra days who now holds powerful dual roles as Secretary of the Central Committee of the PCC and Secretary of the Council of State. In the earlier days of the Revolution, Celia Sanchez was seen more around his apartment and seemed to serve as a housekeeper and aide. Now, with heavier official duties, she is not seen with Fidel as much, but is still the person commonly mentioned as his mate. Fidel refused to answer directly Barbara Walters's inquiry into his marital status, saying it was a private matter. Finally, he said that in the "bourgeois sense of the word," he was not married, leaving the speculation open again that his is a common-law arrangement. For whatever private reasons he has chosen to keep his secret, he has maintained his single status and steadfastly refuses to appear at any function with a female companion.

Such actions may even enhance his appeal to women, who usually find him "sexy," "exciting," or "intriguing." More than once foreign reporters have noticed the unusual attention that Fidel gives to any attractive feminine members of their group. At parties he is always kind, witty, and particularly interested in any beautiful guests. These gestures generate great new rumor outpourings but no tangible evidence that he is anything but a very private person.

Beyond the stature of the man—six feet two inches and over-weight—lies the intangible, that magnetic grasp on the affections of the average Cuban who would gladly follow him anywhere. This incredible ability to lead has been a lifelong gift. Some call it charisma, and there is no question it is there. Few other national personalities can command the appeal or popularity he enjoys. The same confidence he instilled in young men and women who risked their lives at Moncada and in the Sierra persists as he softly tells the waiting half million in the Plaza that things will be bad for a while, and much of the responsibility is his, but he intends to try to do better for them all. They love it, and they continue to love him. Who in one life could have been cursed and cheered by so many for the same acts? Castro has the ability to inspire both reactions, and the sincerity to convince even the dubious that his only concern is to do the right thing. As is not true of other Latin American leaders, no one has ever been able to level a charge that his ambition is to profit from the Revolution. In fact, it is clear that the leaders almost surely live lives that are considerably less privileged than they would be had the Revolution never come. This is not a government for personal gain but one of commitment. Fidel Castro believes in what he is doing and the deepness of that belief comes through to his audiences. He honestly thinks that communism is better for Cuba and for the world. He believes that people would be happier and healthier if they could all live under his system. Obviously, he is a realist too and knows that conditions are currently unsuccessful within his economy. Unfortunately, rather than placing the blame fully on internal reasons, he has chosen to accuse capitalism and imperialism of causing Cuba's problems. Capitalism did not produce the world sugar glut that caused the price collapse (when the price was rising dizzily a few years back, Cuba did not offer any credit to capitalism) or create the top-heavy bureaucracy that socialism suffers under. And capitalism can hardly be blamed for producing the conditions where people choose to work at less than full capacity for the state.

Recently, Fidel has begun describing himself as an internationalist, setting his sights beyond Cuba and including global goals. Recogni-

Taking aim with a new Polaroid SX-70 camera, Fidel practices his hobby when he occasionally relaxes. On his first trip to the Soviet Union, he lined up the Kremlin leaders and took out his first Polaroid, snapped their picture, and showed it to them, saying, "Isn't that an amazing invention? It's American you know."

Tired after his month-long safari to black Africa, Eastern Europe, and the Soviet Union, Fidel returned to Cuba to rest.

tion by the United States would be a major step toward casting him in the role he seeks. Needless to say, he alone has done a considerable amount to enhance that reputation. The spring, 1977, trip to Angola mushroomed into a trans-African safari where he landed in country after country to the enthusiastic cheers of airport crowds. Instead of the junketing leader of a small Caribbean island, he was heralded as the great hope for Black Africa, a new super-salesman, a character more popular than most other international figures on the scene today, and a personality able to outdraw the visiting President of the Soviet Union, who was in several of the same African countries almost simultaneously. Always a consummate showman, Fidel climaxed his month-long safari with a stop in Moscow, rave reviews in hand to cash in at the negotiating table. He has created for himself the unchallenged position as chief proponent of Marxism on the world stage, a new kind of socialist huckster. He probably has surpassed the more complacent Soviets and, according to one diplomatic theory, is actually leading his benefactors into new uncharted international waters. The suspicion is that Castro initiated the Angola experiment and dragged a somewhat reluctant Soviet Union along after he had committed his troops. Surely their pleasure at watching their number one traveling salesman verbally conquer Africa, a continent where they have had only limited successes, is tinged with a little concern as to where Castro might lead them next.

The anxiety is legitimate, since there is nothing more unpredictable than a zealot. And Fidel Castro is a man with a mission. He sees himself in the role of a missionary, and his message is the conversion of the entire world to Marxist-Leninist thought. He believes he has been singled out to deliver this message and lead the way to communism and appears disappointed that the Soviets, who historically should assume this role, have become "soft" on action and are becoming more capitalistic in thinking and in their economy. He also thinks the Chinese, like the Russians, have deviated from the proper road, and in the void left by superpower inactivity, he now thinks he and Cuba will pick up the torch. Sufficient confidence in his own status, Cuba's economy, and governmental institutionalization seems to have convinced him that the time is now. He no longer even fears the presence of large numbers of American tourists on the island and the insidious effects their affluence will have on deprived Cubans.

That confidence comes from what certainly seems to be a proper reading of contemporary Cuban thought. Citizens complain about the lines and waiting, about shortages, and especially about rationing. But they never complain about Fidel. CDR meetings may have grumblings over this or that, but they do not question Fidel. His place is extraordinary. The assumption is that he has made mistakes—and he has admitted most of them—but that his sincerity is unquestioned. No one in Cuba doubts that Fidel is working for what he truly believes. Parents certainly do not like to see their sons go off to an African war to be killed or wounded, but if Fidel tonight asked for more soldiers to launch yet another invasion, the volunteers would line up.

Such power comes from affection as well as respect. One old woman who now lives in Cuba grew up in the United States. Having known a lifetime of American society, she is greatly disappointed and against the Revolution, complaining about many things that she considers wrong. She shows no apprehension about condemning most of the cornerstones of the movement, but draws the line when the conversation turns to Castro. "Ah, Fidel, he's different." And that is the way most Cubans view Fidel—it is different where he is concerned. He remains the glue that holds the entire fabric together.

Naturally, such thoughts lead to the nagging problem of a successor, a circumstance not easily solved in either an on-going Revolution or a traditional Communist society. Fidel says jauntily that it is all solved now and the new government has a provision for electing a new leader. It will not be so simple. The Cuban people have suffered their deprivations largely because Fidel asked them to and they believe him when he tells them it will be better. No one outside Cuba seriously thinks there is another leader who will be able to hold that trust together. Raúl, Fidel's younger brother, is clearly being groomed for the position. Having been present at Moncada, on *Granma*, and in the Sierra, Raúl certainly has the historical credentials. As General of the Army and Second Secretary of the Central Committee of the Party, he also has the proper governmental experience. Raúl also serves as First Vice-President of the Council of State and First Vice-President of the Council of Ministers and heads all Cuba's military forces. In the only interview where an official would actually name names, Enrique Oltuski said, "After Fidel, it should be Raúl. He holds the number two position in our government and that should be respected. He has the prestige, and he has his own history."

However, Raúl obviously lacks the leadership qualities that forged the country's Communist government from a tiny band of mountain guerrillas. Warm, witty, and charming in private, Raúl is stiff and impersonal in public, referred to as "the squirt" behind his back. Depending on when Fidel finally relinquishes power, and whether it is a smooth transition or accompanied by violence, there may be an agonizing period of trying to determine whether the country will remain as it is or fall into the web of a military dictatorship. Raúl clearly controls the military now, and the armed forces are disproportionately large for the population. It may well be impossible for Cuba to escape turmoil after Castro. No one appears to be even a possibility to replace his leadership. Of course, the government is constantly assuring the world that the new Constitution will stabilize any changeover, but the political reality of any country with Cuba's past coupled with the growing unrest that economic conditions are producing may well prove overwhelming. While it is certainly true that there is no overt dissent inside Cuba now, a groundswell of resentment would be normal in the absence of Fidel. As that unrest materialized and grew, the temptation to suppress it with part of the huge military machine just might be impossible to overcome.

Attempting to discuss contemporary attitudes concerning Cuba after Fidel or Cuba without Fidel transports interviewees into a world they would rather not explore. One young intellectual, who describes himself as a socialist and not a Communist, answers, "What a question! Cuba without Fidel would be like imagining the earth without the sun. It is just too much for us to contemplate." Enrique Oltuski, who has known Fidel since the Sierra Maestra days, is filled with sadness at even the thought. "The style and the charisma of Fidel would not be here. The charm, the humaneness, the brilliance of that man will then be lost. Does that mean we will become a dark Revolution—a police state? That will not happen."

For Roberto Fernandez Retamar the prospect is filled with word images that capture the incomprehensibility of the moment. "You cannot replace individuals. You cannot replace your mother or your lover. A man like Fidel has been absolutely determined. He is absolutely irreplaceable. I do hope to disappear before Fidel. He has given the Revolution audacity, style, imagination. Even without Fidel, the Revolution will go on successfully. We have a great many leaders, and the country will create others, and in the long run we won't need leaders. My idea of communism is when the whole country becomes that mature. I do not think of Fidel as a father . . . call him a brother . . . a wise, courageous brother. It does not matter that a country has a Fidel. There will be other Fidels. There was a Martí; there was a Fidel. For the United States to have a Lincoln was

Ramón Castro, Fidel's older brother, entertains guests at his small home on the cattle operation, picadura, he manages east of Havana. Gregarious even beyond his expansive brother, Ramón says everyone on the farm is like one big happy family, and he treats them that way.

something that did not come to the country easily. These things are special. So it is with Fidel." Despite slogans around Cuba that exclaim, "Men die—the Party is immortal!" feelings about Fidel are best summed up by his brother Ramón, who said, "Fidel is going to live a thousand years."

Fidel Castro knows this and is prepared to remain in government perhaps longer than he would like. His personal dream of fewer responsibilities continues to founder, and he is much too committed to become less involved. He is sure he is now winning and will work as diligently as possible to add impetus to any movement. He told the author that socialism is the wave of the future and is gaining all over the world. Only the United States, where capitalism is most entrenched and powerful, will retain its system much longer. He sees the United States as the final capitalist holdout until it too succumbs to the inevitable world communism. If that scenario is conducted, Fidel Castro plans to be one of the orchestrators.

Cuba, the United States, and the World

16

> If I were to have the privilege of living my life over
> again, I would do many things differently from the way I
> have done them up to now; but at the same time I
> can assure you that I would fight all my life with the same
> passion for the same objectives I have fought for up
> to now. COUNTRY OR DEATH—WE SHALL OVERCOME!
>
> —*Fidel Castro*

In the early days of the Revolution, before the full impact of Cuba's conversion to communism had been totally absorbed, one of the leaders of a so-called Central American "banana republic" remarked, "I could understand that happening here where conditions are ripe for a revolt, but why Cuba?"

Why Cuba? The question has been asked thousands of times in the past eighteen years. Why would a country just off the U.S. coast embrace the only political system in the world that is threatening to the leading capitalistic nations? Why would any small island deliberately choose a system that risked war with its gigantic neighbor, and further antagonize that neighbor with expropriations and name-calling attacks? Why would a nation with enormous capitalistic investments, a capitalistic tradition, and prosperity far beyond its Latin counterparts consciously decide, without war, to set those considerations aside for an untried Marxist government whose presence alone might be sufficient cause for its own demise? For eighteen years, historians and political analysts have sought, without complete success, to provide a satisfactory answer to that important question.

The first place to look is in the personality of Fidel Castro. No one forced communism on the Cuban people. No Soviet army occupied their land, as in Eastern Europe after World War II, and imposed a new political order. Fidel Castro decided, after internal turmoil and external suggestions that he alone knows and has chosen thus far to keep secret, and when that decision was made, he almost alone convinced the Cuban population to follow him on his grand experiment. To a large extent, it is a testament to the continued high regard and trust that the people feel for him that the majority of Cubans voluntarily gave up the way they had always lived, to follow Fidel into socialism. Of course, many objected and hundreds of thousands left, unwilling to fight or try to live under the new system. Of those who stayed, there are also many who disapprove of communism. But they too have chosen to go along, partly from fear and partly from the feeling of hopelessness of a tiny minority. Generally, observers agree that most Cubans approve of the experiment and are still willing, with all the hardships, to give it a chance to work.

The rapid and relatively peaceful transformation from capitalism to communism in this hemisphere is what is noteworthy. After trying through elections, Chile has since reverted to a right-wing dictatorship. Jamaica seems to be courting the idea with the United States and Caribbean closely observing any further movement there. But in Cuba, an incredible number of circumstances rushed together to create a charged atmosphere that nurtured revolution first, and then the decision for Marxism. Its island geography no doubt played a role. Had there been bordering neighbors whose systems might have been threatened by communism, there likely would have been a considerably greater reaction against Cuba. (In the same vein, had President Kennedy been more seasoned in the job and more assured in international relations, the Bay of Pigs invasion might have received much greater military support.) Many other factors contributed to Cuba's position as the country of decision. Its role as the last Spanish colony (with Puerto Rico) in the Americas; the unified struggle for freedom that continued for almost half the nineteenth century; a residue of prejudice against the United States that began in 1898 and continued through Batista; the economic exploitation by U.S. and Cuban businesses; an almost unbroken history in this century of dictatorships, oppression, and corruption in government;

grinding poverty across much of the country; a loss of hope and a loss of pride in being Cuban—these things and more all coalesced into the perfect medium for the development of a revolt. When it came, it was coupled with the galvanizing influence of the personality of Fidel Castro, and the resulting reaction was explosive.

Today Cuba is still reeling a bit from the ramifications of a generation of Marxism. Among many fundamental changes is the concept of individualism. More than most other Latin Americans, Cubans formerly were renowned for individual thought and action. Now, as in their economic concept of island industrialization, they are closer to Japan in collective decisions than to their Spanish-heritage neighbors. For vastly different reasons, Japan and Cuba have both subjugated individual action to mass welfare. In the case of Japan, thousands of years of tradition with an enormous population on a small island has meant the necessity of group cooperation simply for survival. One common language, racial heritage, religion, and culture have meant unification and collective decisions for the common good. In business, "Japan, Inc." is more than a slogan; it means that negotiation with a single concern is controlled by government policy. In the case of Cuba, it is not the profit motive that determines policy, but the government's concept of mass benefit. Individuals, as such, are considered unimportant, and only the greatest good for the largest number of Cubans determines policy. At this stage of the country's development, individual workers with their job problems, apartment shortages, and rationing crises are of minor concern to government planners, but the larger considerations of mass support, community welfare, island defense, and Five-Year Plans receive maximum attention. Conceptually, communism cannot tolerate individual thought. The two are opposites. The very notion of a Marxist society implies giving up individual needs and concerns for the greater welfare of the masses. Fidel Castro, who, as an intellectual, has always valued intellectual freedom for himself, told the author, "In the United States there is an overemphasis on the individual. Too much attention to the individual is a bad thing. It leads to the selfishness that is at the heart of the ills of capitalism. If people only think about themselves and their families, there can be no true concern for the society in general. It is only when people put aside such ideas as antiquated and work toward socialism and its concept of selflessness that the world will benefit."

As diplomatic relations between the United States and Cuba are normalized, one nagging problem will arise—negotiating with a nation that uses similar words while giving them opposite meanings. Most Americans could probably agree on very basic definitions for such words as *freedom, democracy, republic, free elections, capitalism, imperialism,* and *aggression.* With Communists in general and Cubans in particular, these words take on meanings that most U.S. students of government would find appalling. The government and Cubans in general insist they are free, even though there is very limited personal travel abroad, domestic movement is restricted by passes and permissions, people are afraid to speak out in public, the press is tightly controlled and prints only heavily biased approved reports, and jobs, apartments, and purchases are severely restricted. There is the freedom to be Cuban socialist and work toward the New Society. Over dinner one evening, Esteban Morales, Dean of Humanities at the University of Havana (a post that should have exposed him to some of the great democratic thought of Greece), said, "In capitalist countries the concern for personal freedom becomes a neurosis. As an abstract concept, freedom does not exist in general. Personal freedom is only determined by a person's role in society. And that role is determined by conforming to society's needs."

Obviously, dealing with and talking to Cubans is likely to be a bit trying for both Cubans and U.S. citizens. An additional problem the new influx of tourists will encounter is that most of them will be coming face to face with a Communist government for the first time. Old habits and set patterns inevitably will create impediments to understanding. For example, one U.S. traveler on an early tour judged Cuba solely by comparison with life back home, saying, "No country can be great without a strong savings and loan institution network." The absurdity of trying to juxtapose this observation with the basic economic premises of communism is apparent. It is an American trait to compare everything foreign to life here. It is unfortunate and perhaps even unfair to judge Cuba by American standards. It is a small country, with an undeveloped economy, and a system almost diametrically opposed to ours. A fair appraisal would consider Cuban progress since the time their new system was introduced and its effect on everyday lives.

A vast number of other daily items of concern will be assimilated only slowly. American professionals will, no doubt, stroll through Old

Havana in amazement as they realize that there's a society without taxes. How can they be expected to see the ramifications of a tax-free society? When we calculate the number of hours a week that we spend on record keeping, tax reports, bank accounts, information for accountants, insurance decisions, and the minutiae of urban living, it is enlightening to find that a developed country can do without those services and have those hours and resources to use elsewhere. There are no business lawyers, no tax accountants, and no securities analysts, nor are there the many other careers that we now consider indispensable. There are a few attorneys who normally work as trial lawyers, appointed by the state in civil and criminal cases. There are still lawsuits for theft, domestic violence, automobile injuries, and such that are settled in court.

Many Americans can grasp the concept that Communist countries have state ownership of all income-producing facilities. It is the realization that whole professional areas are eliminated by such a system that baffles most. The average U.S. citizen seems to have great difficulty believing Cubans pay no income or real estate taxes, keep no monetary records for anyone except their own families, have no insurance of any type, and live from day to day without investments, retirement plans (other than the official government system), stocks, bonds, property other than a home, or vast accumulations of material possessions.

Finally in this look at Cuba's condition today, we find three other major U.S. problems virtually nonexistent in their everday life: street crime, unemployment, and inflation. How blessed Americans would consider themselves if that trio could be eliminated. In Cuba there is some crime, with thefts increasing, but it is still an insignificant problem by Western standards. Black marketeering, more serious, can be considered a social disease instead of a genuine crime. Unemployment is only a minor concern, though again one that may be on the rise. Basically, by guaranteeing jobs and printing money as needed for the low-paid salaries, Communist governments can keep everyone working. Inflation, with the other woes, is increasing, even in the face of tightly controlled prices and wages. Here the cause is external, since Cuba depends to such a large extent on imports, and those imports often come from areas of the world that are suffering from inflation. The result has to be a relentless pressure for higher prices.

Nowhere are Cuban attitudes more confused than in the country's relationship with the United States. For a generation, there have been almost nonstop propaganda barrages against anything originating from here. However, there exists a great reservoir of goodwill toward Americans, which has already been witnessed by the first few travelers. The apparent dichotomy is easily overlooked by Cubans, who quickly point out that they never criticized the American people, only government policy. In the same breath that a local revolutionary will condemn Yankee imperialism, capitalism, and its exploitation, he will likely suggest that the very best products continue to come from the United States and will pay a premium for them on the black market. The fact is that Cubans, in general, like Americans and American things. Perhaps that is one reason why the sudden switch in official attitudes toward opening the country to U.S. tourism and a reinstitution of diplomatic recognition met with so little reaction throughout the island. After the years of anti-American propaganda, many observers felt it would be impossible to turn Cuban feeling around when the time came to trade or establish diplomatic relations. It is another aspect of the belief that had Cuba not had a U.S.A. to kick around, she would have had to invent one. Without a doubt, whipping up fear, anxiety, and hatred have served as effective diversions to very real economic problems. But events have proven such speculation overstated. The Cuban people seem to have accepted the return of Americans with greater warmth than anyone would have expected. After all, they never stopped watching and

At the conclusion of the South Dakota basketball trip, Fidel Castro met with Senator George McGovern to discuss the future of U.S.-Cuban relations.

listening to Florida television and radio stations. There was a continuing relationship and contact, even though the government probably would have preferred reducing it. And many family ties have been sustained across the borders.

Simultaneously with the government's past active campaign to generate animosity toward America, a substantial amount of energy each year went into building up public esteem for the Soviet Union. That program is almost surely a failure. Cubans simply do not like Russians. They are grateful for support and aid, but whenever a clear choice is available, Cubans will ignore their benefactors at every turn. The Soviets are called *bolas,* because the Cubans think they are shaped like bowling pins with small heads and big bodies. Cuban men, acutely aware of everything feminine, constantly joke about the Russian women's shapes. Worse, there is almost universal disdain for the lack of personal cleanliness. The word "Russian" has become a synonym in Cuba for body odor. A person will come into a room and say, "There is a scent of *Russo* in here." Several Cubans will call out to the offending Russian, "Use underarm, it's off-ration." In this regard, women are the most frank and uncompromising. Menstruation is still referred to as the curse. When Cuban women discuss their Russian guests, they often say, "Those women never seem to change their Kotex, bras, or wash their 'privates.' " A shop door will open and someone inside will get a whiff and say, "Oh God, it's a Russian with the curse." Obviously, such things are not the only reasons for general negative feelings. The Soviets have offended the Cubans with their attitudes of superiority. And unquestionably, any attempt to blend the Cuban culture with that from the subartic would produce a very strange mixture. In discussing this, one Cuban said, "We find Russians have such a tragic view of life and that is not our outlook. The two viewpoints do not mix well."

One can reasonably ask why 1977 is the year of movement between the United States and Cuba. From the Cuban side, the answer appears simple. Their system is working, but not very well. Economic problems plague Communist nations generally, and Cuba is trying to do so much so quickly that her thin economy is stretched beyond its limits. Stabilized relations with the United States would be advantageous to Cuba, giving the aura of legitimacy that no other act could duplicate. In effect, it would be a stamp of approval to the Third World, and especially to Latin America, proving it possible to take on the capitalist giant and beat her to a standoff. Castro wants his outlaw past forgotten.

Cuba's Angola adventure most certainly was a shock to the United States and other Western countries. Few leaders would have dared risk what Castro did for the gains he sought. Had the United States chosen to strike, calculating that the Soviet Union would not risk a nuclear war for one African country, Cuba's government and many of its people might no longer exist. Most everyone agrees that, if the United States ever did feel adequately provoked to take military action against Cuba, there would be no large-scale Soviet support for her ally, any more than we chose to go across the ocean to assist Hungary or Czechoslovakia. As it turned out, Castro's evaluation was more accurate. He felt he could gain a military victory in Angola if the United States stayed out, and thought the Vietnam experience would ensure a U.S. reluctance to enter any new wars. He was right.

The book is still open on future U.S. actions if the Cubans seek greater African involvement. Already, Cuban military advisers are dotted across the continent, helping numerous countries. However, their feelings of invulnerability were almost surely shaken by the Zaire experiment, when the invading Cuban-trained troops from Angola were turned back by local soldiers assisted by Moroccans. The real test will come later in South Africa when growing pressure for black rule meets the steadfast resistance of the ruling Afrikaaners. If the Cubans expand their roles now limited to Angola and some guerrilla activity in Namibia, the United States will face a terrible choice of getting involved in a racial war in Africa or sitting by and allowing a white-dominated and strategically important ally to be overcome. Thus far, President Carter and Andrew Young, the U.S. representative to the United Nations, have warned that we will not aid South Africa unless moves are taken to transfer power to the black majority. Refusing to do so may be an open invitation for the Cubans to instigate a move.

From the American viewpoint, it is considerably more difficult to see tangible gains in recognizing Cuba now. For months there has been no particular call for action except by South Dakota's two Senators, George McGovern and James Abourezk. President Nixon was clearly more interested in China, the Middle East, and détente with the Soviet Union than he was in Cuba. President Ford began preliminary talks but stopped them abruptly with the Angolan involvement. One senior White House official told the author that there were few reasons for recognition and many against it. It was described as being an unpopular act, appearing to give in to the Communists, seemingly admitting defeat after a sixteen-year fight to isolate Cuba and bring down the government. Recognition had few proponents and many opponents, including the wildly vocal exile community in south Florida. Even the businesses that might benefit from a lifting of the trade embargo turned out to be relatively limited. A congressional trade hearing determined that the United States now, through overseas subsidiaries, has approved licenses for almost $300 million in trade. All those licenses may not come through, and the recent sugar price plunge has meant curtailing hard currency purchases, but a total annual U.S. trade could easily be in the $200 million range. The U.S. Department of Commerce estimates that, without the embargo, our trade to Cuba could rise to $350 million annually, with about the same value of imports from Cuba, giving a total trade of about $700 million (from a total U.S. world trade of $200 billion). Realistically, a country of only 9½ million people represents a limited market. Then there is the small detail that the 1974 Trade Act limits the "Most Favored Nation" status to those countries offering free emigration. Current legal tariffs on cigars, rum, and nickel would soar for any country unable to qualify as an MFN exporter. It is also doubtful that U.S. public opinion would allow a waiver of this restriction, considering Cuba's reputation for repression and political prisoners, and its hard line against this country over the years. Jimmy Carter's stand on human rights and his desire to normalize relations with Cuba may come into serious conflict.

Considering the obvious problems with recognition, why then did the United States choose 1977 as the time to begin? Certain moves were taken because many people in government simply felt no goals were being served by continuing the isolation. The policy, while not bringing Castro down, might even be giving him fuel for his continuing attacks. It was also believed that more could possibly be gained from working from within a country instead of from outside. Finally, President Carter believes the United States should have diplomatic relations with everyone and that we would be able to do more within the system. He actively sought to improve such relationships where problems existed. Even though the United States had said that we would not cooperate with Cuba until she removed

A significant thaw in Cuban-U.S. relations occurred April 5, 1977, when this basketball team from South Dakota stepped onto the floor at Havana's Sports City Coliseum, carrying an American flag and marching to the "Star-Spangled Banner."

her troops from Angola, stopped aggression everywhere, and paid the approximately $2 billion in compensation for seized properties, the rapid movement to open diplomatic offices belied the prohibition. And Cuba for years had said there would be no talking with the United States until the trade embargo was lifted. She first opened the doors to tourism and then to official relations without getting her demand.

In television interviews in June, 1977, Castro did suggest that the loose arrangement of opening "interest sections" in each country might continue until "President Carter's second term of office." That would seem to indicate that Castro does not expect normalization to occur right away. That too points to a possible continuation of his push to eliminate the trade embargo first. He also announced, as a goodwill gesture related to the U.S. agreements, that Cuba would release a group of Americans held in prison on drug and hijacking charges. Yet to be dealt with is the more sensitive issue of U.S. political prisoners inside Cuba. In addition to the unknown number of Cuban exiles who have been captured while infiltrating the island either for the C.I.A., with the C.I.A.'s support, or completely isolated from the agency, there is a group of ten U.S. citizens who have been held from nine to seventeen years on political charges. All ten of these men were residents of Cuba before the Revolution and either worked for U.S. businesses or had their own firms. All were accused of counterrevolutionary activities and sentenced to twenty- to thirty-year terms (except for one who was sentenced to seven years but attempted escape and had his time extended. He was due to be released in the summer of 1977). They all live together in a new Havana prison and are seen once a year by representatives of the Swiss Embassy, who handle U.S. affairs in Cuba. Four times annually the men are allowed boxes of food, medicine, and reading material printed in Cuba. Except for these brief contacts, the prisoners merely exist, with no sports and no work. They can exercise, eat relatively well, and claim they have not been mistreated. Still, their case may cause a considerable stumbling block to relations when the American people discover that they have been kept confined for a generation without Red Cross or other help. The Carter administration will find it very difficult to criticize other Latin American nations over treatment of their own citizens when U.S. citizens are being imprisoned with minimal considerations for international prisoner agreements.

The whole issue of political prisoners has been a gnawing one for Cuba, with running criticism from much of the free world. Western democracies simply do not jail members of opposing political beliefs. The Communists consider it inefficient and even dangerous to have people critical of the government running around loose causing trouble. In the early 1960s Castro was quoted by photojournalist Lee Lockwood as saying there were about 20,000 political prisoners in Cuba. The country has never allowed Red Cross, Amnesty International, or U.N. groups to visit prisoners to determine either numbers or treatment. When asked about this prohibition, Castro told Barbara Walters in June, 1977, that Cuba considers such matters strictly internal concerns and will not open its doors to observation. The Miami exile groups have been vocal through the years over alleged human rights violations inside the prisons. They claim beatings, starvation, and all sorts of maltreatment. The truth will not be known until prisoners themselves are free to talk. One black American hijacker claimed he was blinded in one eye by guard beatings. Several of the hijackers who talked with the author say they have been in various prisons much of the time they have been in Cuba. Claiming provocations by guards, most tell of beatings and rough treatment and that one hijacker was killed by guards who bashed his head against bars until he was unconscious. (Obviously, hijackers as a lot would not be a representative selection of Americans and, with the thanks of the U.S. flying public, Cuba's imprisonment and harsh treatment of the hijackers virtually eliminated the dangerous practice in this country.) To a man, every interviewed hijacker longed for return to the United States and said he would gladly face jail and even life imprisonment with no parole to living outside jail in Cuba.

At this point, no one really knows whether political prisoners are treated better or worse than common criminals. In any event, Castro now says there are closer to 3,000 political prisoners in Cuba and that the number is diminishing constantly as sentences run out or prisoners recant. Most enter work farms before being set free. Whatever the number, the issue is a volatile one in the United States, where jailing citizens for political activities and mistreating prisoners are almost universally condemned. They will be topics likely to mar U.S.-Cuban relations for years to come.

Of the many other raw issues between the two countries, perhaps none will be more agonizing to overcome than the presence of the Cuban military apparatus. Culver Gleysteen, Coordinator of Cuban Affairs in the U.S. Department of State, says Cuba has more personnel and a better equipped military establishment than any other nation in Latin America. For its size, it has the best in the

Troops from the various military academies and active duty units march before government leaders at the December 2 parade. The event was carried live and in color on nationwide television.

hemisphere. On a per capita basis, Cuba has more people and more equipment in her military forces than any other country in North or South America. The best U.S. estimates at this time are an active Cuban army of about 100,000 people and 60,000 more in the ready reserve. Her air force numbers approximately 12,000 and the navy another 9,000. If it were entirely a defensive force, which is what Cuba claims, it would pose no particular threat to the hemisphere or the world.

However, Angola clearly proved that the "defensive" force could, on extremely short notice, suddenly be placed in a foreign country in an effective offensive role. The Angola episode demanded reappraisal of Cuba's military intentions and abilities. In a Latin blitzkrieg, Cuba transported men, equipment, and supplies by air across the Atlantic, adding the necessary weight to defeat the Western-leaning forces in Angola's civil war. The heady aura of that victory still surrounds the Cubans and is causing many black African leaders to seek their military aid for other racial and political wars.

Now Castro is saying he views his role as an "internationalist," with a duty to support all wars of liberation and spread Marxism wherever he can. His modern, Soviet-equipped armed forces, headed by brother Raúl, are equipped with at least a hundred new tanks (plus all his older models), Mig 21s and Mig 23s, surface-to-air, surface-to-surface, and air-to-air rockets, AK-47 automatic rifles, and a plethora of landing craft, ships, cargo planes, etc. There are Soviet

New Soviet tanks rumble through the Plaza of the Revolution during the *Granma* anniversary parade. Such equipment is the backbone of the Cuban military apparatus, often called the largest and best outfitted in Latin America.

Soviet-built Migs overfly Havana as a supersonic reminder that a dangerous and potentially hostile military force is poised only a few minutes flying time from south Florida. The Soviet Union has maintained Cuban arsenals with reasonably modern weapons.

Although not particularly unusual in Havana streets, this line of twenty Soviet-built armored personnel carriers captured attention because all were driven by Russians, who normally maintain a very low profile in Cuba.

Soviet-provided military hardware is on display at the December 2 parade marking the anniversary of *Granma's* landing. The Cuban Navy's surface-to-surface missiles are trucked before a gigantic mural combining Cuban and Soviet heroes: Máximo Gómez, José Martí, Antonio Maceo with Marx, Lenin, and Engels.

pilots inside Cuba to train flyers, and 9,000–10,000 Soviet forces and advisers based on Cuban soil. Probably 3,000–3,500 of those handle Cuba's up-to-date aircraft defenses. As an indication of the value the Soviet Union places on the effort, she keeps a very senior officer (a Colonel General) on station in charge of her troops. All in all, this situation is more than a small irritant to Pentagon and Latin American leaders. Having a huge military machine is somewhat akin to owning a supercharged sports car—someday the temptation to open it up and see what it can do may become overwhelming.

If Castro thinks his initial African outing has set a pattern, the world may be in for some dangerous days on that continent. As positions solidify more and more in South Africa, in particular, Cuba may see that rich nation as an irresistible target. The wills of many Western countries will be sorely tested if such a confrontation materializes. Admiral Elmo Zumwalt, upon returning from a tour of South Africa, told the author that he felt the whites there had fewer than five years to solve their problems or face war. It is highly likely that a horrifying escalation may develop in such a conflict if the South Africans have acquired nuclear weapons, as many fear, and if they choose to use them on bordering invading countries. Throughout all these convolutions, the United States continues to view Cuba with increasing alarm. As incredible as the notion may have appeared only two years ago, this small island is now practically the leading foreign military and public relations force in all of Africa. Although Castro constantly restates his position about overseas involvements being strictly at the request of a struggling liberation force and in the interest of socialism, more than one government worries that once force is unleashed, it may be very difficult to bring home the victory-tasting generals.

Another awkward problem to conciliate will be that of the Florida exiles trained by the C.I.A. and the role of the C.I.A. in Cuba. After the Bay of Pigs invasion failed, President Kennedy authorized an extensive C.I.A. undercover war against Cuba with the dual aims of bringing down the government and assassinating Fidel Castro. Many of the details of that reasonably public war have been revealed in congressional hearings and in a Bill Moyers television documentary, aired in June, 1977. Congress verified eight known C.I.A. attempts to kill Castro, who says the number is actually twenty-four. It now seems that those assassination plans have been terminated, but the trained exiles remain fervent in their determination. The question that Castro asks is why the all-powerful U.S. government cannot defuse a relatively small bunch of Miami fanatics. As any urban U.S. citizen knows, it is not always simple to contain disorder in a democratic society. People just cannot be picked up and held in jail on suspicion of crimes. However, the situation is now almost completely out of hand in Florida. One Miami newspaper reported that the only city in the world with a greater number of bombings was Belfast, Ireland. Seven exile leaders in Florida have already been murdered for expressing moderate views toward Castro. A radio broadcaster who was saying that the United States and Cuba should begin to talk had his legs blown off in a bomb-rigged car.

The C.I.A.-trained exiles have sworn continued war against Cuba no matter what the U.S. government does toward normalization of relations. They learned their guerrilla tactics when this country wanted to send them ashore in small boats for clandestine operations. Now they are using their bombs, machine guns, planes, boats, and grenades against the wishes of the U.S. government. When the Cubana Airlines plane exploded on takeoff from Barbados in the autumn of 1976 (precipitating Castro's cancellation of the U.S.-Cuban hijack treaty), Miami exiles were quick to accept credit. Other Florida groups claim responsibility for bombing Cuban diplomatic and airline offices around the world. Castro says such terrorism must cease before Cuba and the United States can become good neighbors. The U.S. position is that it cannot assign a policeman to watch every one of the half million exiles in Florida. Obviously, if Bill Moyers can get a television crew into a Miami warehouse filled with weapons and show exiles in training, then U.S. authorities should also be able to identify troublemakers. Naturally, the Cubans are worried that some of the U.S. tourist groups will also include terrorists, arriving by chartered jetliner instead of floating ashore in a raft. Obviously, the entire exile community question needs some serious evaluation. When anonymous inquiries are made in Miami, a majority of the Cubans would like to see improved relations between the two countries. They are afraid to say so in public. There can and should be a legitimate mechanism for venting what are usually very strong emotions in Florida, but it should be apparent that neither the United States nor any other country can allow a lawless group to openly flaunt the law and alter international policy.

Setting the consideration of U.S. involvement aside, many questions remain on the continuing evolution of the Cuba experiment. No governmental system is static. Over the past fifty years the general trend throughout the world has been toward some form of socialism. In Europe the concept is well accepted and established, not only in the all-encompassing welfare states of Scandinavia, but throughout the continent. Naturally, the Communist countries are based on state ownership of production facilities. What has been simultaneously both surprising and logical is the increasing drift toward socialism by the capitalistic nations. Although "socialism" is still practically a synonym for subversion among many in the United States, the reality is that Americans have practically demanded more government involvement in their lives. The Social Security system is a prime example of a federally operated retirement plan. There are Medicare and Medicaid, programs not imposed on an unwilling people but health-care institutions lobbied for by the poor and the elderly. The Carter administration is committed to a national health insurance program to put U.S. citizens under governmental care similar to that which the Cubans enjoy. There are the regulatory agencies, almost laws unto themselves—O.S.H.A, E.P.A, F.D.A.—and a myriad of federal interests touching every American citizen's life many times daily. These are all justified by the public who asks to be protected from its own businesses and citizens. As more law-enforcement roles are controlled from Washington and more centralized computers house records on every person, including income tax, credit, and finance details, so that private lives are revealed by the touch of a keyboard terminal, it must be admitted that socialistic tendencies no longer are crawling but are approaching a stampede. Americans have asked for more social and welfare programs and a series of Democratic congresses have gladly provided them, along with record-setting federal deficits to finance them.

From Castro's viewpoint socialism is the rising star around the world. Either through evolution or "wars of liberation," he thinks the trend is irreversible, feeling that the United States will be the final capitalistic nation to capitulate. While the number of countries in the world has about doubled since World War II, few have chosen democracy in the U.S. mold. For many reasons, when former colonies have been given their freedom, they have most often established socialistic governments. Perhaps Americans should look at that and then at themselves and ask why so many people want to live in the United States but few want a government like ours. Almost everyone wants American products and the U.S. standard of living, but our crime, violence, and the nearly indefinable "quality of life" which values things before people in a society living at breakneck speed are threatening. However we may feel about national intentions, the fact is that much of the world views the United States as immoral, largely as a result of the Vietnam involvement and the operations of multinational businesses, including well-publicized bribery scandals.

Such views are causing the United States to lose the public-relations war with Cuba and communism in general. Castro toured Africa as a hero, assuring his screaming audiences that socialism was the cure for the ills of poverty and that a true Marxist country was not interested in expansion but only in assisting struggling brothers. He reminded the millions of blacks that no Cuban businesses were standing behind the army, waiting to come in and exploit their mineral wealth. As soon as Angola's land was secure, he said, and her government formed on Marxist lines, the Cubans would gladly leave. Emerging countries all too often overlook the Soviet influence in Eastern Europe, where they came and stayed, and Soviet domination of the various nations' economic systems. What they remember are the U.S. Marines in Latin America, U.S. businesses in a dominant role around the globe for decades, Vietnam, and the C.I.A.'s secret wars against opposing governments. We have become very poor salesmen of our system, while Marxism, with all its inherent flaws, is spreading.

Of perhaps even more importance than where Cuba is today are the projections of her future directions. As the United States becomes a trading and tourist partner, it is most likely that the strident attacks on Yankee imperialism will diminish. Unfortunately, the success of normalization will largely depend on the control of the Florida exiles. Looking inside Cuba, as long as Fidel Castro is alive and in power and his contacts with the Soviets remain strong, one has every reason to expect a continuing Communist rule permeating every aspect of Cuban life.

The larger question revolves around Fidel's successor. Every indication would point to Raúl Castro. Certainly there is no one in Cuba who could challenge him for the position if Raúl were alive and wanted it. But Cuba's Revolution was conceived and formed by one

General Raúl Castro, Fidel's brother and Commander of the Armed Forces of Cuba, meets with South Dakota Senators James Abourezk and George McGovern during the visit of the South Dakota basketball team. During this talk, Raúl, who has typically been a hardliner against the United States, for the first time publicly spoke of the time having come when bridges between the two nations should be built.

man, and his loss is going to create a crisis of the first order. Already people are planning for life after Fidel, with few clearly delineated answers. The assumption is that the new Constitution will provide a mechanism for electing Raúl to the posts now held by Fidel. But there is a great gap between such inside elections and acceptance by the people. Dissent will no doubt flourish and the military may tighten its grip to control inevitable problems. Unless someone, or a small group, emerges before Fidel's death as an acceptable alternative, it is highly likely that Cuba will drift toward a military dictatorship after Castro. Although Cuban leaders deny and resent such a prediction, historical precedents abound for such a move at the demise of a primary leader. And Cubans show no great love for communism or deprivations. They do love Fidel and will continue to follow him, but with him gone, it would be difficult indeed to hold them together without force.

For now, assuming no accident or disaster, the concern is not what to do after Fidel, but what to do while he is in control. Fidel's dreams may have outstripped his island's limited ability to perform. A population of over 9 million on a large fertile land should be able to produce a reasonably high standard of living for all. Normally, with stable political institutions and a common effort, it would be possible. However, Cuba wants to leap over systematic development to be a modern force in every area in one generation. There is simply not enough money for that. Thus far, the Soviets have provided sizable sums but are unwilling to subsidize all that Castro wants. Professional Cuba watchers both in Washington and Havana came to similar conclusions regarding Fidel's Africa-Moscow visits in the spring of 1977. The assumption is that appeals were made directly to Libya for money and that it may be forthcoming. In Moscow, Castro probably arrived as the hero who conquered Africa and requested more aid to replace his sugar income losses. He may well have asked also for compensation for Cuba's Angola expenses, even though he insists the Angola experience was conducted at Cuba's initiative and was without Soviet assistance.

Hard currency is short in Cuba, accounting for the sudden impetus toward improved U.S. relations. Cuba is looking for $50 to $100 million in the new tourist trade and sees much of that coming from the United States, which will supplement the already brisk Canadian tourism business. What seems like such a sensible solution to a money shortage is causing the Cuban government considerable internal difficulties. After eighteen years of hard-line anti-U.S. propaganda, the fear now is that improving relations with the United States and allowing thousands of American tourists to enter will, in the long term, soften Cuba's Communist ideology and may appear to the Cuban public as appeasement toward the imperialists. It is a delicate consideration. The basic goodwill toward Americans which is common inside the country is about to conflict with the official line of the state. Some planners fear their propaganda efforts will have been in vain when Cubans and Americans are sharing the same sand and bars at Varadero, enjoying each other and becoming friends.

Cuba is sensitive to such problems, wanting both form and substance simultaneously. The government is concerned that it appear to other nations as a legitimate entry into world politics. U.S. recognition will help , and no matter how much Cuba may resent the importance of the United States's role in granting legitimacy, she has accepted its necessity. The immediate result, she feels, is that other Latin American nations will become more open and available. This is most likely an accurate evaluation. Now, only Guyana and Jamaica have close Cuban ties, although Castro's long defiance of U.S. supremacy in the hemisphere has given him a recognized position as a kind of cult hero. It can be fully expected that his popularity will rise among his Latin neighbors when normalization is complete. On one level, Castro offers an alternative to countries with histories of U.S. influence or military domination. It is reasonable to expect that in the future, with Cuba's actual or tacit aid, there will be more armed struggles around the Caribbean and to the south. Fidel's seeming independence and macho appeal, backed by a higher standard of living than many other areas, may be sufficient enticement for rebel groups to emulate his success. A steady stream of Latin American students, labor leaders, and revolutionaries pours through Cuba as expense-paid guests of the government, to see and learn about communism from its hemisphere prophets.

Beyond this role as proselytizer to a waiting continent, Cuba is developing an industrial complex which it hopes will provide manufactured goods to countries throughout the region. As capitalistic a concept as that seems, Cuba's approach would be as a socialistic society benefiting from a capacity to produce excess goods to sell for much-needed hard currency. Such development could come, but not for years, since current plants are insufficient to supply even internal demands. If the government can maintain consumer peace and use its income to further expand production, Cuba might well achieve its dream of being the "Japan of the Caribbean." Castro told one of the endless groups of American businessmen sniffing at the possible new market that he could visualize Cuba's becoming a "service" nation for the United States and other industrial powers. Using Cuban factories, Cuban workers would turn imported raw materials into finished products. Such a startling possibility would necessitate considerable rethinking on the part of U.S. corporations, the U.S. government, and Cuban Marxists. The resulting interdependency could conceivably provide the model relationship able to terminate hostilities more quickly than all the negotiating teams combined.

In view of all that has been said, one feels compelled to ask, has Cuba's Communist experiment been beneficial? As disappointing as such answers inevitably are, a qualified "maybe" in this case seems appropriate. As usual, it depends on whose viewpoint is used. For the U.S. government, having a Communist government, often openly hostile, just off Florida's coast has to be a negative factor. The entire ugly saga of the C.I.A.'s intrigue with the Miami exiles leaves a legacy of deceit and violence which will linger for decades. On the positive side, Cuba has forced the United States to reconsider Latin America and pay it some of the attention it deserves. Even though we are told constantly that the Communist aim is to "bury" us all, Cuba is beginning to show Americans that it is possible to live, for the first time in our 200-year history, next door to a hostile neighbor and survive the experience. We may, as China did for thousands of years, not depend on armed conflicts to overwhelm our enemies, but simply consume them with our size. How long, a good capitalist may ask, can Cuba remain truly committed to communism when her people are buying U.S. blue jeans and TV sets, making electronic components for us in their own factories, and selling us fruits and vegetables?

In south Florida answers are harder. The former "Gold Coast" resort community has been forever altered by the influx of over half a million Cuban exiles. More than half the businesses in Dade County are now owned by Cuban-Americans. Racial and language problems abound in the area which once prided itself on being America's winter playground. People are afraid to express their views openly for fear they or their businesses will be bombed. Just after Mackey Airlines, a Fort Lauderdale-based concern, applied to the C.A.B. for permission to be the first scheduled carrier between Florida and Cuba, its offices were blasted, and the application was withdrawn. Although many Miamians feel the Cubans contribute to the stability of the community and have made it more of a year-round city, old-time residents deeply resent the Latinization. Beyond the local issue, the large concentration of dissidents who are ready and willing to bomb their way to recognition makes the exiles a group to be reckoned with in any settlement. For most of them, the professional class of pre-Castro Cuba, the past eighteen years have been a nightmare with total losses of homes and property and reestablishing lives in a new, sometimes unfriendly country. Their misery in one of history's greatest political exoduses will long be remembered.

Before Castro, Cuba was a corrupt and miserable little island filled with people lacking particular hope or prospects for the future. Now the Miami exiles will have us believe it was a tropical paradise with prosperous workers happily cutting cane and dancing in nightclubs. That deception serves no one at this time. Havana was Mafia-infiltrated, police killings and payoffs were as common as prostitutes soliciting outside the Nacional, and threats of violence held the fabric together. The countryside was poverty-wracked, with disease, illiteracy, and despair rampant. There were prosperous and beautiful parts, but they were the exceptions. Most people were not proud of themselves or their country and held little hope for the future of either.

Castro changed that in traditional Communist fashion. He pooled all the country's wealth, which was not much, and divided it among the workers. Now no one has very much, but everyone has something, that small share equal to almost everyone else's. So when one asks whether Cubans have benefited, the answer is that many have. All the poor Cubans who had never gone to school before learned to read and write. The impoverished sick were treated for the first time in their lives. The malnourished received rations consistent with others, no matter what salary was paid. And people who felt, somewhere deep within them, racially inferior because of their Spanish, Negro, and Indian blood were told they were Cubans and could stand alone against the world and be proud of their heritage. From the Plaza Fidel Castro told his spellbound audience that their small country would no longer be America's whorehouse and gambling den but that he and they would transform it into a model Marxist state the world would have to notice and respect. The Cubans loved it all, and loved him for telling them.

Have Cubans benefited? Yes, they have, and in ways that may be impossible for Americans ever to grasp. For the first time in their tortured history, they feel in control of themselves, their island, their homeland, and their destiny. The United States scoffs at this idea, feeling Cuba is controlled by the Soviet Union and cannot move without approval. Such an idea indicates a lack of understanding of Castro's nature or the Cuban drive for independent action. Cuba is delighted to accept Soviet aid, but does not intend to be a Russian pawn. There is every indication that Castro's instigation took troops to Angola and only afterward did the Soviets support the effort. Cuba's new Constitution established the precedent allowing Castro to be both head of the Communist Party and also President of the Council of State, which is the chief executive officer in the country. Seven months later the Soviets made a similar move and, for the first time, gave their principal leader (the First Secretary of the Communist Party) the additional title of President. One can ask, who is following whom?

Taking a longer view, one can feel sorrow for Cuba, for she has chosen a system that will serve her poorly. Plato was one of the earliest writers on the subject of the efficiency of dictatorships. In decision making and execution, certainly tyrannies and tight centrally controlled Communist states offer advantages over slower-moving democracies. But always the core question remains: at what cost? We are unquestionably in a period of world socialism at the expense of democratic capitalism. As any student of history knows, there are cycles to all human endeavors, compressed somewhat now with the extraordinary advances in global communications. Capitalism may slumber because it is not perfect and is only one more idea in an endless sequence of men's attempts to govern themselves while meeting basic needs. But communism will not prevail either. Given a conceivable combination of circumstances, the West's loss of a will to compete and the Marxists' consolidating sufficient resources and might to overcome any resistance, there could be a period of Communist domination. But it would be short-lived. If the study of the past teaches anything, it is that human will cannot be restrained forever. Freedom is a powerful force, fulfilling some basic and not clearly understood need for independence. Every parent has experienced it in his teen-age offspring. The spirit to fly free is one of man's most precious and indomitable characteristics. People may be suppressed, but not for long.

Communism will fail in Cuba and throughout the world, but it may take decades or even hundreds of years. It is to be hoped that it will be resolved short of a catastrophic confrontation between East and West that would leave the world unsafe for habitation. Instead, if time is allowed, it will probably change by evolution, with small relaxations here and there, succumbing to citizen pressures, until the Communist nations are no more radically socialistic than the socialist-democracies.

Communism is a threat to the United States not because of any inherent superiority, but because it can centralize its decision-making process and military power to single-minded long-term goals. American policy hardly exists from one administration to another. Without military confrontations, the Communist systems are practically self-defeating. After leaving office, Henry Kissinger described communism by saying, "In Eastern Europe, boredom, intellectual emptiness, inefficiency, and stultifying bureaucracy have been obvious for decades." Cuba inherited all those problems and more when it embraced Marxism. It imported an entire system that denies freedom of expression and all the ideas, inventions, and human advancement that such expression brings. It also imported the self-righteousness of Marxism with its assumption of superiority and lack of any capacity for dissent. And Cuba instituted the hypocrisy of Communist ideology, which vigorously claims high democratic principles while denying them all.

To focus only on the negative accomplishments would be a disservice to the achievements of the Soviet Union and Cuba, and also to anyone who might be misled into thinking there is no danger from what Americans feel is an inferior system. Even with its economic woes, Cuba is moving forward with her plans and her development. By any measurable standard, the Soviet Union under communism has been one of the major success stories in history. Formerly one of the world's most backward nations, she now has the number two economy and perhaps the number one military complex. She is a giant, and that growth occurred when a corrupt and regressive system was thrown aside and communism instituted. It is the Soviet model which Cuba has chosen and, as ponderous as it may seem, there have been great accomplishments.

The ultimate failure of communism, already a problem with Cuba's workers, lies in the self-centered nature of mankind. (A less kind or cynical definition might be greed or selfishness.) Communism is based on the premise that people will work to their fullest purely for the welfare of society. This sounds noble but reality proves the average worker reacts differently. When a political and economic system denies the individual any ability to succeed, to own, to advance, or to gain rewards for creativity, then incentive suffers. If communism can reverse these historical precedents, its contribution to mankind will be ensured. People work hard, for long hours, at night, on weekends, in their garages, and on multiple jobs because they foresee returns for themselves and their families. The great inventions that have forever altered our lives and planet were mainly created by people who could envision human benefits, had the freedom to express their thoughts, and saw a personal profit potential for their work. When society limits expressive freedom and eliminates the possibility for profits, creativity practically ceases. No one cares, work production falls, and the entire social structure becomes lethargic. That, of course, is what is happening inside Cuba. The enthusiasm that marked the early days of the Revolution is slowly giving way to less interest and an unwillingness to work hard six or more days a week for minimal pay. The entire system is slowly unraveling. Simple services take two or more months. Water and electricity are often interrupted. Lines to obtain goods are the norm. The government, like its Soviet model, is top-heavy with a bureaucracy that is lead-footed and unwieldy. Everyone knows things are stale, but there is no mechanism for correction. Since the government controls everything and makes all the decisions, when it is the government itself that is at fault, there is no one to expedite action. Only if someone inside starts corrective measures are any ever taken.

One possible means of correcting this basic flaw in communism is already being tested. Cuba is adding "monetary incentives" to the already existing "moral incentives." In a clear return to capitalistic principles, Cubans are being rewarded with money for extra work, overtime, high production records, etc. Also, the service industries are so hopelessly backlogged and inefficient that private individuals have recently been given the right, for a small license fee, to perform service tasks for other citizens and retain the income. Such revisions have come much faster in Cuba than they did in the Soviet Union. In order to get the economy moving, the next step will be foreign investments and working out a system where people can actually profit from extra endeavors. Artists gained this right in 1977 with a ruling that they can sell their works outside the system. Little by little, the strictures of communism are eroding.

Cuba, however, is very much a committed Communist nation, and it would be a mistake for Americans to believe that her status will soon be altered just because we are dealing with her again. Such changes probably will occur, but in a more distant future. For now, the most important concern is that the doors are opening and people are traveling between the two countries, a move that should bring understanding and cooperation to end a most unfortunate generation of differences. The histories of the United States and Cuba are forever linked by geography and past involvements. The question now is whether two opposing ideologies can tolerate such proximity and begin to forge a relationship based on positive considerations. To an extent, the future peace and harmony of the hemisphere will depend on the outcome.

Abourezk, James, 135, 287
Africa, 78–79, 275–76, 287, 294, 297
Agrarian Reform laws, 195–96, 268
Agriculture
    coffee, 212–13
    fruits and vegetables, 213–14
    private farms, 196, 215
    tobacco, 194, 196–200
    See also Sugar industry
Agrupación Genetica de la Havana, 210–11
Alamar Housing Project, 36–38, 123
Alonso, Alicia, 146–47, 149
Angola, 78, 92, 287, 292
Apartments. See Housing
Appliances, home, 23–24, 36, 38
Arts, the, 139–54, 245
    See also specific arts
Automobiles, 3–5, 24, 25

Balart, Mirta Días, 261
Ballet, 146–49
Banks, 17, 85
Baseball, 133–35, 137–39
Basketball, 135–36
Batista, Fulgencio, 252–53, 264–68
Bay of Pigs invasion (1961), 72, 173
Begging, 8, 163, 164
Bender, Mr. (CIA agent), 63
Billboards, 6–7
Birth rate, 2–3
Black market, 26, 28, 284
Brú, Carlos, 230–31
Bureaucrats, 16, 69, 84, 237

Calculators, manufacture of, 105
"Cantata de Chile" (film), 152
Capitalism, 68–69, 81–83, 86, 180
Carter, Jimmy, 287, 288
Castro, Angel, 259–60
Castro, Fidel, 5, 55, 59, 68, 92, 102, 116, 118, 172, 239–40,
    244, 254–79
    on art and censorship, 139, 140
    attempts on life of, 271–72
    background of, 259–62
    cattle raising and, 207, 256, 257
    communism (socialism) and, 60–65, 281, 282
    on Communist Party's policy-making powers, 66–67
    on education, 110, 111
    on government of Cuba, 235–37
    History Will Absolve Me, 60, 179, 264–65
    international role of, 274–76, 292
    on leadership, 257–58
    Moncada attack and (1953), 60, 65, 172, 175–76, 262–64
    popular view of, 242–43, 270–71, 273–74, 276–77, 281
    private life of, 272–73
    in revolutionary war, 266–69
    succession to, 277–79, 297–98
    sugar industry and, 180–82, 193, 256
    in United States (1959), 61–63
    See also specific topics
Castro, Ramón, 16, 51
Castro, Raúl, 75, 240, 262–67, 277–78, 292, 297–98
Catholic Church, 51–54
Cattle and dairy farming, 206–11
Central Intelligence Agency (CIA), 63, 77, 80, 271, 289, 294
Céspedes, Father Carlos Manuel de, 54, 247
Céspedes, Carlos Miguel, 252
Children, 45–47, 52, 54–58
    See also Education; Schools
Cienfuegos, Camillo, 267
Cigar industry, 194, 196–200
Citrus cultivation, 107–8, 211–12

Clothes, 22–24, 49
Coffee, 92, 212–13
Columbus, Christopher, 13, 106, 198
Committees for the Defense of the Revolution (CDRs), 55,
    69–75, 78, 80, 172, 238
    origin of, 69–70
    public-health role of, 121
    tasks of, 70–72
    vigilance role of, 72, 74
Communism, 60–61, 63, 68–69, 280–82, 300–305
Communist Party (PCC), 49, 51–52, 55, 59–68, 237, 239–42,
    244
    as elitist, 67–68
    membership of, 65–66
    policy-making process of, 66–67
    in prerevolutionary period, 60
Constitution, Cuban, 60, 66–67, 237–38, 244–46
Construction, 9–10, 36–40
Corral, Jesús Perea, 123–25
Cosmetics shortages, 49–50
Crime, 28, 72, 74, 284
Cuba, physical geography of, 10–14, 41
Cuban economy
    excess savings, 33–34, 84–85
    full employment, 83–84
    inflation, 81–83, 284
    long-range goals, 90
    ownership in, 88
    planning in, 86–87
    sugar dependency, 90–92, 193, 214
    See also specific topics
Cuban exiles, 77, 80, 230–31, 294–95, 297, 301
Cuban Institute of Cinematic Arts and Industries (ICAIC),
    151–54
Cuban Revolution, 61, 280–82
Cuban Women's Federation (FMC), 55, 75–76, 121
Cult of personality, 270–71
Curbelo, Hermenegildo, 210–11
Currency, 84, 85, 299

Dairy farming, 206–11
Dance, 146–51
Day care, 45–47
Dentistry, 117, 118
Diet, 26, 203–4, 213
Dissent, 78–80
Doctors, 2, 17, 31, 93, 117–18, 122–23, 125
Droller, Mr. (CIA agent), 63
Dufty, William, 183
Duran, David, 72

Economy. See Cuban economy
Education, 95–114
    adult, 112–13
    Castro on, 110
    of doctors, 125
    universalization of, 111–14
    See also Schools; Teachers; University of Nation
Eisenhower, Dwight D., 61
Elections, 237–41
Electricity, 41–42, 225
England, 182–85
Exiles, Cuban, 77, 80, 230–31, 294–95, 297, 301

Family Code, 36, 49
Fernandez, Victor, 42–45
Figueroa, Max, 97–98, 112–13
Film industry, 151–54
Fishing industry, 200–206
Five-Year Plan, 10, 91, 113, 188, 219, 237
FMC. See Cuban Women's Federation
Food rationing, 18–22, 26

Fruits, 213–14
Full employment, 83–84

Government, 235–53
  attitude of Cubans toward, 16–17, 76–77
  ministries, 242
Granma (boat), 7, 170, 266
Granma (newspaper), 7, 272–73
Graphic arts, 140–43
Grau, Ramon, 252
Guantánamo Bay, U.S. Naval Station at, 226–34, 244
Guevara, Alfredo, 151, 153, 262
Guevara, Ernesto (Che), 58, 222, 223, 266

Havana, 1–8
Havana Libre Hotel, 161, 162
Havana's Pearl Harbor (pamphlet), 63–64
Health. *See* Public health
Hemingway, Ernest, 167–69
Hernandez, Ebemito, 136–37
High schools. *See* Secondary schools
History Will Absolve Me (Castro), 60, 179, 264–65
Hospitals. *See* Polyclinics
Hotels, 158, 161–63, 172–73, 176–77, 194, 198–200
Housing 8, 9, 28–29, 36–43
  rural, 42–44
Human rights, 68, 242–43

ICAIC (Cuban Institute of Cinematic Arts and Industries),
  151–54
Illiteracy, 111
Incentives, moral vs. material, 15–16
INDER (sports ministry), 130–32
Individualism, 282
Industry, 87, 90, 219–25, 300
  nickel mining, 216–18
Inflation, 81–83, 284
INIT (National Institute of Tourist Industries), 22, 164–65
INRA (National Institute of Agrarian Reform), 25, 42, 83,
  195–96, 198, 213
Isle of Pines, 95, 97, 98, 105–8, 161, 211–12

Jamaica, 183–86
José Martí Pioneer Camp, 55–58
Juantorena, Alberto, 133
Juventud Rebelde (newspaper), 7

Kissinger, Henry, 303
Krause, Monica, 75, 76

L'Aiglon Restaurant, 84, 164
Las Américas Restaurant, 160
Las Ruinas Restaurant, 165
Latin America, 246–47, 299–300
Law, Jason, 233–34
Lenin Park, 170–71
Lenin Vocational School, 102–5, 114
Literacy, 111
Lobster fishing, 204–6
Lockwood, Lee, 290
Lopez, Alfredo, 85–86, 109
Lopez, Jorge, 7

McConnell, John, 230, 234
McGovern, George, 135, 287
Machado, Gerardo, 251
Macho attitude, 47–49, 75
McKinley, William, 249
Maine incident, 247–49
Malnutrition, 26
Marazul, 161–63
Marriage, 24, 34–36
Martí, José, 247
Matanzas, 98, 192

Matos, Hubert, 63–64
Matthews, Herbert, 267
Medicine. *See* Doctors; Public health
Mental health, 126–28
Micro-brigades, 36–38
Military, the, 58, 291–94
Milk rationing, 211
Ministries, 242
Modern dance, 149, 150
Moncada Barracks, attack on (1953), 60, 65, 172, 175–76,
  262–64
Moral incentives, 15–16
Morales, Esteban, 283
Motels, 173–74
Motion pictures, 151–54
Municipal assemblies, 237–39, 242
Music, 139–41

National Assembly, 67, 235–42, 245–46
National Ballet of Cuba, 147, 149
National Institute of Agrarian Reform (INRA), 25, 42, 83,
  195–96, 198, 213
National Institute of Tourist Industries (INIT), 22, 164–65
National School of Art, 141, 148
Neuvitas, 224–25
Nickel mining, 216–18
Nightclubs, 149–51, 155–56, 159, 171
Nixon, Richard, 62, 268, 287

Oil refineries, 221
Old Havana, 5–6, 168
Oltuski, Enrique, 29–31, 65, 91, 179, 201–3, 207, 277, 278
Olympics, 130, 131
Ordoñez, Cosme, 121–22
Organizaciónes Revolucionarias Integradas (ORI), 64
Organization of American States, 128

Padilla, Heberto, 140–41
Painting, 140–43
Pais, Frank, 266
Paz, Hector, 55–56
PCC. *See* Communist Party of Cuba
Pinar del Río, 10, 176, 197–98
Pioneers, 52, 54–58
Pirate's Cave Nightclub, 155–56, 159
Poder Popular (Popular Power), 22, 84, 237–42
Political prisoners, 289–91
Polyclinics, 121–26
Presidential Palace, 168–70
Press, the, 7–8, 243–45
Prio (President), 252, 265–66
Professionals, 4, 17, 88–89, 94
Prostitution, 8–9, 163–64
Provincial assemblies, 237–41
Psychiatric care, 126–28
Public health, 115–28
  polyclinics, 121–26
  preventive medicine, 121
  rural, 115–17, 119
  See also Doctors

Radio, 145–46
Rationing, 18–26
  clothing, 22–24
  coffee, 92
  dairy products, 211
  food, 18–22, 26
  household products, 23–24
Reed, Walter, 249–50
Religion, 51–54, 245
Restaurants, 20, 22, 84, 160, 164–66
Retamar, Roberto Fernandez, 53, 76, 139, 278
Retirement, 31

Revolutionary Museum, 80
Riviera Hotel, 161, 162, 164
Roca, Blas, 60, 64, 237
Rodriguez, Carlos Rafael, 60, 64, 65
Roman Catholic Church, 51–54
Roosevelt, Franklin D., 251–52
Roosevelt, Theodore, 228, 249–50
Rural areas, 42–45
  public health in, 115–17, 119
Russians in Cuba, 79, 80

Sabatier, Ilidio, 25–26
Salaries and wages, 17, 25, 123
Salutations (greetings), 51, 58
Sanchez, Celia, 273
Santiago de Cuba, 11–13, 175, 249
Savings, excess, 33–34, 84–85
Schools, 10, 52, 53
  prerevolutionary, 97, 100
  primary, 112
  secondary. See Secondary schools
  See also Education; Teachers
Secondary schools, 95–108, 125
  daily routine, 95–97
  Isle of Pines, 95, 97, 98, 105–8, 211–12
  study-work programs in, 99–102
  vocational-technical, 102–5
Service businesses, 28–31
Sex, extramarital, 34
Shipbuilding, 223–24
Shopping, 171–72
Shortages, 25–26, 86
  electricity, 41–42
  housing, 36
  water, 41
  See also Rationing
Sierra Maestra, 11, 42–45, 110, 116, 175, 266–67
Slavery, 182–85
Slums, 8
Socialism, 60–61
  See also Communism
South Africa, 287, 294
Soviet Union, 105, 276, 304
  aid from, 87–88, 200, 292–94
  dance influenced by, 147–49
  sports influenced by, 130–31
  sugar purchases by, 87, 91–92, 192–93
Spanish-American War, 247–49
Spanish rule, Cuba under, 13–14, 182–87, 247
Sports, 129–39, 145, 244
Stevenson, Teófilo, 129, 132–33
Sugar industry, 85
  Castro and, 180–82, 193, 256
  economy's dependence on, 90–92, 193, 214
  harvest, 86, 180–82, 187–89, 192–93
  history of, 14, 182–87
  mechanization of cutting cane, 187–89
  mills, 190–92
  prices, 91–92, 179, 189, 192–93, 212

refining, 190–92
  Soviet purchases, 87, 91–92, 192–93

Taxes, 284
Teachers, 112–14
Technical schools, 102–5
Television, 104, 143–45
Theft, 28, 74, 160–61
Thomas, Hugh, 246
Tobacco industry, 194, 196–200
Tourism and tourists, 155–77, 283, 299
  entertainment, 159, 171. See also Nightclubs
  hotels, 158, 161–63, 172–73, 176–77, 194, 198–200
  motels, 173–74
  package tours, 157–61
  shopping, 171–72
  sightseeing excursions, 173–77
Travel, freedom of, 243
Trinidad, 174–75
Tropicana nightclub, 149–51, 171
26 of July Movement, 60–64, 267–68

Unemployment, 83–84, 93, 284
Union of Young Communists (UJC), 7, 52, 54, 55, 58–59
United States
  Castro's 1959 visit to, 61–63
  Cuban attitudes toward, 82–83, 145, 284–86
  films from, 153
  Isle of Pines and, 106–7
United States-Cuban relations:
  exiles and, 294–95, 297, 301
  fishing rights, 203
  Guantánamo naval base, 226–34
  normalization of relations (recognition), 287–89
  political prisoners and, 289–91
  prerevolutionary, 93, 216–17, 247–53
  trade, 87, 220, 256, 288
University of the Nation (formerly University of Havana), 108–9, 118, 122, 251, 260
Upmann's, H., 194, 198–200
Utilities, 38, 41–42

Varadero Beach, 155–60
Vegetables, 213–14
Velázquez, Diego, 13, 174
Vocational-technical schools, 102–5

Wages and salaries, 17, 25, 123
Walters, Barbara, 273, 290
Water, 38, 41
Welles, Sumner, 251–52
Women
  equality of, 48–49
  macho attitudes and, 47–49
  in work force, 45, 49, 76, 84
  See also Cuban Women's Federation
Worker-student program, adult, 112, 113
Work-study programs, secondary schools', 99–105
Working conditions, 218–19